William S. Loomis.
Sixty-second birthday.
October 7" 1902.
"Vrow".

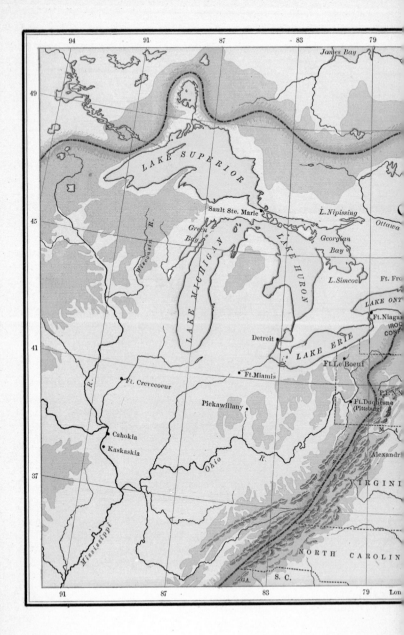

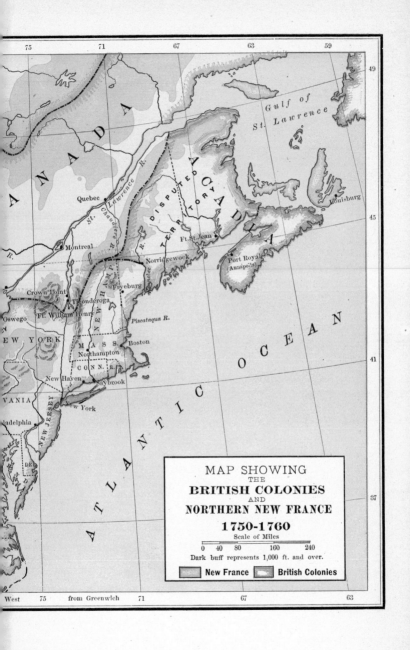

MAP SHOWING
THE
BRITISH COLONIES
AND
NORTHERN NEW FRANCE
1750–1760
Scale of Miles

0   40   80   160   240

Dark buff represents 1,000 ft. and over.

New France   British Colonies

NEW FRANCE AND
NEW ENGLAND

BY

JOHN FISKE

BOSTON AND NEW YORK
HOUGHTON, MIFFLIN AND COMPANY
The Riverside Press, Cambridge
1902

Published September, 1902

PUBLISHERS' NOTE

THE place of the present volume in the series of Mr. Fiske's books on American history may best be indicated by a few words from his preface to " The Dutch and Quaker Colonies in America." That work, it will be remembered, comes next in order after " The Beginnings of New England," and in describing its scope Mr. Fiske remarks: " It is my purpose, in my next book, to deal with the rise and fall of New France, and the development of the English colonies as influenced by the prolonged struggle with that troublesome and dangerous neighbour. With this end in view, the history of New England must be taken up where the earlier book dropped it, and the history of New York resumed at about the same time, while by degrees we shall find the histories of Pennsylvania and the colonies to the south of it swept into the main stream of Continental history. That book will come down to the year 1765, which witnessed the ringing out of the old and the ringing in of the new, — the one with Pontiac's War, the other with the Stamp

v

Act. I hope to have it ready in about two years from now." This preface bears the date of May-day, 1899.

It will be seen that " New France and New England " completes the story of the settlement and development of the colonies up to the point where Mr. Fiske's "American Revolution " has already taken up the narrative. It therefore gives a final unity to the sequence of remarkable volumes which he has devoted to American history.

The lamented death of the brilliant author prevented him from giving the final touches to his work. Most of the material for it was delivered as lectures before the Lowell Institute during the last winter of his life ; but only the first two chapters received his definite revision for the press. The third chapter was unfinished, but has been completed by a few pages, enclosed in brackets, and prepared in accordance with Mr. Fiske's own memoranda indicating what incidents he proposed to include in the remaining paragraphs. The other chapters were in the form of carefully prepared lectures, but were not equipped with the side-notes and annotations calling attention to authorities, such as Mr. Fiske supplied freely in his " Discovery of America " and other volumes. From the third chapter onward, it has been thought best to provide such topical notes and references as may prove helpful to the reader. These notes are enclosed in brackets.

The text of all the chapters has been printed as it left his hand. Though he doubtless would have touched it here and there either for adornment or for a more exact precision of detail, it will on that account possess no less interest for the readers of that notable series of historical writings to which this volume now gives the desired continuity and unity.

4 PARK STREET, BOSTON
Autumn, 1902

CONTENTS

I

FROM CARTIER TO CHAMPLAIN

II

THE BEGINNINGS OF QUEBEC

III

THE LORDS OF ACADIA. — LATER HISTORY OF CHAMPLAIN

IV

WILDERNESS AND EMPIRE

V

WITCHCRAFT IN SALEM VILLAGE

VI

THE GREAT AWAKENING

VII

NORRIDGEWOCK AND LOUISBURG

VIII

BEGINNINGS OF THE GREAT WAR

IX

CROWN POINT, FORT WILLIAM HENRY, AND TICONDEROGA

X

LOUISBURG, FORT DUQUESNE, AND THE FALL OF QUEBEC

LIST OF ILLUSTRATIONS

NEW FRANCE AND NEW ENGLAND

I

FROM CARTIER TO CHAMPLAIN

AMONG the seafaring people of Europe there are perhaps none more hardy and enterprising than the inhabitants of the picturesque little towns along the coasts of Normandy and Brittany. In race characteristics there is a close similarity to their neighbours of the opposite British shore. The Welsh of Armorica are own brethren of the Welsh of Cornwall, and as long ago as the reign of the Emperor Julian the regions about the mouth of the Seine were commonly known as a *Litus Saxonicum*, or Saxon shore. There to this day you will find the snug enclosed farmsteads so characteristic of merry England, while the map is thickly dotted with Anglo- Saxon names. Thither a thousand years ago flocked the Vikings from the fjords of Norway and settled down over the north of Gaul as over the east of Britain. The geographical position

Norman sailors

was favourable to the indulgence of inherited
proclivities, and throughout the Middle Ages
the French and English shores of the Channel
were famed for their hardy mariners. Their
ships thronged side by side in the Icelandic
waters, in quest of codfish, and even the chase
of the whale was not unknown to them. When
at the beginning of the fifteenth century the
Norman knight Jean de Béthencourt conquered
and colonized the Canary Islands, for which in
return for aid and supplies he did homage to
the king of Castile,[1] his company was chiefly
composed of Bretons and Normans, who have
left their descendants in those islands to the present day. As early as 1364 we find merchants
from Dieppe trading on the Grain Coast, between Sierra Leone and Cape Palmas ; and by
1383 these bold adventurers had established
themselves upon that shore, which they held
until 1410.[2] They were thus in advance of the
On the coast   pioneers of Henry the Navigator,
of Africa   and for a moment it might have
seemed as if the Guinea coast were likely to become French rather than Portuguese, when the
civil war between Armagnacs and Burgundians
and the invasion of France by Henry V. of
England put a new face upon the matter, and
the hold of the French upon Africa was lost.

[1] See my *Discovery of America,* i. 321.
[2] Shea's *Charlevoix,* i. 13.

A substantial monument of their early activity in that quarter is furnished by the fortified town of Elmina, upon the Gold Coast, whence in these British days runs the direct road to Kumassi. Elmina was founded in the fourteenth century by men of Dieppe, and the trade in elephants' tusks then inaugurated gave rise to the ivory manufactures which still flourish in the little Norman seaport.[1]

Under these circumstances it is not strange that the voyages of Columbus and the Cabots should have met with a quick response from the mariners of northern Gaul. Local traditions of a patriotic sort have asserted that Normandy and Brittany did not wait for the Cabot voyages to be taught the existence of the New-foundland fisheries, but had learned the lesson for themselves even before the crossing of the Sea of Darkness by Columbus.[2] There is no reason why fishing voyages to the Newfound-land banks might not have been made before 1492, but on the other hand there is no respect-able evidence that any such voyages had been made. The strong impression made upon John

---

[1] Gaffarel, *Étude sur les rapports de l'Amérique et de l'ancien Continent avant Christophe Colomb*, Paris, 1869, p. 316.

[2] Such claims are to be found in the extremely uncritical book of Desmarquets, *Mémoires chronologiques pour servir à l'histoire de Dieppe*, Paris, 1785.

Cabot by the enormous numbers of codfish off the coasts of Labrador and Newfoundland[1] indicates that the western stretches of the ocean were by no means familiar to the fishermen of the English Channel. The first authentic record Breton ships we have of Breton ships in New-on the banks foundland waters is in the year 1504, and from that time forward we never lose a year. The place once found was too good to be neglected, and thus a presumption is raised against any date earlier than 1504.

From catching fish in these waters to visiting the neighbouring coasts the step was not a long one, and presently the name Cape Breton makes its appearance, the oldest surviving European name upon the Atlantic coast of North America. It is asserted by Dieppese writers that a chart of the Gulf of St. Lawrence was made in 1506 by Jean Denys of Honfleur, and that two years later Thomas Aubert ascended the great river for eighty leagues, and brought back to Alleged dis- Europe seven tawny natives who were covery of the Gulf of St. exhibited at Rouen and perhaps else-Lawrence where in 1509. We are furthermore assured that upon this voyage Aubert was accompanied by a Florentine mariner destined to win great renown, Giovanni da Verrazano. The

[1] See his conversation with the Milanese ambassador in Harrisse, *John Cabot, the Discoverer of North America, and Sebastian his Son*, London, 1896, p. 54.

authority for these statements is not such as we
could desire, being found chiefly in uncritical
documents collected by the uncritical editor
Desmarquets, who lets slip no opportunity for
glorifying Dieppe. There is strong collateral
evidence, however, of a voyage into the Gulf
of St. Lawrence at about this time. Not only
does the exhibition of the kidnapped Indians
rest upon independent evidence, as early as
1512,[1] but in the edition of Ptolemy brought
out in 1511 by Sylvanus, there is a map containing a square-looking gulf to the west of a
spacious island which is unquestionably intended for Newfoundland, and the outlines of
this gulf seem to have originated in actual exploration and not in fancy. There is a map
preserved in the government archives at Ottawa,
which purports to be a copy of that of Jean
Denys, and may well be so, for, although the
names upon it belong to a later period, there is
some reason for believing that they are a subsequent addition. If the outlines are those of
Denys of Honfleur, we have in them a satisfactory explanation of the strange map of Sylvanus. Moreover, some weight must attach to
the fact that both the voyages of Denys and of
Aubert are mentioned under the years 1506 and
1508 by Ramusio.[2] There can be little doubt

[1] *Eusebii chronicon*, Paris, 1512, fol. 172.
[2] Ramusio, *Navigationi e viaggi*, Venetia, 1550, iii. 423;

that the attention of Frenchmen was, to an appreciable extent, drawn toward the New World during the reign of Louis XII.

Under his successor, the gay, gallant, and ambitious Francis I., attention was still further drawn to these strange shores. The jovial lawyer, Marc Lescarbot of Vervins, writing in 1612, tells us that about the year 1518 a certain Baron de Léry made an unsuccessful attempt at establishing a colony upon Sable Island, and left there a stock of cattle and pigs which multiplied apace, and proved comforting and toothsome to later adventurers.[1]

The French had sturdy rivals in these Atlantic waters. That was the golden age of Portuguese enterprise, and one of the first results of the Cabot voyages was to stimulate the curiosity of Portugal. The voyage of Cabral in 1500 proved that the Brazilian coast in great part falls east of the papal line of demarcation, and therefore belonged to Portugal, and not to Spain. In that same year a voyage in the northern waters by Gaspar Cortereal raised hopes that the same might be proved true of Newfoundland, and

The Portuguese voyages to North America

2d ed., Venetia, 1606, iii. 355. Ramusio speaks of Aubert as the first who brought Indians to France, "il primo che condusse quì le genti del detto paese."

[1] Lescarbot, *Histoire de la Nouvelle France*, Paris, 1612, i. 22; De Læt, *Novus orbis*, p. 39.

Portuguese vessels sailed often in that direction. Their fishing craft were to be seen off the coast, in company with Norman, Breton, and Biscayan vessels, and sometimes an elaborate attempt at exploration was made. Such was the voyage of Alvarez Fagundes in 1520. In accordance with an old custom the king of Portugal promised this mariner a grant of such new lands as he might discover upon this expedition. In March, 1521, after the return of Fagundes and his report to the king, the grant was duly issued. From the descriptions in the grant, supplemented by a map made forty years later by Lazaro Luiz, we may draw conclusions, somewhat dubious, as to just what was accomplished by Fagundes ; but there can be little doubt that he explored more or less thoroughly the coasts of the Gulf of St. Lawrence.[1]

But the Portuguese were becoming too deeply absorbed with their work in the Indian Ocean to devote much attention to North America. And in like manner in 1517–21 the discovery of Mexico and the astonishing exploits of Cortes quite riveted the minds of their rivals, the Spaniards, in that direction. It was just at

[1] The voyage of Fagundes is discussed in Harrisse, *The Discovery of North America*, pp. 180–188 ; Bettencourt, *Descobrimentos, guerras, e conquista dos Portugueses em terras de Ultramar nos seculos xv. e xvi.*, Lisbon, 1881, i. 132–135, etc.

this moment, and through these circumstances, that French interest in America received a fresh stimulus. After the capture of the city of Mexico an immense store of gold and silver was shipped for Spain, in charge of Alonso de Avila; but Avila, with his ships and his treasure, was captured by the famous Verrazano and carried off to France, probably to Dieppe, where the Florentine navigator seems for many years to have had his headquarters. In the course of the same cruise Verrazano captured another Spanish ship on its way from San Domingo, heavily laden with gold and pearls, so that he was enabled to make gorgeous presents to King Francis and to the Admiral of France. The delightful chronicler, Bernal Diaz, who tells us these incidents, adds that the whole country was amazed at the stupendous wealth that was pouring into the treasury of Charles V. from the Indies. The first great war between Charles and Francis was raging, and the latter did not need to be told that Mexican money could be used to pay the troops that were defeating his army in Lombardy. He sent a bantering message to Charles, asking if it were really true that he and the king of Portugal had parcelled out the earth between them without leaving anything for him. Had Father Adam made those two his only heirs?

Verrazano

Francis I. and the demarcation line

If so, he wished they would show him that patriarch's last will and testament.[1] Until they could do so he should feel at liberty to seize whatever his good ships might happen to meet upon the ocean, and forthwith he concerted with Verrazano fresh raids upon the enemy's sinews of war.

The result of these meditations was the great voyage of 1524, which first placed upon the map the continuous coast-line of the United States, from North Carolina to the mouth of the Penobscot River. The purpose of this Verrazano's voyage was twofold: first, to ascertain purpose if any more countries abounding in precious metals, like Mexico, or in pearls, like Venezuela, were to be found within or near the longitudes traversed by Columbus and Cabot; secondly, to find some oceanic route north of Florida from European ports to the Indian Ocean. In other words, this voyage of Verrazano was the first one which had any reference to a northwest passage. Columbus had believed the shores on which he landed to be parts of Asia, either continental or

---

[1] " Y entonces dize que dixo el rey de Francia, o se lo embiò a dezir a nuestro gran Emperador, Que como auian partido entre el y el rey de Portugal el mundo sin darle parte a el ? Que mostrassen el testamento de nuestro padre Adan, si les dexò a ellos solamente por herederos," etc. Diaz, *Historia verdadera,* Madrid, 1632, cap. clxix.

insular, and his last voyage was an attempt to find the Strait of Malacca at the Isthmus of Panama. Subsequent explanations, however, had disclosed an unbroken coast-line all the way from Florida to Patagonia ; and the recent return in 1522 of the wornout remnant of Magellan's expedition brought convincing evidence that the voyage to India by his southerly route was so long and difficult as to be practically useless. Thus the New World coasts were coming to be recognized as a barrier on the route to Asia, and an important part of Verrazano's business was to discover a northern end to this long barrier, or a passageway through it somewhere to the northward of the regions already examined.

This is not the best place for giving a detailed account of Verrazano's voyage, inasmuch as it was confined to portions of the American coast over which France has never held sway. I have given the principal details of it in treating of the Dutch and Quaker Colonies,[1] and need not repeat them here. Let it suffice to say that besides delineating the coast of the United States from North Carolina to Maine, Verrazano entered the Hudson River and Narragansett Bay, and saw from his ship's deck the distant peaks of the White Mountains. He found no gold mines nor beds of pearl, neither did he anywhere detect

[1] [*The Dutch and Quaker Colonies*, i. 68–78.]

what seemed to him a feasible waterway into the
Indian Ocean, but he did discover in this connection one of the most extraordinary mare's
nests on record. He seems to have gone ashore
upon the Accomac peninsula and tramped across
it until his eyes rested upon the waters of Ches-
apeake Bay, which he mistook for the Pacific
Ocean. For soon after his return to Europe
two maps were issued, one by his own brother,
Girolamo Verrazano, one by Vesconte Maggiolo,
which exerted a great influence upon the geographical ideas of the next three generations of
Europeans. These maps show a solid continental mass connecting Florida with Mexico, and
another solid mass to the northward, such as
would naturally have been suggested to Verrazano by the presence of such large The Sea of
rivers as the Hudson and the Penob- Verrazano
scot. But between these masses the whole central region of the United States is represented
as an immense sea continuous with the Pacific
Ocean; while the Virginian coast is shown as a
very narrow isthmus, with an inscription by Verrazano's brother, informing us that here the
distance from sea to sea is not more than six
miles. A full century elapsed before this notion
of the Sea of Verrazano was eliminated from
men's minds, and without taking this fact into
the account it is impossible to understand the

movements of navigators who ascended rivers like the Hudson and the St. Lawrence in the hope of finding passageways into the western sea.

When Verrazano arrived in Dieppe in July, 1525, the king, who had been taken prisoner at the battle of Pavia in February, was a captive at Madrid. His demand for a sight of Father Adam's will had met with a rude response. He purchased his freedom in January, 1526, by signing a disastrous treaty, but no sooner had he leaped upon his goodly steed, on the French side of the Pyrenees, than he renounced all intention of keeping promises thus made under duress. The worthy Verrazano fared much worse than his royal master. In the year 1526 he entered into an arrangement with Jean Ango and other important citizens of Dieppe for a voyage into Death of the Indian Ocean for spices, but in the Verrazano course of the following year he was overhauled by Spanish cruisers, who took him prisoner and hanged him as a pirate.[1]

There enters now upon the scene a man of whose personality we have a much more distinct conception than we have of Verrazano. As that accomplished Italian is one of the chief glories of the town of Dieppe, so the Breton seaport of

[1] Barcia, *Ensayo chronologico para la historia general de la Florida*, 1735, p. 8, since confirmed by documents in the archives of Simancas.

St. Malo is famous for its native citizen, Jacques
Cartier.   His portrait hangs in the town hall.
Unfortunately its authenticity is not   <small>Jacques</small>
above question, but if it is not surely   <small>Cartier</small>
a true likeness it deserves to be ; it well ex-
presses the earnestness and courage, the refine-
ment and keen intelligence of the great Breton
mariner.[1] He had roamed the seas for many
years, and had won — and doubtless earned —
from Spanish mouths the epithets of " corsair "
and " pirate," when at the age of three and forty
he was selected by Philippe de Chabot, Admiral
of France, to carry on the work of Denys and
Aubert and Verrazano, and to bring fresh tidings of the mysterious Square Gulf of Sylvanus.

On April 20, 1534, Cartier sailed from St.
Malo with two small craft carrying sixty-one
men, and made straight for the coast of Labrador, just north of the Straits of Belle Isle, a region already quite familiar to Breton and Norman fishermen. Passing through the straits he
skirted the inner coast of Newfoundland southward as far as Cape Ray, whence he crossed to
Prince Edward Island, and turned his prows to
the north. The oppressive heat of an American
July is commemorated in the name which Cartier gave to the Bay of Chaleur. A little further
on, at Gaspe, he set up a cross, and with the

---

[1] The best and most critical biography is Longrais, *Jacques
Cartier*, Paris, 1888.

usual ceremonies took possession of the country
in the name of Francis I. Thence he crossed to
the eastern end of Anticosti, and followed the
north shore of that island nearly to its western
point, when he headed about, and passing
through Belle Isle made straight for France,
carrying with him a couple of Indians whom he
had kidnapped, young warriors from far up the
St. Lawrence, who had come down to the sea to
catch mackerel in hemp nets.

With this voyage of reconnoissance the shad-
owy Square Gulf of Sylvanus at once becomes

The explora-
tion of the
St. Law-
rence

clothed with reality. Enough interest
was aroused in France to seem to justify another undertaking, and in May,
1535, the gallant Cartier set forth once more,
with three small ships and 110 men. Late in
July he passed through the Strait of Belle Isle,
and on the 10th of August, a day sacred to the
martyred St. Lawrence, he gave that name to a
small bay on the mainland north of Anticosti.
Whales were spouting all around his course as
he passed the western point of the island and
ploughed into the broad expanse of salt water
that seemed to open before him the prospect of
a short passage to the Indian Ocean. Day by
day, however, the water grew fresher, and by the
September morning when he reached the mouth
of the Saguenay our explorer was reluctantly
convinced that he was not in a strait of the ocean,

but in one of the mightiest rivers of the earth.
To these newcomers from the Old World each
day must have presented an impressive spectacle; for except the Amazon and the Orinoco it
may be doubted if there be any river which gives
one such an overwhelming sense of power and
majesty as the St. Lawrence ; certainly the Mississippi seems very tame in comparison.

As the Frenchmen inquired the names of the
villages along the banks, a reply which they commonly received from their two Indian The name
guides was the word *Canada*, which is " Canada "
simply a Mohawk word for " village." [1] Hence
Cartier naturally got the impression that Canada
was the name of the river or of the country
through which it flowed, and from these beginnings its meaning has been gradually expanded
until it has come to cover half of a huge continent. Presently on arriving at the site of Quebec, Cartier found there a village named Stadacona, with a chieftain called Donnacona. Painted
and bedizened warriors and squaws came trooping to the water's edge or paddling out in canoes
to meet the astounding spectacle of the white-
winged floating castles and their pale-faced and
bearded people. In the two kidnapped interpreters the men of Stadacona quickly recognized
their kinsmen ; strings of beads were passed
about, dusky figures leaped and danced, and

[1] Beauchamp, *Indian Names in New York*, p. 104.

doleful yells of welcome resounded through the
forest. Was this the principal town of that country ? No, it was not. The town in question was
many miles up-stream, a great town, and its name

Hochelaga

was Hochelaga, but it would be rash
for the bearded visitors to attempt to
go thither, for they would be blinded with falling
snow, and their ships would be caught between
ice-floes. This ironical solicitude for the safety
of the strangers has the genuine Indian smack.
The real motive underlying it was doubtless
" protection to home industry ; " why should
the people at Hochelaga get a part of the beads
and red ribbons when there were no more than
enough for the people at Stadacona ? Recourse
was had to the supernal or infernal powers. On
a fine autumn morning a canoe came down the
river, carrying three scowling devils clad in dog-
skins, with inky-black faces surmounted by long
antlers. As they passed the ships they paddled
shorewards, prophesying in a dismal monotone,
until as the canoe touched the beach all three
fell flat upon their faces. Thereupon forth issued
from the woods Donnacona's feathered braves,

An Indian
trick

and in an ecstasy of yelps and groans
seized the fallen demons and carried
them out of sight behind the canopy of leaves,
whence for an hour or so their harsh and guttural hubbub fell upon the ears of the Frenchmen. At last the two young interpreters crawled

out from the thicket and danced about the shore
with agonized cries and gestures of lively terror,
until Cartier from his quarter-deck called out to
know what was the trouble. It was a message,
they said, from the mighty deity Coudouagny,
warning the visitors not to venture upon the
dangerous journey to Hochelaga, inasmuch as
black ruin would surely overtake them. The
Frenchman's reply was couched in language dis-
respectful to Coudouagny, and the principle of
free-trade in trinkets prevailed.

With a forty-ton pinnace and two boats carrying fifty men Cartier kept on up the river,
leaving his ships well guarded in a snug harbour
within the mouth of the stream now known as
the St. Charles. A cheerful voyage of a fortnight
brought the little party to Hochelaga, Cartier
where they landed on a crisp October arrives at
morning. There came forth to meet Hochelaga
them — in the magniloquent phrase of the old
narrator — "one of the principal lords of the
said city," [1] with a large company of retainers,
for thus did their European eyes interpret the
group of clansmen by whom they were wel-
comed. A huge bonfire was soon blazing and
crackling, and Indian tongues, loosened by its
genial warmth, poured forth floods of eloquence,

[1] "L'un des principaulx seigneurs de la dicte ville."
Cartier, *Brief recit de la nauigation faicte es ysles de Canada,*
etc., p. 23.

until presently the whole company took up its march into the great city of Hochelaga. A sketch of this rustic stronghold was published in 1556 in Ramusio's collection of voyages. The name of the draughtsman has not come down to us, but it was apparently drawn from memory by some one of Cartier's party, for while it does not answer in all details to Cartier's description, it is a most characteristic and unmistakable Iroquois town. It was circular in shape. The central portion consisted of about fifty long wigwams, about 150 feet in length by 50 in breadth, framed of saplings tightly boarded in with sheets of bark. Through the middle of each wigwam ran a passageway, with stone fireplaces at intervals coming under openings in the high bark roof whereby some of the smoke might escape. Kettles of baked clay hung over most of the fires, and the smoky atmosphere was redolent of simmering messes of corn and beans and fowl, or, if it were a gala day, of boiled dog, while the fumes of tobacco were omnipresent. On either side were the rows of shelves or benches covered with furs, which served as beds ; while here and there, overlooking sheaves of stone arrows and scattered tomahawks, there dangled flint knives and red clay pipes and dried human scalps. These spacious wigwams were arranged about a large central square, and outside of them a considerable inter-

Hochelaga a typical Iroquois town

val or boulevard intervened between habitations and wall. Such a town might have held a population of from 2500 to 3000 souls, but the actual number was apt to fall short of the capacity. The town wall was ingeniously constructed of three concentric rows of stout saplings. The middle row stood erect in the ground, rising to a height of twelve or fifteen feet ; and the two outer rows, planted at a distance of five or six feet on either side of it, were inclined so as to make a two-sided tent-shaped structure. The three rows of saplings met at the top, and were tightly lashed to a horizontal ridge-pole, while at the bottom, and again about halfway up, they were connected by diagonal cross-braces, after the herring-bone pattern, thus securing great strength and stability. Around the inside of this stout wall, and near the top, ran a gallery accessible by short ladders, and upon the gallery our explorers observed piles of stones ready to be hurled at an approaching foe. Outside in all directions stretched rugged half-cleared fields clad in the brown remnant of last summer's corn crop, and dotted here and there with yellow pumpkins.

The arrival of the white strangers was the cause of wild excitement among the bark cabins and in the open square of Hochelaga. Their demeanour was so courteous and friendly that men, women, and children allowed curiosity to prevail over fear; they flocked about the Frenchmen and felt of their steel weapons and stroked their beards. Sick Indians came up to be touched and cured, trinkets were handed The name about, polite speeches were made, and Montreal at length amid a loud fanfare of trumpets the white men took their leave. Before they embarked the Indians escorted them to the summit of the neighbouring hill, which Cartier named *Mont Royal*, a name which as *Montreal* still remains attached to the hill and to the noble city at its foot.

It was getting late in the season to make further explorations in this wild and unknown country, and upon returning to Stadacona the Frenchmen went into winter quarters. There they suffered from such intensity of cold as the shores of the English Channel never witnessed, Distresses of and presently scurvy broke out with the winter such virulence that scarcely a dozen of the whole company were left well enough to take care of the rest. In vain were prayers and litanies and genuflexions in the snow. The heavenly powers were as obdurate as when Cassim Baba forgot the talismanic word that opened the robbers' cave. But presently Cartier learned from an Indian that a decoction of the leaves of a certain evergreen tree was an infallible cure for scurvy. The experiment was tried with re-

sults that would have gladdened Bishop Berkeley, had he known them, when he wrote his
famous treatise on the virtues of tar water.[1]
Whether the tree was spruce, or pine, or bal-
sam fir, is matter of doubt, but we are told that
Cartier's men showed such avidity that within
a week they had boiled all the foliage of a tree
as big as a full-grown oak, and had quaffed the
aromatic decoction, whereupon their cruel distemper was quickly healed.

The ranks had been so thinned by death
that Cartier was obliged to leave one of his
ships behind. Further exploration must be
postponed. It was the common experience.
A single season of struggle with the savage continent made it necessary to return to Europe
for fresh resources. So it was with Cartier.
The midsummer of 1536 saw him once more
safe within the walls of St. Malo, and confident
that one more expedition would reveal some at
least of the wonders which he had heard of,
comprising all sorts of things from gold and
diamonds to unipeds. As we are confronted
again and again with these resplendent dreams
of the early voyagers to America, we are re-

[1] On its specific use in scurvy, see Berkeley's *Siris*, pp.
86–119, in Fraser's edition of his works, Oxford, 1871, ii.
395–408. The bishop's interest in tar water seems to have
been started by his experiences in America, iv. 262.

minded not only that the wish is father to the thought, but also that the stolid-looking red man is the most facetious of mortals, and in his

Indian tales

opinion the most delightful kind of facetiousness, the genuine epicure's brand of humour, consists in what English slang calls " stuffing," or filling a victim's head with all manner of false information. In Cartier's case one effect was to lead him to kidnap Donnacona and several other chiefs, and carry them to France, that they might tell their brave stories before the king.

Five years elapsed before another expedition was ready for Canada. King Francis made up his mind that a little more flourish of trumpets, such as the crowns of Spain and Portugal indulged in, would not come amiss. Columbus and Gama had been admirals and viceroys ; it was high time for the king of France to create a viceroyalty in the New World. To fill this eminent position he selected Jean François, Sieur de Roberval, a nobleman who held large estates in Picardy. This man he created Lord of Norumbega and Viceroy over Canada, Hochelaga, Saguenay, Newfoundland, and so on through a long string of barbaric names. At

Roberval

the same time Cartier was made captain-general, and in his commission the king declares that the lands of Canada and Hochelaga " form the extremity of Asia toward

the west." [1] The flourish of trumpets was loud
enough to reach the ears of Charles V., but the
Spaniards had become convinced that the codfish coasts contained no such springs of sudden wealth as Cortes and Pizarro had discovered for them, and the Spanish ambassador
at Paris advised his master that the soundest
policy was to let Francis go on unmolested and
waste his money in a bootless enterprise.

The event seemed to justify this cynicism.
It was a dismal tale of misdirected energies. So
little commercial interest was felt in the voyage
that volunteers were not forthcoming and had
to be sought in the jails. So much time was
consumed in getting ready that it was decided
to send on a part of the expedition   Cartier's voy-
in advance, and so in May, 1541, Car-   age, 1541
tier started with three ships, expecting soon to
be overtaken by Roberval. In this expecta-
tion he tarried six weeks on the Newfoundland
coast, until the arrival of August determined
him to wait no longer, and he pushed across
the Gulf of St. Lawrence and up the river. Of
this voyage we have no such full report as of
its predecessor. Very little seems to have been
accomplished in new explorations; at Hochelaga there were rumours of hostile plots on the
part of the red men; and then there was another

---

[1] Harrisse, *Notes sur la Nouvelle France,* " De par le
roy," 17 Oct. 1540.

wretched winter near the site of Quebec; and then a forlorn retreat to the ocean and to France. At one of the harbours on the Newfoundland coast the little fleet of Cartier met that of Roberval, whose detention of a whole year has never been accounted for. Our authorities are here so confused that it is impossible to elicit from them a coherent story. It seems clear, however, that the meeting between the two commanders was not a pleasant one, and that Cartier kept on his way to France, leaving Roberval to shift for himself.

The Lord of Norumbega was not left helpless, however, by this departure. He had sturdy pilots on board, already familiar with these coasts, and one of his three ships was commanded by a veteran navigator who was thought to be unexcelled by any other seaman of France. This was Jean Allefonsce, of the province of Saintonge, over which sweep the salt breezes of the Bay of Biscay. In forty years or more of life upon the ocean he is likely to have visited more than once already these northern waters, such a haunt of Biscayan fishermen. He was now entrusted with an important enterprise. In the Gulf of St. Lawrence the expedition was divided, and it seems clear that while Roberval undertook the task of exploring the river he sent Allefonsce on an ocean trip to find a passage

Jean Alle-fonsce tries to explore the Sea of Verrazano

into the Sea of Verrazano. This voyage is usually mentioned in such terms as to be unintelligible; as for example by the Recollet friar, Sixte le Tac, writing in 1689, who says that Roberval sent Allefonsce northward to Labrador in quest of a passage to the East Indies, but that Allefonsce was so beset with floating ice that he was fain to rest contented with discovering the strait between Newfoundland and the continent in latitude 52°,[1] or, in other words, the Strait of Belle Isle. Now this is of course absurd, for the Strait of Belle Isle had long been familiar to mariners and was a favourite route for entering the Gulf of St. Lawrence. In one of the most recent books, the late Justin Winsor's "Cartier to Frontenac," we get a reverberation of this statement when we are told that " Allefonsce went north along the Labrador coast to find, if possible, a passage to the west. The ice proved so dense that he gave up the search."[2] But while most writers have repeated this state-

[1] "Ce fut lui [Roberval] aussy qui envoya Alphonse très habile pilote xaintongeois vers la Brador pour essayer de trouver un passage aux Indes Orientales, mais il se contenta de decouvrir seulement celuy qui est entre l'isle Terreneuve et la grande Terre du Nord par les 52 degrès, les glaces l'empeschant d'aller plus loing." Sixte le Tac, *Histoire chronologique de la Nouvelle France, publiée pour la première fois d'après le manuscrit original de 1689, par E. Réveillaud*, Paris, 1888, p. 45.

[2] *Cartier to Frontenac*, p. 41.

ment, it is to be observed that the careful and
thoroughly informed Hakluyt, writing in 1589,
Errors in re-
gard to the
voyage of
Allefonsce knows nothing of any such northern
voyage of Allefonsce. The truth
is, that eminent sailor, after returning from his expedition with Roberval, wrote
an account of his voyages, in which he was
aided by a friend, Paulin de Secalart, a geogra-
pher of Honfleur. This narrative, written in
1545, still remains in manuscript, a folio of 194
leaves, and is preserved in the National Library
at Paris.[1] But in 1559, shortly after the death
of Allefonsce, and during that brief period of
quickened curiosity about the man which is
wont to come at such a time, a book was published at Poitiers, entitled "The Adventurous
Voyages of Captain Jean Allefonsce," and this
book ran through at least seven editions. It
was compiled by a merchant of Honfleur
named Maugis Vumenot, and is a thoroughly
uncritical and untrustworthy narrative.[2] It omits
much that Allefonsce tells, and weaves in such
interesting material as Master Vumenot hap-

[1] Its description is *Cosmographie avec espere et regime du
Soleil et du Nord en nostre langue françoyse par Jehan Allefonsce,* Bibliothèque Nationale, MSS. français 676. An
account of it is given in Harrisse, *Découverte de Terre-Neuve,*
p. 153, and *Notes sur la Nouvelle France,* p. 7. See also De
Costa, *Northmen in Maine,* etc., pp. 92–122.

[2] Cf. Weise, *The Discoveries of America,* New York,
1884, p. 352.

pened to have at hand, without much regard to
its historic verity. Such were the naïve methods
of sixteenth century writers.

If we consider what Allefonsce himself tells
us, although his allusions to places are often far
from clear, we cannot fail to see that his voyage
in quest of a western passage in the summer of
1542 was directed not northward but The true direction of Allefonsce's voyage
southward from the Gulf of St. Law-
rence. He seems to have entered
Massachusetts Bay, and may have passed
through Long Island Sound and Hell Gate ;
at all events he has much to say about the town
of Norumbega, which Mercator's map of 1569
places upon Manhattan Island ; and he tells us
that the river of Norumbega is salt for more
than ninety miles from its mouth, which is true
of the Hudson, but not of any other river which
men have sought to associate with Norumbega.
Moreover our good pilot feels confident that
this great river, if followed far enough to the
northward, would be found to unite with the
other great river of Hochelaga, that is, the St.
Lawrence.[1] This notion, of a union between
the Hudson and the St. Lawrence, became a
very common one, and found expression upon
the famous map of Gastaldi in 1553, and upon
other maps.

[1] Cf. Weise, *The Discoveries of America*, New York,
1884, p. 352.

If we were to allow a little free play to our fancy, it would not be difficult to assign a suitable explanation for this voyage of Allefonsce in connection with the expedition of Roberval. There is no longer any doubt that the Hudson River was first made known to Europeans by Verrazano in 1524, and was called by various names, of which perhaps the Grand River was the most common. At the Indian village on Manhattan Island French skippers traded for furs, and in 1540 a French blockhouse was built near the site of Albany for the purpose of protecting such traffic with the red men of the Mohawk valley. The name Norumbega unquestionably first appears with Verrazano's voyage, and for forty years thereafter it was closely associated with the neighbourhood of the Hudson. In reading the string of Roberval's titles — which begin with Norumbega and run through Canada, Hochelaga, Saguenay, etc., down to Newfoundland — it is clear that the king meant to concentrate under his rule the various regions which Verrazano and Cartier had discovered. When the expedition arrives on the American coast it seems not unnatural that the viceroy should send his lieutenant to Norumbega while he himself should prosecute the journey to Hochelaga. Possibly, as some believed, the watery channels pursued by the two might unite. At

Allefonsce visits the Hudson

all events a passage into the Sea of Verrazano
was more likely to be found at the fortieth par-
allel than at the fifty-second.

It is a pity that these amiable old skippers,
in telling of their acts and purposes, should
have paid so little heed to posterity's craving
for full and exact knowledge. Just how far the
good Allefonsce ever got with his Norumbega
voyage, or what turned him back, we are not
informed. We may safely say that he did not
succeed in sailing into the Sea of Verrazano, and
the next summer we find him once more with
Roberval on the St. Lawrence. Thither that
captain had proceeded at the outset after part-
ing company with Allefonsce. Of his fortunes
during the next seventeen months our accounts
are but fragmentary. Hakluyt is unusually brief
and vague, and we have to rely largely upon a
manuscript of 1556,[1] written by the somewhat
mendacious André Thevet, who seems to have
been an intimate friend of Roberval and a boon
companion of the irrepressible buffoon Rabelais.
Provokingly scanty as Thevet often is, there are
times when he goes into full details, and one of
his romantic stories is worthy of mention, since
it probably rests upon a basis of fact.

The expedition of Roberval was intended
not only for exploring the wilderness but for
founding a colony. Homes were to be estab-

[1] See Harrisse, *Notes sur la Nouvelle France*, p. 278.

lished in the New World, and many of the
company brought along with them their wives
and children. Among the young women was
Marguerite Roberval, niece of the Lord of
Norumbega, and on the same ship was a gallant chevalier, and the twain loved one another
not wisely but too well. Roberval
was a man of stern and relentless disposition, and forgiveness of sins
formed no part of his creed. He set his niece
ashore on a small barren island, with an old
Norman nurse who had been in her confidence,
and left them there with a small supply of food
and guns for shooting game or noxious beasts.
As the ship sailed away, the lover leaped into
the sea and by dint of frenzied exertion swam
ashore. The place was dreaded by sailors, who
called it the Isle of Demons, but bears and
wolves were more formidable enemies. On that
island was born, during the year 1542, the first
child of European parents within the vast region
now known as British America, but one after
another, child, father, and nurse, succumbed
to the hardships of the place and died, leaving
the young mother alone in the wilderness.
There for more than two years she contrived
to sustain life, on three occasions shooting a
white bear, and at all times keeping the demons aloof by the sign of the cross, until one
day she was picked up by a fishing vessel and

The charac-
ter of Rober-
val

carried back to France. There Thevet tells us
that he met her a little later, in a village of Peri-
gord, and heard the story from her
own lips. At all events it was much
talked of in France, and forms the
subject of the sixty-seventh tale in the famous
collection of Queen Margaret of Angoulême,
sister of Francis I.[1] The Isle of Demons was
often called by sailors the Isle of the Damsel.

The romance
of Roberval's
niece

Ascending the great river to Cap Rouge,
near the site of Quebec, where Cartier had win-
tered, Roberval made it his headquarters. Little is known as to the course of events, save
that in the following summer Allefonsce had returned, and a trip was made up the Saguenay.
There were severe hardships and many died.
The sternness of Roberval is conspicuous in
the narrative, and may have been called forth
by apparent necessity. There were occasions on
which both men and women were shot for an
example, and the whipping-post was frequently
in requisition, " by which means," observes the
worthy Thevet, " they lived in peace." This is
about all we know of the mighty viceroyalty of
Hochelaga, etc. Lescarbot tells us that in the
course of 1543 the king sent out Cartier once

---

[1] See *Heptameron: Les Nouvelles de Marguerite, Reine
de Navarre*, Berne, 1781, tom. iii. pp. 179–184. In my
copy of this *edition de luxe* the superb engraving by Freu-
denberg represents the lovers seated under palm-trees !

more, who brought home to France the wretched
survivors of the company.[1] About this time
Cartier received from the king a grant of a
manor on the coast of the Channel, not far from
St. Malo, and there we lose sight of the navigator, except for the mention of his death at
that place in 1557. Allefonsce seems to have
been killed in a sea fight about ten years before,
and we are told that Roberval was assassinated
one evening on the street in Paris.

After the failure of this expedition there was
a partial cessation of French enterprise upon
the high seas. The reign of Henry II. was
clouded by the disastrous wars with Spain, in
which France lost the three bishoprics of Metz,
Toul, and Verdun, and French armies were so
woefully defeated at St. Quentin and Gravelines.

Suspension of   The death of the king in 1559 was
French ex-   the signal for the rise of the Guises
ploration   and the pursuance of a policy which
brought on one of the most disastrous civil
wars of modern times. From 1562 to 1598
some historians enumerate eight successive wars
in France, but it is better to call it one great
civil war of thirty-six years, with occasional
truces. It is still more instructive to regard it
all as a phase of the still mightier conflict which
was at the same time raging between Spain and
the Netherlands, and which presently included

[1] Lescarbot, ii. 416.

Queen Elizabeth's England among the combatants. It was not a favourable time for expending superfluous energy in founding new states beyond sea. During the latter half of the century we witness two feeble and ill-starred attempts at planting Huguenot colonies in America, — the attempt of Villegagnon in Brazil in 1557–58, and that of Ribaut in Florida in 1562–65. The latter of these was Ribaut in formidable in purpose; it represented Florida the master thought of Coligny which led Sir Walter Raleigh to plan the founding of an English nation in America. The violent destruction of this Huguenot colony was the last notable exhibition of Spanish power beyond sea in that century of Spanish preëminence. Spanish energy, too, was getting absorbed in the conflict of Titans in Europe.

The affair of Florida was essentially military in purpose and execution. Attempts at planting commercial colonies on the St. Lawrence must wait for some more favourable opportunity. Yet French fishing vessels steadily plied to and fro across the Atlantic. Investigations in the local account-books of such towns as Importance Dieppe and Honfleur lead to the con- of Dieppe in clusion that as many as 200 ships were the sea equipped each year in French ports for fishing in American waters.[1] It was no uncommon

[1] Winsor, *Cartier to Frontenac*, p. 74.

thing for these craft to bring home furs and
walrus ivory. But we hear of little in the way
of exploration. Dieppe, indeed, boasted something like a school of seamanship. It was a city
to which astronomers, geographers, and map-
makers were drawn in order to profit by the
experiences of practical navigators, and where
questions connected with oceanic exploration
were likely to be treated in a scientific spirit.
In those days such men as Pierre Desceliers,
who has been called the creator of French hy-
drography, and whose beautiful maps are now
of great historical importance, made his headquarters at Dieppe. It was a time of keen intellectual curiosity and bold commercial activity;
and nothing was needed but relief from the
oppressive anarchy that had ruled so long to see
France putting forth new efforts to plant colonies and to prepare for maritime empire. The
end of the century saw a new state of things,
the military strength of Spain irretrievably
broken, the policy of France in the hands of
the greatest and wisest ruler that France ever
had, with England and the Netherlands loom-
ing up as powerful competitors in the world beyond seas. Before the rivals lay the American
coasts, inviting experiments in the work of
transplanting civilization. It remained to be
seen how France would fare in this arduous
undertaking.

II

THE BEGINNINGS OF QUEBEC

THE year 1598 was a memorable one in the history of France, for it witnessed the death of that insatiable schemer, Philip II. of Spain, supporter of the Guises, and it also saw the end of the long wars of religion and the promulgation of the Edict of Nantes. The time seemed to be more propitious than before for commercial enterprises, and the thoughts of a few bold spirits turned once more to the St. Lawrence. One of these was the Marquis de la Roche, a Breton noble-man, who obtained from Henry IV. a commission very similar to that under which Roberval had sailed. But so little popular interest was felt in the enterprise that volunteers would not come forward, and it became necessary to gather recruits from the jails. The usual scenes of forlorn and squalid tragedy followed. Roche was cast ashore on the Breton coast in a tempest, and was thrown into a dungeon by the king's enemy, the Duke de Mercœur ; [1] while his convicts were landed on Sable

Voyage of the Marquis de la Roche

---

[1] The "Duke Mercury" of John Smith's *True Travels*, chaps. v., vi.

Island, and only saved from starving by the wild cattle descended from Léry's kine of four-score years before.

While these things were going on there was a skipper of St. Malo, a man of good family and some property, François Gravé, Sieur du Pont, commonly known as Pontgravé, who had made up his mind that the Canada fur-trade was some-thing that ought to be developed. He had sailed up the St. Lawrence as far as Three Rivers, and had feasted his eyes upon the soft glossy pelts of mink and otter, lynx and wol-verene. The thing to do was to get a monopoly of the trade in furs, and with this end in view Pontgravé applied to a friend of the king, a wealthy merchant of Honfleur named Pierre Chauvin and a staunch Huguenot withal. An-other man of substance, the Sieur de Monts, became interested in the scheme, and the three formed a partnership; while the king granted

Pontgravé and Chauvin secure a mo-nopoly of the fur-trade

them a monopoly of the fur-trade on the condition that they should establish a colony. This privilege awakened fierce heart-burnings among the gal-lant skippers of St. Malo, who declared that they had done more than anybody else to maintain the hold of France upon the St. Law-rence country, and there was no justice in sin-gling out one of their number for royal favour, along with merchants from Honfleur and else-

where. Similar complaints were heard from
Rouen, Dieppe, and Rochelle; the parliaments
of Normandy and Brittany took up the matter,
and a fierce outcry was made because Chauvin
and Monts were Protestants. But this argument
naturally went for little with Henry IV., and
the monopoly was granted.

Pontgravé and Chauvin made their headquarters at Tadousac, where the waters of the
Saguenay flow into the St. Lawrence. The traffic in furs went on briskly, but the business of
colonization was limited to the leaving of miserable garrisons in the wilderness to perish of
starvation and scurvy. So things went on from
1599 to 1603, when Chauvin on his third voyage died in Canada. The partnership was thus
broken up, and the monopoly for the moment
went a-begging.

It was only for a moment, however. The
governor of Dieppe since 1589 was Aymar de
Chastes, a stout Catholic of the national party
and a friend of Henry IV. On the great day
of Arques in 1589, when the Leaguers boasted
that their fat Duke of Mayenne,[1] with his army
of 30,000, would make short work of the king
with his 7000, when the fashionable world of
Paris was hiring windows in the Faubourg St.

[1] Mais un parti puissant, d'une commune voix,
Plaçait déjà Mayenne au trône de nos rois.
Voltaire, *La Henriade*, vi. 61.

Antoine, to see the rugged Bearnese brought in tied hand and foot, it was largely through the aid of Chastes that Henry won his brilliant victory and scattered the hosts of Midian.[1]   It was therefore not strange that when, upon the death of Chauvin this scarred and grizzled veteran asked for the monopoly in furs, his request was promptly granted.

De Chastes
succeeds
Chauvin

Chastes soon found an able ally in Pontgravé, but even with the allurements of rich cargoes of peltries it was hard to get people to subscribe money for such voyages. Loans for such purposes were classed on the market as loans at heavy risk, and the rate of interest demanded was usually from 35 to 40 per cent.[2]

While the preparations were briskly going on a new figure entered upon the scene, the noble figure of the founder of New France. Samuel Champlain was now about six and thirty years of age, having been born in or about the year 1567, at Brouage, a small seaport in the province of Saintonge, not many miles south of Rochelle. The district, situated on the march between the Basque and Breton countries, was famous as a

[1] Michelet, *Histoire de France*, xii. 286 ; Gravier, *Vie de Champlain*, p. 6.

[2] Toutain, " Les anciens marins de l'estuaire de la Seine," in *Bulletin de la Société normande de Geographie*, 1898, xx. 134 ; Bréard, *Le vieux Honfleur et ses marins*, Rouen, 1897, p. 59.

nursery of hardy sailors, and the neighbourhood of Rochelle was one of the chief centres
of Huguenot ferment. Champlain's father was
a seafaring man, but nothing is positively
known as to his station in society or as to his
religion. One local biographer calls   The early life
him an humble fisherman, but the   of Champlain
son's marriage contract describes him as of
noble birth. The son was often called by contemporaries the Sieur de Champlain, but that
was chiefly perhaps after he had risen to eminence in Canada. The baptismal names of the
father and mother, Antoine and Marguerite,
indicate that they were born Catholics ; while
Samuel, the baptismal name of the son, affords
a strong presumption that at the time of his
birth they had become Huguenots. In later
life Champlain appears as a man of deeply religious nature but little interested in sectarian disputes, a man quite after the king's own heart,
who realized that there were other things in the
world more important than the differences between Catholic and Huguenot. Champlain was
to the core a loyal Frenchman, without a spark
of sympathy with those intolerant partisans
who were ready to see France dragged in the
wake of Spain.

The early years of this noble and charming
man were mostly spent upon the sea. He was
a true viking, who loved the tossing waves and

the howling of the wind in the shrouds. His strength and agility seemed inexhaustible, in the moment of danger his calmness was un-ruffled as he stood with hand on tiller, calling out his orders in cheery tones that were heard above the tempest.[1] He was a strict disciplina-rian, but courteous and merciful as well as just and true ; and there was a blitheness of mood and quaintness of speech about him that made him a most lovable companion. In the whole course of French history there are few person-ages so attractive as Samuel Champlain.

For several years until the peace of 1598 Champlain served in the army of Henry IV. as deputy quartermaster-general. One of his uncles was pilot major of the Spanish fleets, and after the peace Champlain accompanied him to Seville. A fleet was on the point of sailing for Mexico, under the Admiral Francisco Colombo, and Champlain obtained, through his uncle's influence, the command of one of the ships.

Champlain in the West Indies
The voyage, with the journeys on land, lasted more than two years, and Champlain kept a diary, from which after returning to France he wrote out a narra-tive [2] which so pleased the king that he granted

[1] Champlain, *Traité de la marine et du devoir d'un bon marinier*, pp. 1-7.

[2] An English translation from this MS. was published by the Hakluyt Society in 1859 under the title *Narrative of a*

him a pension. In this relation Champlain described things with the keen insight and careful attention of a naturalist. Shores, havens, and mountains lie spread out before you, with the wonderful effects of snow-clad peaks rising from the masses of tropical verdure, birds of strange colour sing in the treetops, while hearsay griffins, with eagles' heads, bats' wings and crocodiles' tails lurk in the background ; and worse than such monsters, our traveller thinks, are the spectacles of Indians flogged for non-attendance at mass, and heretics burned at the stake. While making a halt at the Isthmus of Panama it occurs to him that a ship-canal at that point would shorten the voyage to Asia even more effectually than the discovery of a northwest passage.

When Champlain returned to France he found Aymar de Chastes preparing to send Pontgravé upon a voyage to Canada. The veteran Pontgravé was brave and wise, resourceful and light-hearted, just the sort of man whom Champlain would be sure to like. It is therefore not strange that we find him embarking in the

Voyage to the West Indies and Mexico. The original MS. was first published in 1870 as the first volume of Champlain's works edited by Laverdière : *Brief discours des choses plus remarquables que Samuel Champlain de Brouage a reconnues aux Indes occidentales au voyage qu'il en a faict en icelles en Lannee mil v^c iiij^{xx} xix,* etc.

enterprise with Father Pontgravé, as he used
affectionately to call him. The two sailed from

Champlain's
first voyage
to Canada

Honfleur on the 15th of March, 1603,
and seventy days later they were
gliding past the mouth of the Saguenay. As they approached the St. Charles they
saw no traces of the Iroquois town of Stadacona.
On they went, as far as Hochelaga, where Cartier had been entertained sixty-eight years before, but not one of its long bark cabins was
left, nor a vestige of its stout triple palisade,
nor a living soul to tell the story of the dire
catastrophe. No Iroquois were now to be met
upon the St. Lawrence except as invaders, nor
were the accents of their speech to be heard
from the lips of the red men who emerged from
the thickets to greet Champlain and Pontgravé.

The disap-
pearance of
the Iroquois
village of
Hochelaga

Another name than " Canada " would
have become attached to that country
had these explorers been the first to
penetrate its wilds. No doubt, whatever, can attach to the facts. There is no doubt
that in 1535 Iroquois villages stood upon the
sites of Montreal and Quebec, or that the
Iroquois language was that of the natives who
dwelt along the shores of the St. Lawrence;
while in 1603 the villages with their people and
their language had vanished from these places,
and instead of them were found Algonquin villages of a much lower type and a ruder people,

known as Adirondacks, and speaking an Algonquian language. The visits of our good Frenchmen have placed dates upon a portion of one of those displacements or wanderings of people that have commonly gone on in barbaric ages alike in the Old World and in the New. Just as we find Hunnish hordes in one age breaking their strength against the great wall of China and in another age mowed down by the swords of Roman and Visigoth in the valley of the Marne, just as we see the Arab smile and hear the Arabic guttural in Cordova and in Lucknow, so in the New World we find Dacotahs or Sioux strayed afar into the Carolinas with their identity veiled under the name "Catawbas," and we recognize in the brave and intelligent Cherokees of Georgia pure-blooded Iroquois, own cousins of the Mohawks.

Now the Iroquois, as we know them, while preëminent in power of organization, have not been a numerous family. Within our historic ken, which is so provokingly narrow, the most fruitful and abounding Indian stock has been that of the Algonquins. They include the Blackfeet of the Rocky Mountains and the Crees of the Hudson Bay country along with the Powhatans of Old Virginia, and Eliot's version of the Bible for the natives of Massachusetts Bay is to-day for the most part intelligible to the Ojibways

The Iroquois displaced by the Algonquins

of Minnesota. Obviously within recent times, that is to say since the fourteenth century, the Algonquins have been for a period of some duration a rapidly multiplying and spreading race, and their weight of numbers for a time proved too much for the more civilized but less numerous Iroquois to withstand. Thus in the Appalachian region we find the mound-building Cherokees retiring from the Ohio valley into Georgia before the advancing swarms of Shawnees ; and we see the Tuscaroras, another band of Iroquois, pushed into Carolina by the expansion of the Algonquin Powhatans and Delawares.

From the time when white men first became interested in the Five Nations of New York, it was a firmly established tradition among the latter that their forefathers had once lived on the St. Lawrence, and in particular that they had a stronghold upon or hard by the site of Montreal ; but that they had been driven to the southward of Lake Ontario by the hostility of a tribe of Algonquins known as Adirondacks.[1] Their first movement seems to have been up the St. Lawrence and across Lake Ontario to the mouth of the Oswego River, where for some time they had their central strongholds. Thence they spread in both directions. Those

[1] Colden's *History of the Five Indian Nations*, London, 1755, i. 23.

who settled at the head of the Canandaigua lake became known by the Algonquin name of Senecas, which has been variously interpreted. Those who stopped at a lake to the eastward, with a marsh at its foot, called Cayuga, or "mucky land," were known by that name. Those who kept up the ancestral council fires, and spread over the divide between the Oswego and Mohawk watersheds, and so on over the gentle rolling country eastward of the Skaneateles or "long lake," have ever since been known as Onondagas, or "men of the hills." Eastward from this central region the people were called Oneidas, or "men of the boulders" (or perhaps "men of granite"), from the profusion of erratic blocks strewn over their territory. Furthest to the east, and most famous of these confederated warriors, were the people who called themselves, or were called by their kinsmen, Caniengas, or "people of the flint" that was used in striking fire; they are best known to history, however, by the name of Mohawk, or "man-eater," bestowed upon them by their Algonquin foes, and which all the Iroquois seem abundantly to have earned by their cannibal propensities.[1]

The driving of the Iroquois up the St. Law-

[1] Beauchamp, *Indian Names in New York*, passim; Morgan, *League of the Iroquois*, pp. 51–53; *Ancient Society*, p. 125.

rence valley into central New York by their Algonquin assailants had remarkable consequences. For military and commercial purposes the situation was the best on the Atlantic slope of North America. The line of the Five Nations stretched its long length between the treasures of beaver and otter on the great lakes and the wampum beds on the coast of Long Island ; but if an enemy, from any quarter of the compass, ventured to attack that long line, forthwith it proved to be an interior line in following which he was apt to be overwhelmed.

Along with this singular advantage of geographical position the Five Nations soon learned the value of political confederation in preserving peace among themselves while increasing their military strength. It was a common thing for Indian tribes of allied lineage to enter into confederation, but no other union of this sort was so artfully constructed, harmonious, and The Iroquois enduring as the League of the Iroconfederacy quois. The date of the founding of this confederacy seems to have been not far from 1450, and we may suppose the great movement from the valley of the St. Lawrence to the lakes of central New York to have occurred about a century earlier. This group of Iroquois, which became the Five Nations, was an overgrown tribe which underwent expansion and segmentation. From the expanding Onondagas the extreme wings first broke off as Senecas and Mohawks; afterward the Onondagas again threw off the Cayugas, while a portion of the Mohawks became marked off as Oneidas. To abolish war throughout their smiling country by referring all affairs of general concern to a representative council was the great thought of the Onondaga chief Hiawatha, who, after bitter opposition in his own tribe, found a powerful ally in Dagonoweda, the Mohawk.[1] Soon after the middle of the fifteenth century the work of these sagacious statesmen was accomplished, and thenceforth the people of the five tribes, from Canandaigua, "the chosen settlement," to Schenectady, "the plain beyond the opening," were proud to call themselves Hodenosaunee, or "Kinsmen of the Long House." Thenceforth they found themselves more than a match for the Algonquin foe, and able to go forth and assail him.

But there were yet other Iroquois kinsmen beside those of the Long House. To the north of the St. Lawrence and of Lake Ontario as far west as the Georgian Bay of Lake Huron one might have encountered the populous tribe of Hurons. In blood and speech they differed no more from Mohawks than a Frank from a Frisian, or a Welshman of Wales from a Welshman of Cornwall. They were the rear of the

---

[1] Hale, *The Iroquois Book of Rites*, chap. ii.

retiring Iroquois host, the buffer that took the
first brunt of the Algonquin onsets. They were
probably the last to leave the valley of the St.
Lawrence. In all probability the towns of
Hochelaga and Stadacona, visited in
1535 by Cartier, were Huron towns,
which in the course of the next half
century were swept away by the last advancing
Algonquin wave. In Champlain's time the
Huron boundaries all stopped west of the
meridian of Niagara, and their population of
20,000 souls was to be found mostly between
Lake Simcoe and the Georgian Bay. Between
these Hurons and Lake Erie, west of the Niagara River, dwelt another tribe of identical
blood and speech, known as the Attiwendaronks ; and south of Lake Erie came the Eries ;
while down in the pleasant valley of the Sus-
quehanna were the villages of the powerful tribe
variously called Susquehannocks, Andastes, or
Conestogas. All these were Iroquois, and were
severely blamed by the Five Nations for refusing to accept Hiawatha's " Gift of Peace " and
join the confederacy. They were scorned as
base and froward creatures, so bent upon having
their own way that they held aloof from the only
arrangement that could put a curb upon the per-
petual slaughter ; such, at least, was the purport
of the solemn speeches that used to be made before the council fires at Onondaga. The Five

Outlying
tribes of
Iroquois

Nations were bound to be peace-makers, even at the cost of massacring all the human population of America. They fully appreciated the injunction " Compel them to enter in." In the course of the seventeenth century we find them annihilating successively the Hurons, Attiwendaronks, Eries, and Conestogas, and after the customary orgies of torment and slaughter, adopting the remnants into their own tribes. In Champlain's time the hatred between the Five Nations and the Hurons had come to such a pass that the latter forgot their ancient hostility to the Algonquins of the St. Lawrence, and were wont to make common cause with them against the dreaded Long House. In these ways, when Champlain arrived upon the scene, a situation had been prepared for him and for France, of which he understood absolutely nothing.

Five years were to pass, however, before the gallant Frenchman was to taste the first fruits of the true significance of the disappearance of Hochelaga. When in the autumn of 1603 the returning ships arrived at Havre, they were met by the news that Chastes was dead. Once more the business must be reorganized, and this time it was the Sieur de Monts, already mentioned, who took the lead. This nobleman turned his thoughts a little to the southward, perhaps with a view to milder winters, and obtained from the king a grant

Designs of the Sieur de Monts

extending from about the latitude of Montreal
as far south as that of Philadelphia.   There is
a Micmac word, Acadie or Aquoddy, which
means simply " place " or " region," and which
appears in such names as Passamaquoddy. In
French it has a romantic flavour, which is perhaps
slightly enhanced in the English Acadia. To the
country since famous under that name the Sieur
de Monts brought his little company in the
spring of 1604. There had been indignant out-
cries over the circumstance that this gentleman
was a Huguenot, but the king laughed at these
protests. He insisted that Monts should so far
defer to public opinion as to take a Romish
priest with him to preach the gospel to the heathen ; but he allowed him also to take a Calvinist minister for his own spiritual solace and en-
livenment. Hardly had the French coast-line
sunk below the horizon when the tones of envenomed theological discussion were heard upon
the quarter-deck. The ship's atmosphere grew
as musty with texts and as acrid with quibbles
as that of a room at the Sorbonne, and now and
Homeric   then a scene of Homeric simplicity
quarrels   was enacted, when the curate and the
parson engaged in personal combat. " I forget
just now," says Champlain, "which was the hard-
est hitter, but I leave you to imagine what a fine
spectacle they made, aiming and dodging blows,
while the sailors gathered around and backed

them according to their sectarian prejudices," [1] some shouting " Hang the Huguenot ! " and others " Down with the Papist ! " On shore similar scenes recurred, with an accompaniment of capering and yelping Indians, to whom it was quite enough that a scrimmage was going on, and who were perhaps scarcely worse fitted than the combatants themselves to understand the issues involved. It happened that amid the hardships which assailed the little company these two zealous men of God succumbed at about the same time, whereupon, says one of our chroniclers with a shudder, the sailors buried them in the same grave, expressing a hope that after so much strife they would repose in peace together.[2]

In our brief narrative there is no need for entering into the details of this first experience of white men in Acadia. The experiment Occupation extended over three years, during of Acadia which there were voyages back and forth across the ocean with reinforcements to offset the losses from disease. Among the company, besides its leaders, were two men of rare and excellent quality, the Baron de Poutrincourt and Marc Lescarbot, an advocate and man of letters who was seized by a sudden inclination for wild life. Among Lescarbot's accomplishments was a knack of turning off long Alexandrine verses by

[1] Champlain, *Voyages*, 1632, i. 46.
[2] Sagard, *Histoire du Canada*, 1636, p. 9.

the yard, but what was of far more value, he wrote a shrewd and pithy prose, abounding in good sense and cheer. After the priceless writings of Champlain himself there are few books about the beginnings of New France with which we should be so loath to part as the three teeming volumes of Lescarbot.

The first attempt at settlement was made at the mouth of the river Ste. Croix, but the fancy of Poutrincourt was captivated by the beautiful gulf to which the English in later days gave the name of Annapolis. He obtained from Monts a grant of the spot with its adjacent territory, Founding of and called it Port Royal. There after Port Royal, later Anna- a while the work of these colonists was polis concentrated, while Champlain spent much time in exploring and delineating the coasts. Of making charts he was never weary, and in following sinuous shore-lines he found delight. One of his first discoveries was the grand and picturesque island which he called " isle of the desert mountains," " L'Isle des Monts Déserts," a name which to this day by its noticeable accent on the final syllable preserves a record of this French origin. A little further to the west he entered and explored for Champlain some distance the Penobscot, which explores the New Eng- fishermen often called the river of land coast Norumbega, but he found no traces of the splendid city into which popular fancy had magnified Allefonsce's Indian village upon the island of Manhattan.[1] Farther on he ascended the Kennebec, and was correctly told by Indians of the route to the St. Lawrence by the valley of the Chaudière, the route which was traversed with such bitter hardship by Benedict Arnold and his men in 1775. As the French navigator passed Casco Bay he began to notice a marked superiority in the Indians over the squalid Micmacs and Etetchemins of Acadia. The wigwams were better built, and the fields of maize, beans, and pumpkins wore a kind of savage cheerfulness under the scorching July sun. Champlain entered the Charles River, and mistook it for the great stream which was soon to be explored by Henry Hudson. After duly astonishing the natives of the triple-peaked peninsula, he passed on to Plymouth, sailed around Cape Cod, and proceeded as far as Nauset Harbour, where the supplies began to give out, and a direct return was made to the Bay of Fundy.

The object of this coasting voyage was to see if any spot could be found for a settlement that would be preferable to those already visited in Canada or on the Bay of Fundy. For a moment the Charles River seems to have tempted these worthy Frenchmen, but they decided to go fur-

[1] In Gravier's *Vie de Samuel Champlain*, Paris, 1900, pp. 40–49, the reader will find more or less uncritical speculation connected with this little summer voyage.

ther. Their narrative indicates a much greater
coast population of red men than was found by
the Mayflower Pilgrims fifteen years later, and
enables us to form some idea of the magnitude
of the pestilence which in the interval nearly de-
populated the shores of Massachusetts Bay. In
1605 all the best spots seemed to show Indian
villages. The next summer Champlain made

A second ex-
ploration of
the Massa-
chusetts
coast

another reconnoitring voyage from
Port Royal, in company with Poutrincourt. They lost but little time in
getting to Cape Cod, and then in
rounding Cape Malabar they had a singular experience. At a distance of a league and a half
from the shore they found the depth of water
rapidly diminishing to less than a fathom, while
on every side the waves leaped and gambolled
in the wildest confusion. They got their bark
across this ugly shoal with a broken rudder, little dreaming that only four years before the same
spot, proudly rearing its head above the sea, had
been described by Bartholomew Gosnold under
the name of Nauset Island. It had lately been
beaten down and submerged by the angry waters, but nearly three centuries were consumed in
washing away the fragments. The sea is now six
fathoms deep there.[1]

After getting clear of this dangerous place
Poutrincourt put into Chatham Harbour for re-

[1] De Costa, *Pre-Columbian Discovery of America*, p. 97.

La grande baye

Croix blanche

Brest

Belle isle
Isle sichet
Cap de grat
Cap rouge

Groye

Baye dorge

Les isles a Chauaux
Baye blanche

C St Iean

Isles des sougues
Isle de moy
C. de bonne vst

Le Golphe St Laurens

Antycosty

Terre neuue

Bayes

Baye de l

Cap S^{te} Fr.

Isle aux oyseaux

Cap de ray

romee

70

Ste Claire

Rocher

Finouse
Isles despoirs
Cap de raga

I. St Paul
C. St Laurens

Niganis
Cap Enfumé

Gransibou

Cap breton
Port aux Anglois

Cap St Antoine

Canceau
Port de soualette
Iles

32

Isles St Pierre

4

68

B
C. Ste Marie

66

C

Ban uuert

Banquereaux

Isle de sable

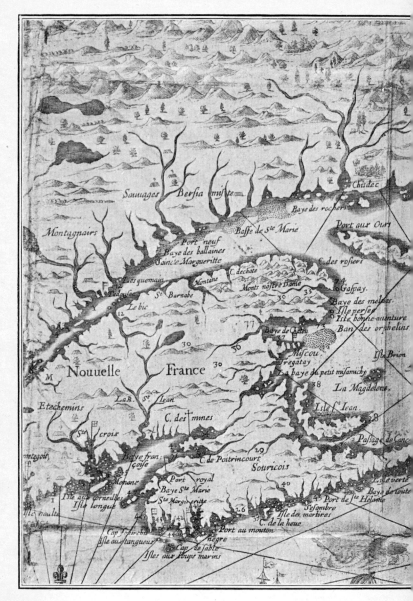

Sauuages Bersia misite

Chisdec

Baye des rochers

Port aux Ours

Basse de Ste Marie

Montagnairs

Port neuf
Baye des ballaines
Saincte Margueritte

C. des rosiers

Lesquemain

C. dechate

Montane

Monts nostre Dame

Gaspay

Tadousac

St Barnabe

Baye des meltes

Isle perse

Le bic

Isle bonne-auenture

12

Ban des orphelins

77

Baye de Chalu

Isle Brion

30

50

Miscou
tregatay

Nouuelle   France

La baye du petit misamichy

38

30

La Magdelene

Etechemins

LaB. St Iean

Isle St Iean

8

Ste croix

C. des mnes

Passage de Canc

29

Baye fran
çoise

C. de Poitrincourt

Souricois

Menane

Port royal

40

Isle aux corneille

Baye Ste Marie

Isle verte

Isle longue

Ste Margrrite

Port de Ste Helene

Baye de toute

46

Isle multa

Isle des martires

Desombre

26

C. de la heue

Cap Fourchu

Port au mouton

Isle au tangueur

negre

Cap de sable

Isles aux Loups marins

THE GULF OF ST. LAWRE

pairs, and there he remained a fortnight, closely watched from the bushes by peering red men who one morning before daybreak came swarming about a party of sleeping Frenchmen, and killed several. Thence our voyagers kept on to Hyannis, and from that neighbourhood descried a shore-line to the southward, which must have been either Martha's Vineyard or Nantucket. By this time Poutrincourt had made up his mind that Port Royal was the best place for his colony after all, and so the prow was turned in that direction.

Things went well enough with them until in a stress of weather near Mount Desert their rudder broke, and their last hundred and fifty miles were far from comfortable. As they entered the harbour of Port Royal a singular spectacle greeted them. That fortress consisted of a large wooden quadrangle enclosing a court-yard. At one corner, which came down to the water's edge, was an arched gateway flanked by rude bastions mounting a few cannon. One side of the quadrangle comprised the dining-room and officers' quarters, on the second side were the barracks for the men, on the third the kitchen and oven, and on the fourth A picturesque the store-rooms. Now on the No- welcome vember evening when Champlain and Poutrincourt sailed into the harbour they saw the buildings brightly lighted and the arch surmounted

by the royal arms supported on either hand by
the heraldic emblems of Baron Poutrincourt
and the Sieur de Monts. While the weary voyagers were admiring the pageant there stepped
forth from the gateway no less a personage than
old Neptune, Lord of the Ocean, with a pom-
pous retinue of Tritons, who marched with
measured step to meet the ship, declaiming long
Alexandrine rhymed couplets of praise and
welcome. Thus was the tedium of the wilderness relieved by the ingenious Lescarbot, whose
active brain was never idle, but in the intervals
of work was sure to be teeming with quips and
quirks and droll conceits. During the summer,
he had kept the men at work to good purpose,
and not only raised a crop of maize, but made
a respectable beginning with barley, wheat, and
rye. It was to a well-stocked home that he
politely ushered the voyagers, after wanderings
which he would refrain from comparing with
those of Æneas and Ulysses, inasmuch as he
did not like to soil their holy missionary enterprise with unclean pagan similitudes. In such
whimsicalities there was a strong sympathy
between the mariner of Saintonge and the lawyer of Vervins. Champlain praised Lescarbot's
thrifty housekeeping, and devised a plan whereby
their table might be always well supplied. The
magnates at Port Royal, who occupied the
dining-room, were fifteen in number; Cham-

plain formed them into an order of knighthood, which he called " The Order of Good Times," and each member in regular rotation was Grand Master of the Order for one day, during which he was responsible not only for the supply of the larder but for the cooking and serving of the meals. The result was a delicious sequence of venison, bear, and grouse, ducks, geese, and plover, as well as fresh fish innumerable, to go with their bread-stuffs and dried beans. Lescarbot boasted that the fare could not be excelled in the best res-taurants of Paris, and they had brought more-over such a generous quantity of claret that every man in the colony received three pints daily. Under such circumstances we need not wonder that there was no scurvy, or that there were only four deaths during the winter. Such comfort and immunity were unusual in those improvident days.

It was with high hopes that these blithe Frenchmen hailed the approach of spring, but its arrival brought unwelcome news and re-minded them of the flimsiness of the basis on which such hopes had been sustained. The merchants and fishermen of Normandy and Brittany had never approved of the monopoly granted to Monts; on the contrary they had never ceased to fight against it at court with money and personal influence, and now at last they had procured a repeal of the monopoly. Monts had spent on the enterprise a sum exceeding $100,000 of our modern money; he was allowed an indemnity of $6000 provided he could collect it from fur-traders. The blow was decisive. If it proved so hard to found colonies even with the advantages of a monopoly, clearly there was no use in going on without such aid. The good Poutrincourt could not be induced to give up his plans for Port Royal, but three years elapsed before he was enabled to renew his work there. Meanwhile we must follow the fortunes of Champlain and Monts after their return to France.

Collapse of De Monts' monopoly

They first betook themselves to Paris, to confer with the king; and Champlain tells us how day after day he walked the streets of the great city like a man in a dream. In early days he had loved the ocean and felt suffocated in an air that was not spiced with adventure. He had now left his heart in the wilderness, a subtle robber that in such matters never makes restitution. He longed to follow up each entrancing vista in the woodland, and to improve his acquaintance with its denizens, four-footed or winged as well as human. Especially was his curiosity whetted by the recollection of the mighty river which he had once ascended for so many miles. At

Champlain turns his attention to Canada

Hochelaga, or rather upon the shore where that barbaric town had once stood, he had heard of oceans to the westward, by which his informants doubtless meant the great lakes, and he had been told of a cataract a league in width, down which leaps a mighty mass of water, which certainly sounds to our ears like a reference to Niagara Falls. Champlain wished to see such things for himself, and he believed that the St. Lawrence fur-trade would prove a source of great wealth ; nor was he at all lacking in missionary zeal. He was more than once heard to say that the saving of a soul is worth more than the conquest of an empire. Here then was important work which he felt that Frenchmen were called upon to do. He consulted with his comrades Monts and Pontgravé, and found in them abundant sympathy. Henry IV. was inclined to look with favour upon such schemes, but his able minister Sully took a different view. The European schemes of these two statesmen were far-reaching and of the utmost importance, and Sully believed that France had need at home of all the able-bodied men she could muster ; it was poor economy, he thought, to be wasting lives in Canada. There was also the cry against monopolies, but Henry nevertheless yielded so far as to renew to Monts the monopoly in furs for one year, a concession which was far from showing the king's customary soundness of judgment, since it was too brief to be of much use. The grantee and his friends, however, could go on in the hope of further renewals; and so in fact they did.

In April, 1608, the expedition sailed from Honfleur, Champlain following Pontgravé at a

The expedition of 1608

week's interval. On arriving at Tadousac our French adventurers got into further trouble in the matter of Father Adam's will. Pontgravé found a party of Basques trading with the Indians, and so far were they from taking his remonstrance in good part that a tussle ensued in which they boarded his ship, killing and wounding some of his men, and seized all his fire-arms. But on the arrival of Champlain the strangers became more peacefully inclined, and an agreement was made by which the whole matter was referred to the courts of justice in France.

Champlain then pursued his way up-stream past the island of Orleans to the narrow place where a mighty promontory rears its head over

Quebec founded

opposite Point Levi. The French continued calling it by its Algonquin name *Quebec*, or " The Narrows," [1] and there, in what is now the Lower Town, they speedily reared a stack of buildings enclosed by a wooden wall mounting a few cannon and loopholed for musketry. While the building was going on

[1] Parkman, *Pioneers of France*, p. 329.

there was a leaven of treason at work in the company. A locksmith, named Duval, took it into his head that more was to be gained from playing into the hands of the Spaniards who had not yet left Tadousac than from loyally serving his own country. What private motives may have urged him we do not know. The plan was to murder Champlain and hand over the new fortress and all the property to the Basques. But the secret was entrusted to too many persons, and so came to Champlain's ears. Just as he had learned all the details a pinnace sent up from Tadousac by Pontgravé arrived upon the scene, and in it was a man whose fidelity was above suspicion. Champlain instructed him to invite Duval and three accomplices Treachery to a social evening glass in the cabin, foiled telling them that the wine was a present from some Basque friends. The bait was eagerly swallowed, and no sooner had the plotters set foot aboard the pinnace than to their amazement they were seized and handcuffed. It was not clear just how far the plot had spread, but it mattered little now. In the middle of the summer night the little colony was aroused from its slumbers, and many a heart quaked with fear as the announcement was made of the detection of the plot and the arrest of the ringleaders. The long rays of the morning sun revealed the severed head of the locksmith Duval adorning the wooden gateway of the courtyard; his three accomplices were sent to France to work in the galleys; and a proclamation of pardon without further inquiry put everybody else at his ease. Treason and assassination had suddenly become unpopular.

A terrible winter followed. When Pontgravé set sail for France in September with a magni-

The first winter at Quebec

ficent cargo of furs he left Champlain at Quebec with twenty-eight men. At the end of May only nine of these were left alive. At last the good Pontgravé appeared with reinforcements and supplies, and it was arranged that he should carry on his trading at Quebec while Champlain should explore the country. This was a task the meaning of which was to be learned only through harsh experience, but it was obvious from the first that it would involve penetrating the forest to a great and unknown distance from any possible civilized base of operations. It was work of immense difficulty. To carry on such work with an army had well-nigh overtaxed the genius of such commanders as Soto and Coronado, with the treasury of the Indies to back them. For Champlain, without any such resources, different methods must be sought. He must venture into the wilderness with a handful of followers and as little encumbrance as possible of any sort. There seemed to be but one feasible way of approaching this problem, and this was to cultivate the friendship of such native tribes as might be most ser- viceable to him on his long routes. By assimilating these expeditions to journeys through a friendly country the risks might be greatly diminished, and the solid results indefinitely increased.

Friendship with the In- dians the con- dition of successful ex- ploration

It was such considerations as these that started French policy in America upon the path which it was destined thenceforth to follow to the end. It was a choice that was fraught with disaster, yet it would be unjust to blame Cham- plain for that. Nothing short of omniscience could have looked forward through the tangle of wilderness politics that seems so simple to us looking backward. For Champlain's purposes his choice was natural and sagacious, but as to the particular people with whom he should ally himself he can hardly be said to have had any choice. Grim destiny had already selected his allies. The valley of the St. Lawrence was the route for the fur-trade, and friendship must be preserved with the tribes along its banks and in- ward on the way to those great seas of which Champlain had heard. The tribes on the St. Lawrence were Algonquins whom the French called Montagnais, but who were afterward known as Adirondacks to the English of New

This condi- tion deter- mines the subsequent French policy

York. They were less intelligent and more barbarous than the Iroquois.   Agriculture and

Character of
the Indians
of Canada

village life were but slightly developed
among them, they were more dependent upon hunting and fishing, and as
they showed less foresight in storing provisions
for the winter their numbers were more frequently depleted by famine and disease. Farther
up the great river and commanding the northwestern trails were the Ottawas, another Algonquin people considerably more advanced than
the Montagnais ; while southerly from the
Ottawas and bordering on the Georgian Bay,
as already observed, were the Hurons, who
rather than join the league of their Iroquois
brethren preferred to maintain a sullen independence, and to this end kept up an alliance
with their Algonquin neighbours. For such
conduct the Hurons were denounced by the
confederated Iroquois as the vilest of traitors.

Thus the allies marked out for Champlain
and his colony were . the neighbouring Algonquins and the Hurons. It was absolutely necessary that friendship with these tribes should be
maintained. In the autumn of 1608 Champlain

Champlain
allies himself
to the Ot-
tawas and
Hurons

learned that it was in his power to
do them a signal favour.   A young
Ottawa chief who happened to visit
Quebec was astounded at its massive
wooden architecture and overwhelmed with awe

at the voice of the cannon and the distant effects wrought by their bullets. Could not these weird strangers be induced to hurl their thunders and lightnings at the insolent enemy of the Algonquins? The suggestion suited Champlain's love of adventure as well as his policy. It was an excellent means of getting access to the Ottawa's country. Late in the following June the woods about Quebec resounded with the yells of three hundred newly arrived Hurons and Ottawas impatient to start on such an expedition as these forests had never witnessed before. It is a pity that we have no account of it from the red man's point of view; it is fortunate, however, that we have such a narrative as Champlain's own.

On the 28th of June, 1609, after the customary feast and war dance, they started from Quebec, some three to four hundred barbarians in bark canoes, and Champlain A war party with eleven other Frenchmen, clad in doublets protected with light plate armour, and armed with arquebuses, in a shallop, which the Indians assured Champlain could pass without serious hindrance to the end of their route. The weapons of the red men were stone arrows, lances, and tomahawks, but already there were many sharp French hatchets to be seen which had been bought with beaver skins. Their route lay across that broad stretch of the St. Lawrence known as Lake St. Peter to the river which a generation later received the name of Richelieu. There they paused for some fishing and feasting, and something happened which has been characteristic of savage warfare in every age. A fierce quarrel broke out among the Indians, and three fourths of the whole number quit the scene in a towering passion and paddled away for their northern homes. The depleted war party, taking a fresh start, soon reached the rapids and carrying-place above Chambly, and there it was found that the shallop could go no further, since she could not stem the rapids, and was too heavy to be carried. Why the Indians had misinformed their white ally on this point it would be hard to say. Perhaps the inborn love of hoaxing may have prevailed over military prudence, or perhaps they may have entertained misplaced notions of the Frenchman's supernatural powers. At all events the shallop must go back to Quebec, but Champlain decided to go forward in a canoe, and from his men he selected two volunteers as companions. After they had passed the portage there was a grand roll-call, and it was found that the total force was four and twenty canoes carrying sixty feathered warriors and the three white men.

As they approached the noble lake which now bears the name of Champlain, but was long known as Lake of the Iroquois, their movements became more circumspect, they sent scouts in advance, and occasionally they consulted the tutelar spirits of departed Algonquin and Huron heroes. To the pious Champlain this sort of invocation seemed like an uncanny attempt to raise the Devil, but he observed it narrowly and described it fully, according to his custom. A small circular tent was raised, of saplings covered with deerskins, and into it crawled the medicine-man, with shudders and groans, and drew together the skins which curtained him off from the spectators. Then the voice of the tutelar spirit was heard in a thin shrill squeak, like that of a Punch and Judy show, and if the manifestation were thoroughly successful the frail tent was rocked and swayed hither and thither with frantic energy. This motion was thought by the awe-struck spectators to be the work of the spirits, but the scoffing Champlain tells us that he caught several distinct glimpses of a human fist shaking the poles, — which would seem to be a way that spirits have had in later, as in earlier times.

As the war party came nearer and nearer to the enemy's country they took more pains in scouting, and at last they advanced only by night. As the sky reddened in the morning they would all go ashore, draw up their canoes under the bushes, and slumber on the carpet of moss and pine-needles until sunset; then they would stealthily embark and briskly ply the paddles until dawn. It was on the 29th of July, a full month after leaving Quebec, that they were approaching the promontory since famous under its resounding Iroquois name of Ticonderoga, or "meeting of the waters," since there Lake George is divided only by a thin strip of land from Lake Champlain; as they were approaching this promontory late in the evening they descried a dark multitude of heavy elm-bark canoes which were at once recognized as Iroquois. Naval battles are not to the red man's taste. The Iroquois landed at once and began building a barricade, while the invaders danced a scornful jig in their canoes, and the very air was torn asunder with yells. All night the missiles in vogue were taunts and jeers, with every opprobrious and indecent epithet that the red man's gross fancy could devise. Early in the morning the invaders landed, all except the Frenchmen, who lay at full length, covered with skins. There was no thought of tactics. The landing was unopposed, though the enemy were at least three to one. There were as many as 200 of them, all Mohawks, tall, lithe, and many of them handsome, the best fighters in the barbaric world. In the ordinary course of things the invaders would have paid dearly for their rashness. As it was, their hearts began to quake, and they called

War dances

aloud for Champlain. Then he arose and coolly stepped ashore before the astounded Mohawks, while his two comrades moving to a flank position stationed themselves among the trees. Half palsied with terror at this supernatural visitation, the Mohawks behaved like staunch men, and raised their bows to shoot, when a volley from Champlain's arquebus, into which he had stuffed four balls, instantly slew two of their chiefs and wounded another. A second fatal shot, from one of the other Frenchmen, decided the day. The Mohawks turned and fled in a panic, leaving many prisoners in Algonquin hands. Most of these poor wretches were carried off to the Huron and Ottawa countries, to be slowly burned to death for the amusement of the squaws and children. There was an intention of indulging to some extent in this pastime on the night following the victory, but Champlain put a stop to it. The infliction of torture was a sight to which he was not accustomed ; at the hissing of the live flesh under the firebrand he could not contain himself, but demanded the privilege of shooting the prisoner, and his anger was so genuine and imperative that the barbarians felt obliged to yield. After this summer day's work there was a general movement homewards. It was a fair average specimen, doubtless, of warfare in the

The Mohawks panic-stricken by fire-arms

Stone Age; a long, desultory march, a random fight, a few deaths on the field and a few more at the stake, and nothing definitely accomplished.

This last remark, however, will not apply to Champlain's first forest fight. A specimen of the Stone Age in all other particulars, it was in one particular — the presence of the three Frenchmen — entirely remote from the Stone Age. In that one particular it not only accomplished something definite, but it marked an epoch. Of the many interesting military events associated with Ticonderoga it seems the most important. There was another July day 149 years later when a battle was fought at Ticonde-

This battle began a deadly hostility between the French and the Iroquois

roga in which 20,000 men were engaged and more than 2000 were killed and wounded. That battle, in which Americans and British were woefully defeated by the Marquis de Montcalm, was a marvellous piece of fighting, but it is now memorable only for its prodigies of valour which failed to redeem the dulness of the English general. It decided nothing, and so far as any appreciable effect upon the future was concerned, it might as well not have been fought. But the little fight of 1609, in which a dozen or more Indians were killed, marks with strong emphasis the beginning of the deadly hostility between the French in Canada and the strongest Indian power on the continent of North America. In all human probability the breach between Frenchmen and Iroquois would in any case have come very soon; it is difficult to see what could have prevented it. But in point of fact it actually did begin with Champlain's fight with the Mohawks.

On the July day when the Frenchman's thunder and lightning so frightened those dusky warriors, a little Dutch vessel named the Half-Moon, with an English captain, was at anchor in Penobscot Bay, while the ship's carpenter was cutting and fitting a new foremast. A few weeks later the Half-Moon dropped anchor above the site of Troy and within the very precincts over which the warriors of the Long House kept watch. How little did Henry Hudson imagine what a drama had already been inaugurated in those leafy solitudes! A few shots of an arquebus on that July morning had secured for Frenchmen the most dangerous enemy and for Dutchmen and Englishmen the most helpful friend that the mysterious American wilderness could afford.

THE LORDS OF ACADIA. — LATER HISTORY OF CHAMPLAIN

WE must now turn our attention for a moment from Quebec to the Bay of Fundy, where it will be remembered that the withdrawal of the monopoly once granted to Monts had for the moment brought things to a standstill. While Monts and Champlain had forthwith renewed their labours on the banks of the St. Lawrence, Poutrincourt had clung to his beloved settlement at Port Royal. Thither he returned in 1610 with a good priest who converted and baptized the squalid Micmacs of the neighbourhood, and then found it hard to restrain them from testing the efficacy of their new religion by sallying forth with their tomahawks against the nearest heathen tribes. A certified list of baptisms was drawn up, and Poutrincourt's son, usually known by the family name of Biencourt, returning next year to France for assistance, carried with him this list as a partial justification of the enterprise. Arriving

Poutrincourt returns to Port Royal, 1610

in Paris the gallant young sailor found the world turned topsy-turvy. The great Henry had been murdered by Ravaillac. "Never was king so much lamented as this," says James Howell in one of his letters.[1] The effects upon Europe were far-reaching, and in the New France, which had as yet been scarcely more than half ushered into existence, a new and unexpected turn was given to the course of events.

The society of the Jesuits, which began in the year 1534 with seven members, had now come to number not less than 7000, and it was everywhere recognized as one of the most powerful agencies of the counter-reformation. In many directions its influence was beneficial, but there can be no doubt as to its disastrous results in France. The dagger of Ravaillac pointed the way to the discontinuance of the States-General, the expatriation of the Huguenots, the wasting warfare of the last days of Louis XIV., the degrading despotism of the next reign, and the ruthless surgery of the guillotine. Such were the cumulative results of the abandonment of the broad and noble policy inaugurated by Henry in 1598. At the time of his death they were of course too remote to be foreseen, but it was clear to everybody that the power of the

Remoter consequences of the death of Henry IV.

[1] Howell's *Familiar Letters*, i. 49.

Jesuits was rapidly growing, and it was dreaded by many people for its ultramontane and Spanish tendencies.

At that time the spirit of propaganda was very strong among the Jesuits; they aimed at nothing short of the conversion of the world, and displayed in the work such energy, such ability, such unalloyed devotion as the world has never seen surpassed. As early as 1549 St. Francis Xavier had penetrated to the remotest East and set up a flourishing church in Japan. Before the death of Claudio Aquaviva in 1615 they had made their way into China. They had already established Christian communities in Brazil, and about this time began their ever memorable work among the Indians of Paraguay. It was quite in the natural course of things that they should include New France in their far-reaching plans. From Henry IV. they obtained but slight and grudging recognition, but his death for a moment threw the reins quite into their hands. There is something irresistibly funny in the alliance of the three women who made the success of the Jesuits their especial care, when one thinks of their various relations with the lamented king, — Marie de Medicis, the miserable and faithless queen; Henriette d'Entraigues, the vile mistress; and Antoinette, the admirable Marchioness de Guercheville, whom

The far-reaching plans of the Jesuits

Henry had wooed in vain. The zealous fathers might well believe that Satan and the good angels were alike enlisted in their behalf. Young Biencourt soon learned that resistance was useless. It was in vain that the merchants of Dieppe, who were fitting out a new expedition for America, protested that they would have no Jesuit priests, or other agents of the king of Spain, on board. Madame de Guercheville forthwith raised money by subscription, and bought a controlling interest in the business. So the Jesuits came to Port Royal, and bitter were the disputes which they had with Poutrincourt and his high-spirited son Biencourt. An Indian sagamore of the neighbourhood, who loved these old friends, the grantees and true lords of Port Royal, came forward one day with a suggestion for simplifying the situation and securing a quiet life. Provided he could be sure it would be agreeable, he would take great pleasure in murdering the newcomers! To his surprise this friendly service was declined. The grantees found that there was no contending against money. Loans were offered to Poutrincourt in emergencies when he had not the courage to refuse them, and thus a load of debt was created with the result that on his next visit to France, in 1613, he was thrown into prison.

At that juncture a ship bearing the inau-

They secure an interest in Acadia

spicious name of Jonas was fitted up with
Jesuit money and manned by persons entirely
in the interest of that order. Madame de
Guercheville had bought out all the rights and
claims of Monts to lands in Acadia, and she

*Madame de
Guercheville
obtains a
grant of the
coast from
Acadia to
Florida*

had also obtained from the boy king,
Louis XIII., a grant of all the territory between the river St. Lawrence
and Florida. Here was a grant that
came into direct conflict with that
which James I. of England had given only six
years before to his great double-headed Virginia Company. According to this new French
charter the settlers at Jamestown were mere
trespassers upon territory over which Madame
de Guercheville was lady paramount ! Would
she venture to claim their allegiance ?

Nothing nearly so bold was attempted ; but
when the Jonas arrived on the Acadian coast,
the chief of the expedition, a gentleman of the
court named La Saussaye, set up a standard
bearing Madame de Guercheville's coat of
arms. At Port Royal he picked up a couple of
Jesuits and thence stood for Penobscot Bay,

*La Saussaye
in French-
man's Bay*

but first he entered Frenchman's Bay
at Mount Desert, and dropped anchor
there, for the place attracted him.
Presently a spot was found so charming that it
was decided to make a settlement there. It was
on the western shore of Somes Sound, between

Flying Mountain and Fernald Cove. Scarcely had work begun there when a sloop of war came into the sound, carrying fourteen guns, and at her masthead was flying the little red flag of England. She was commanded by young Captain Samuel Argall, who had come all the way from James River to fish for cod, but incidentally Sir Thomas Dale, who was then governing Virginia under the title of High Marshal, had instructed him to look out for any Frenchmen who might have ventured to trespass upon the territory granted by King James to the Virginia Company. Argall had picked up some Indians in Penobscot Bay who told him of the white men at Mount Desert, and from their descriptions he recognized the characteristic shrugs and bows of Frenchmen. When his flag appeared in Somes Sound, the French commander La Saussaye, with some of the more timid ones, took to the woods, but a few bold spirits tried to defend their ship. It was of no use. After two or three raking shots the English boarded and took possession of her. The astute Argall searched La Saussaye's baggage until he found his commission from the French government, which he quietly tucked into his pocket. After a while La Saussaye, overcome by hunger, emerged from his hiding-place and was received with extreme politeness by Argall, who ex-

The French captured by Argall

pressed much regret for the disagreeable necessity under which he had laboured. It was a pity to have to disturb such estimable gentlemen, but really this land belonged to King James and not to King Louis. Of course, however, the noble chevalier must be acting under a royal commission, which would lay the whole burden of the affair upon the shoulders of King Louis and exonerate the officers who were merely acting under orders. So spake the foxy Argall, adding with his blandest smile that, just as a matter of formal courtesy, he would like to see the commission. We can fancy the smile growing more grim and Mephistophelean as the bewildered Frenchman hunted and hunted. When at length it appeared that La Saussaye could produce no such document Argall began to bluster and swear. He called the Frenchmen pirates, and confiscated all their property, scarcely leaving a coat to their backs. Then as he had not room enough for all the prisoners, he put La Saussaye, with one of the Jesuit fathers and thirteen men, into an open boat and left them to their fate, which turned out to be a kindly one, for after a few days they were picked up by a French merchant ship and carried back to the Old World.

As for the other Jesuit father with thirteen other men, Argall carried them to Jamestown,

Argall's trick

where that great stickler for martial law, Sir Thomas Dale, was inclined to hang them all without ceremony; but the wisdom of Master Reynard was Argall's, and he saw that this would be going too far. It might make serious trouble between the two Crowns, and would tend to reveal his trickery in a way that would be awkward. So he revealed it himself to Sir Thomas Dale, pulled La Saussaye's commission from his pocket, saved the lives of the captives, and remained master of the situation. Presently he sailed for the north again with three ships and burned the settlement at Port Royal, destroying the growing crops and carrying away the cattle and horses. *Argall returns and burns Port Royal* At the moment of the catastrophe Biencourt and most of his armed men were absent, and when they returned they were too few to engage with Argall; so after a fruitless parley and much recrimination the English skipper sailed away. Next year the Baron de Poutrincourt was slain in battle in France, and his steadfast son Biencourt, succeeding to the barony and the title, still remained devoted to the father's beloved Port Royal. He obtained fresh recruits for the enterprise, and the little wooden town rose Phœnix-like from its ashes. At the French court there was grumbling over the conduct of Argall, and complaint was made to King James; and there the matter rested.

The death of the elder Poutrincourt occurred in 1615. We must now return for a moment to 1609 and take up the story of Champlain after his memorable experience at Ticonderoga. In June, 1610, he was called upon to repeat it on a larger scale. A party of 100 Mohawks had advanced as far as the site of Contrecœur, on the peninsula formed there by the St. Lawrence and the Richelieu, a few miles above the mouth of the latter river, and there they were overwhelmed by a large force of Algonquins aided by a dozen Frenchmen. The Mohawks, driven to bay, fought until only fifteen were left alive. These were taken prisoners, and one of them was surrendered to Champlain, while another was chopped into fragments and eaten. The rest were put to death with slow fires by the Algonquin women, who in this respect, Champlain tells us, are much more inhuman than the men, "for they devise by their cunning more cruel punishments, in which they take pleasure, putting an end to their lives by the most extreme pains." [1]

After this second taste of Indian warfare Champlain returned to France, and in the following December married a young girl, Helen Boullé, daughter of one of the late king's private secretaries. Clearly Champlain was now no

[1] *Voyages of Champlain*, ed. Slafter, ii. 246.

Huguenot, for as this young lady was somewhat too much of a Calvinist he left her for
a while in the following spring at an Ursuline
convent, where she might learn more wholesome opinions. At a later time she accompanied
him to Canada, but he was not yet quite ready to
bring her to such a place. On his next return,
in 1611, he began building a Chris- Beginnings
tian city on the site of the old Hoche- of Montreal
laga. Both in the interests of the fur-trade and
of his proposed western explorations he thought
it best to have an available station higher up
the river than Quebec. The site where building
operations were begun he called Place Royale,
and on a part of it the Hospital of the Gray
Nuns was afterwards erected. Scarcely was the
work well begun, and a few substantial walls
built, when Champlain again crossed the ocean.
His old colleague Monts had been appointed
governor of Pons, an important place near
Rochelle, and could no longer pay attention to
things in America. He therefore entrusted
everything to Champlain, and it was agreed that
in order to give to his enterprise the requisite
dignity and protection it was desirable to secure
as patron some personage of great social influence. Such a person was found in Charles de
Bourbon, Count of Soissons, a prince of the
blood royal, who was made viceroy over New
France, with Champlain for his lieutenant. To

the latter was given full control over the fur-trade. This arrangement was scarcely made when Soissons died and a still greater magnate was found to succeed him, — namely, Henri de Bourbon, Prince of Condé, a man celebrated, as Voltaire says, for having been the father of the great Condé, but eminent for nothing else save petty ambition and greed. Champlain had come to doubt the wisdom of too exclusive a policy of monopoly, and he sought to organize a numerous association of merchants in the sea-port towns. During this arduous work, when-ever some little assistance at court was wanted the Prince of Condé was always ready to absorb the spare cash as a retaining fee.

The Count of Soissons and the Prince of Condé suc-ceed Monts

There was so much to be done that Cham-plain could not leave France in 1612, but a young man appeared in Paris with such a story about his experiences in the New World that fashionable society had an unwonted sensation. The name of this youth was Nicolas de Vignau. Two years before Champlain had let him go home with a party of Ottawas, in order to learn what he could about their country and perhaps to inculcate a few civilized ideas into the heads of their warriors. Now Vignau strutted about Paris with the story that he had seen with his own eyes the western ocean; at all events, he had followed the river Ottawa

A traveller's tale

up to its origin in a lake, whence a river flowing
northward had carried him down to the sea. On
its shore he had seen the wreck of an English
ship and the heads of eighty Englishmen who had
been massacred by the natives! It is not likely
that this story was pure invention. The Ottawa
River has its sources in a chain of small lakes,
and from these a group of rivers, such as the
Moose and Abbittibi, flow northward into James
Bay, the southeasternmost portion of the vast
Hudson Bay. Vignau may very well have heard
of this route and have coupled with it some
vague rumour of the mutiny and disaster at
James Bay in which Henry Hudson lost his
life in June, 1612. The plausibleness of his
story and his straightforward manner carried
conviction to everybody, to Champlain among
others; and Champlain resolved to make the
visiting of that western sea the chief work of the
summer of 1613.

Late in May he started from the island opposite Montreal, which in honour of the wife
he had left behind he called Helen's Island.
He had two canoes, carrying, besides himself
and Vignau, three other Frenchmen and one
Indian. Far up the Ottawa River   Champlain
they made their way, with fierce and   among the
sanguinary opposition from the mos-   Ottawas,
quitoes, of which Champlain writes with most   1613
lively disgust, but otherwise without unpleasant

experiences. At Allumette Island they came to
a thriving Ottawa village, many of the inmates
of which had never seen any white man except
Vignau. After the usual formalities of feasting
and smoking, Champlain addressed the warriors
in the kind of speech which he had learned that
they liked, and concluded by asking for canoes
and guides to take him further on, even to the
country of the Nipissings. But here he read
in the faces of his hearers that he had touched
an unpleasant chord ; they were not on good
terms with the Nipissings. The old chieftain
Tessouat, who replied, gently rebuked Champlain for not having been at Montreal the preceding summer to take part once more in a
fight against the Iroquois. As for the canoes, of
course if Champlain wanted them he should have
them ; but oh, those Nipissings ! what could
he be thinking of in wishing to go to them ?
They would be sure to kill him ! and what
a day of mourning for every true Ottawa that
would be ! On Champlain's further representations the canoes and guides were promised, and
he stepped out of doors to get a breath of fresh
air. No sooner was his back turned than the
assembled warriors reconsidered the subject and
decided not to grant the canoes. A message to
this effect brought him back into the wigwam,
and once more he had to listen to the tale of
Nipissing depravity. Naturally he pointed to

Vignau and observed that here was a man who had been to the Nipissings and had not found them quite so black as they were painted. " Ah ! " exclaimed old Tessouat, turning upon the wretched impostor, " Nicolas, did you tell him that you had been to the Nipissings ? " It was a terrible moment for that silly young man, before that scowling company, with all those pairs of little snakelike eyes fixed savagely upon him. It mattered little whether he answered yes or no ; but after some moments of silence he replied stoutly that he had been there. Angry shouts of " Liar ! " arose ; for Vignau had really spent his whole winter in this very village, and everybody present knew it. Effrontery was of no avail ; he was plied with sarcastic queries which left him dumb and bewildered. Then quoth Champlain, " Look here, Vignau, if you have told me lies I will forgive what is past, but I insist that you tell the truth now, and if you fail me you shall be hanged on the spot." For a moment more the young rascal hesitated, then fell upon his knees and confessed the whole. The Indians begged to be allowed to kill him, but Champlain kept his word and the worthless life was spared. There was no further talk of canoes and guides, and our hero returned somewhat crestfallen to Montreal.

[Later in the season Champlain took ship

Vignau's imposture discovered

for France where he enlisted the interest of the Recollet friars in the establishment of missions among the Indians. Armed with a royal patent

Champlain returns from France with the Recollets and the authorization of the Pope, he returned to Canada in the spring of 1615, accompanied by four friars, whose singular garb at first greatly astonished their prospective flock.

One of these missionaries, Le Caron, leaving his brethren at Quebec went on to Montreal, where he found the yearly gathering of Indian fur-traders. Champlain appeared a few days later, and was then besought by the throng of Hurons to join them in an attack upon the Iroquois. Yielding to these solicitations he returned to Quebec for equipment. In the mean time Le Caron went on with Indians, making his way in a northwesterly direction until he,

Le Caron reaches Lake Huron the first of white men, gazed on the great Fresh Water Sea of the Hurons. Not many days later, Champlain arrived at the Huron villages and rejoined Le Caron, and on August 12 the first Christian service was held.

Hardly was the work of the church in this abode of evil spirits begun with these solemn rites before attention was directed to the worldly project which the Hurons had most at heart. Champlain reached the chief village of the Hurons, Cahiagué, the 17th of August. Feasts and war dances filled the hours of waiting till all the bands were gathered, and then, crossing Lake Simcoe, the Indians, accompanied by a handful of Frenchmen under the intrepid Champlain, pushed on rapidly by lakes and the river Trent to Lake Ontario.

Boldly venturing upon this inland sea in their frail craft they safely reached the other shore. A few days' march brought them to the Iroquois village,[1] where their first rash attack was successfully repelled, but at the sound of French muskets and the hissing of the bullets the pursuing Iroquois fell back and sought protection within the palisades of their town.

The attack on the Iroquois

To enable an effective assault to be made upon these defences Champlain had a movable tower built, from which sharp-shooters could pick off Iroquois behind the palisades; and also large shields to protect the assailing party from arrows and stones, in their efforts to set fire to the palings. But the excitement of battle was too much for these undisciplined hordes. They threw away the shields, rent the air with cries which made it impossible for Champlain to be

[1] [The situation of this fortified town of the Iroquois has been the subject of no little discussion. For the various views, see Winsor, *Narr. and Crit. Hist.*, iv. 125; Parkman, *Pioneers of France in the New World*, p. 402.]

heard, and in their haste lighted the fires on the lee side of the stockade, where they were quickly put out by the water poured down by the defenders. After three hours of aimless and ineffectual struggle, the Hurons fell back discouraged. Nor was Champlain able to rouse them to another set attack. They refused to stir unless they should be reinforced by some expected allies. These failing to arrive, the defeated Hurons gave up the contest and stole off, carrying their wounded in baskets upon their backs. They found their canoes unharmed, and safely recrossed the lake, but Champlain, greatly to his chagrin, was unable to induce the leaders to fulfil their promise to conduct him back to Quebec. At the last he was fain to accept the shelter of the lodge of a Huron chief. After some months spent in hunting, exploration, and the observation of Huron manners, Champlain returned to Quebec, where he was received as one from the dead.

Champlain's military engines

Champlain's plans to found a colony were in conflict with the commercial interests of the company of merchants who controlled the fortunes of New France. For them the fur-trade was the chief concern, and the growth of settlement could but diminish the profitableness of this commerce. As a trading-post Quebec was a success, but the lapse of eight years from its beginnings saw only two farms in cultivation, one by the Recollet friars, the other by Louis Hébert, who brought his wife and Rivalry of interests children to Quebec in 1617, and established the first Christian household in Canada. In 1620 Champlain brought his own young wife to Quebec, where she devoted herself with the zeal of a young convert to the spiritual welfare of the Indian women and children. These four years of missionary apprenticeship seem to have kindled her piety to such a flame that nothing would satisfy her but retirement from the world, and after her husband's death she became a nun.

In 1621 the merchants of St. Malo and Rouen, owing to repeated complaints, were ordered to give place to two Huguenot merchants named De Caen. Their refusal brought on quarrels between the rival traders, and in weariness at these discords Montmorency sold his viceroyalty of New France to his nephew the Duke of Ventadour, whose interest in the welfare of Canada was wholly religious. It was through him that the order of the The coming of the Jesuits Jesuits embraced New France in the world-wide field of their labours. In 1625 Lalemant, Massé, and Brébeuf began the work which was to place their names so high in the history of Canada. The far-seeing eye of Richelieu was now directed to the possibilities for the extension of French power in the New World, and the wasted opportunities of eighteen years devoted to the conflicting interests of trade and religion, which had left Quebec with only one or two self-supporting families, and at most a motley population of little over one hundred persons, convinced the great minister that a radical change was necessary. He abolished the privileges of the De Caëns, and formed the company of New France, to consist of one hundred members with himself at their head. To this body, commonly known as the "One Hundred Associates," were granted the political control of all of New France, the commercial monopoly of the fur-trade forever, and of other commerce, except whaling and cod-fishing, for fifteen years, for which period the trade of the colony was to be exempt from taxation. In return, the Associates must settle in Canada during these fifteen years not less than four thousand men and women, who were to be provided with cleared lands after three years' residence. In contrast to the lax unconcern with which for the most part England saw her colonies peopled with all sorts and conditions of men, German Protestants and English Catholics, English Puritans and Irish Papists, New France was henceforth to be open only to

The One Hundred Associates

Catholics and Frenchmen. To attain the ideal of religious unity the strongest inducement for an energetic and progressive population to migrate was relinquished, and the inter- Religious esting possibility of the growth of a uniformity Huguenot New France side by side with a Puritan New England was rejected.

Hardly had this reorganization been effected, when, through the outbreak of war between England and France, these plans were interrupted, and not only the possession but even the existence of the colony hung in the balance. The new company despatched four armed vessels in April, 1628, under Roquemont, one of their number, to succour the distressed colonists, and simultaneously Charles I. of England authorized a private expedition, patronized by London merchants and commanded by the three sons of their associate, Gervase Kirke, to dislodge the French from Acadia and Canada. The English fleet arrived first, but Champlain's sturdy resolution and the apparent strength of his position disconcerted them, and they turned back. But if the Kirkes failed to capture Quebec, the blow they did inflict was hardly less serious, for they overwhelmed the expedition of relief led by Roquemont, and the feeble garrison dragged through another year in such misery that Champlain meditated the desertion of Quebec and the capture of some Iroquois village where they would find a buried store of corn. Before so desperate a plan was resolved upon, Captain Kirke reappeared, this time to secure the surrender of Quebec, not through the valour of his attack, but through the despair of its holders. The English possession, however, was short-lived. Three years later, in accordance with the treaty of St. Germain-en-Laye, Canada and Acadia were restored to France in response to a demand which the honour of France, the personal pride of Richelieu as the head of the One Hundred Associates, and the pious urgency of Champlain for the conversion of the savages, all combined to press. In 1633 Champlain returned to Quebec as governor under commission from the One Hundred Associates. For a brief two years more he guided the destinies of New France. His days of exploration were over, and his mind turned more and more to the development and extension of the missions, to which all other interests were now subordinate. On Christmas day, 1635, the father of New France passed away. Like Bradford and Winthrop, his contemporaries, he was not only the brave, patient, and wise leader of an epoch-making enterprise, but also its honest and dispassionate historian. Yet this was not all, for to-day he is not less remembered as the

The capture of Quebec by the English

Champlain's last days

adventurous and indefatigable explorer and the curious observer of savage life and manners.[1]

Recurring now to the rivalry between France and England for the possession of Acadia, the next stage to be noticed is the grant of that region in 1621 by King James I. to Sir William Alexander, a member of the newly organized Council of New England, to be held under the name Nova Scotia as a fief of the Crown of Scotland. The first obstacle to the establishment of his sway Sir William found in the French occupants under the leadership of Biencourt. At Biencourt's death about the year 1623 his possessions and claims fell to his friend and companion, Charles de la Tour. In 1627 Charles de la Tour petitioned the king of France to be appointed commandant of Acadia. His messenger was his own father, Claude de la Tour, who, upon his return with Roquemont's Quebec relief expedition, was captured by the Kirkes and carried to England. Here, being a Protestant, he renounced his French allegiance and entered the

James I. grants Acadia to Sir William Alexander

Claude and Charles de la Tour

---

[1] [Champlain's works are easily accessible in the scholarly collected edition of the Abbé Laverdière, 6 vols., Quebec, 1870. An English translation of his *Voyages* by C. P. Otis has been published by the Prince Society under the editorial charge of Rev. E. F. Slafter, who has added a memoir and extensive notes.]

service of Sir William Alexander, who made him a baronet of Nova Scotia in 1629.

The return of the father with a commission from England after he had been despatched to

Legend of secure one from France produced a
La Tour's situation which has appealed alike to
fidelity to
France poet, historian, and novelist, who have depicted the son sternly rejecting the father's solicitations to change his allegiance. The story is a doubtful one, and the facts seem to be that La Tour adapted himself to the changes in the political world with the readiness of the Vicar of Bray.[1]

The restoration of Canada and Acadia to France in 1632 forced the La Tours to trim their sails again, and Charles de la Tour succeeded in getting a grant of lands and a command from the French king. He soon found himself confronted by a shrewd and tireless ri-

La Tour and val, D'Aunay Charnisay, the heir of
D'Aunay the authority of Claude de Razilly, whom the king had sent over in 1632 to receive back Acadia from the English. The rivalry of these two chieftains revived in Acadia the petty warfare of the feudal ages. Ensconced in their rustic castles, first on opposite sides of the peninsula of Acadia, — D'Aunay at Port Royal and

---

[1] [Roberts, *History of Canada*, p. 50 ; and Rameau, *Une Colonie Féodale en Amérique*, Paris, 1877, p. 57.]

La Tour at Cape Sable, — and later, on opposite sides of the Bay of Fundy, where La Tour established his Fort St. Jean, — contesting each other's holdings, capturing each other's retainers, now proposing common action against the English interlopers, now appealing to Boston for assistance, they carried on the struggle intermittently for years.[1]

Appeals to the king of France at first only complicated matters because of the uncertainties of Acadian geography, but in 1641 D'Aunay's superior influence at court prevailed. La Tour's commission was recalled, and he was ordered to report to the king in France. At the same time D'Aunay was authorized to take possession of La Tour's forts. La Tour refused obedience, and D'Aunay was ordered to seize him. La Tour, now finding himself in the dangerous plight of a rebel, had recourse to Boston for help, and convinced the leaders of the Puritan colony that his cause was just, and that D'Aunay was an intruder. Their help, however, was of little lasting advantage, and in 1645 D'Aunay captured Fort St. Jean and hanged most of the prisoners. Five years later the tide turned, when

[1] [For the vicissitudes of this struggle the reader may be referred to Murdoch's *History of Nova Scotia*, to Rameau's *Une Colonie Féodale*, and to Parkman's *The Old Régime in Canada*.]

D'Aunay was drowned, leaving a widow and eight children. The skies then brightened for

Death of D'Aunay

La Tour, and he came back to Acadia, having succeeded in getting a new commission from the king. Madame D'Aunay was now overwhelmed with misfortune; her claims and those of La Tour seemed incapable of adjustment, and, urged by the necessities of her children, she accepted La Tour's proposal to merge them with his by marriage.[1] Hardly had this promising settlement been effected when a force of New Englanders under Major Robert Sedgwick of Charlestown, following secret instructions received from Cromwell, suddenly attacked and conquered Acadia. Again La Tour's adroitness served him well. In 1656 he secured for himself, in conjunction with Thomas Temple and William Crowne, a grant of all of Acadia, but apparently he had now had enough of the labours and vicissitudes of founding a people, for in less than two months he relinquished

La Tour gives place to Sir Thomas Temple

his share to Temple, who devoted himself with great energy to building up the colony. Temple successfully weathered the change in government at the Restoration, reminding Charles II. that he had been faithful to his father, and " that one of the last commands that he whispered to Kirke on

---

[1] [Murdoch prints the marriage contract, i. 120–123.]

the scaffold was to charge this king to have a care of honest Tom Temple." [1] The injunction was heeded so far as to allow Temple to retain Acadia, but it was not heeded to the extent of indemnifying him for his losses when Acadia was transferred again to France in 1667.

The Lords of Acadia, from Sir William Alexander to Sir Thomas Temple, and not least the two indefatigable rivals, La Tour and D'Aunay Charnisay, had learned to their cost how great a labour it is to found a state.]

[1] [*Calendar of State Papers, Colonial,* i. 496. This volume contains many items on these Lords of Acadia.]

IV

WILDERNESS AND EMPIRE

WE must now return to the lifetime of Champlain and note some of the principal steps by which the French acquired control of the central portion of North America. Among the young men whom Champlain selected to send among the Indians to fit themselves for the work of interpreters was a Norman named Jean Nicollet. This was in 1618, and for the next sixteen years Nicollet's time was chiefly spent among the Ottawas and Nipissings, engaging in their various expeditions, and encountering with them the privations and hardships of the forest. In 1634 Champlain sent Nicollet upon a western expedition. The object was to find out, if possible, what was meant by the repeated stories of large bodies of water to the westward, and of a distant people without hair or beards who did all their journeying in enormous tower-like canoes. Nicollet thought that this must be an Oriental people, and in order that he might not present too strange an appearance when he should have arrived among them, he took along with him a

Jean Nicollet

Chinese gown of rich brocade embroidered with flowers and birds.

Nicollet's route lay up the Ottawa River to Lake Nipissing, and thence to the Georgian Bay. On that broad expanse of water the party launched their canoes for a journey to the Sault Ste. Marie and the Ojibway tribe which dwelt in its neighbourhood. It does not appear that Nicollet gained any positive knowledge of Lake Superior, but he entered Lake Michigan, and followed its western shores as far as Green Bay, where he met with Indians of strange speech who had never before set eyes upon a white man. These were Winnebagoes, belonging to the great Dacotah family, and in their presence the robe of brocade was put to uses quite different from those which its owner had intended. The amazed redskins beheld in its wearer a supernatural being, and were more than confirmed in this belief when they heard the report and saw the flash of his pistol.[1] From Green Bay our explorer pushed on up the Fox River, where he fell in with a tribe of Algonquins famous for their valour, under the name of Mascoutins. These Indians told him of the existence of a " great water " in the

Nicollet explores Lake Michigan

[1] [On this expedition, cf. *Jesuit Relations,*Thwaites's ed. xxiii. 275–279, and the monograph of C. W. Butterfield, *History of the Discovery of the Northwest by John Nicolet,* Cincinnati, 1881.]

neighbourhood, and inasmuch as their speech was Algonquin, the words which they used were in all probability Missi-Sippi. Whether Nicollet entered the Wisconsin River or not is uncertain, but it seems probable that he went further to the south than Green Bay, to reach the country belonging to the Algonquin tribe of the Illinois. He also established friendly relations with the Algonquin Pottawattamies. After this he retraced his course, and reached Three Rivers in July, 1635, just about one year from the time of starting.

Of course the " great water " to which Nicollet's Indian informants alluded was the Mississippi River, but it was an easy and natural mistake to identify it with the western ocean, for which everybody had been so long and so eagerly looking. Many years elapsed before this and its kindred questions were correctly solved. The Jesuit influence, which after Champlain's death was long supreme in the colony, was not especially favourable to western exploration. The scientific zeal of Champlain, which studied geography for its own sake, was not theirs, but their missionary zeal took them to great lengths, and Father Jogues near Lake Superior in 1641 we find Father Jogues preaching the gospel to a concourse of red men hard by the outlet of Lake Superior.[1] It is possible that the movements in

[1] [*Jesuit Relations*, xx. 97 ; xxiii. 19.]

that direction might have been more vigorously prosecuted but for the terrible Iroquois war resulting in the destruction of the Hurons in 1649. Ten years later the journey of two Frenchmen, Radisson and Groseilliers, is worthy of mention because they reached a stream Radisson and Groseilliers which they called Forked River " because it has two branches, the one towards the west, the other towards the south, which we believe run towards Mexico." [1] This, of course, might be meant for the Mississippi and Missouri. Within the next three or four years Ménard and Allouez explored portions of the Lake Superior coast, and again heard enticing stories about the "great water."

About this time a marked change came over Canada. In 1661 the youthful Louis XIV. assumed personal control of the gov- Accession of ernment of France, and it cannot be Louis XIV. said of him that either then or at any later time he was at all neglectful of the interest of Canada. As our narrative will hereafter show, if Canada suffered at his hands, it was from excessive care rather than from neglect. In 1664 and the following year the king sent three very able men to America; the first was the Marquis de Tracy, to be military commander of New France, the Sieur de Courcelle, to be governor

---

[1] [Radisson's narratives of his travels have been printed by the Prince Society, Boston, 1885.]

of Canada, and Jean Baptiste Talon, to be intendant of Canada. The intendant was an of-

His changes in Canadian administration

ficer charged with the duty of enfor-
cing a minute system of regulations in
the colony, and incidentally of keeping a watch upon the governor's actions, according to the universal system of surveillance
for which the old régime in France was so notable. With these men came as many as 2000
fresh colonists, together with 1200 veteran infantry, as fine as anything Europe had to show;
so that there was now some hope that the Iroquois nuisance might be kept at arm's length.
Talon was a man of large views; he had an
inkling of what might be accomplished by such
extensive waterways as those of North America;
and it was his settled intention to occupy the
interior of the continent, and to use the mouths
of its southern rivers as places from which to
emerge in force and threaten the coast of Spanish Mexico. So aggressive was the mood of the
French at this moment that Courcelle projected
an invasion of the Long House, and in January
and February, 1666, he proceeded as far as
Schenectady, whence he retired on learning that

Two expeditions against the Iroquois, 1666

the English had taken possession of
New Netherland. In the ensuing autumn another expedition was undertaken, and Courcelle, accompanied by Tracy,
penetrated the greater part of the Mohawk val-

ley. It was a singular spectacle, that of 600 French regulars in their uniforms, marching through the woodland trails to the sound of drum and trumpet. At a later period such bold-ness would have entailed disaster, but at that time white men and their ways were still suffi-ciently novel to inspire a great deal of whole-some terror. It is not easy to calculate the death-dealing capacity of the unknown, and accordingly our Mohawks, though thoroughly brave men, retired in confusion before the con-fident and resonant advance of the Gallic chiv-alry.[1] The moral impression thus produced was reinforced so effectively by Jesuit missionaries that the Long House was kept comparatively quiet for twenty years. Indeed, fears were en-tertained at times in New York that the French might succeed in winning over the Iroquois in spite of the past, but any such result was averted by the far-sighted policy of Sir Edmund An-dros and Thomas Dongan, and the ascendancy acquired over the Mohawks by the Schuylers at Albany.

The remotest western frontier of French mis-sionary enterprise was now the northern portion of Lake Michigan from the Sault Ste. Marie to Green Bay. The French names dotted with

[1] [For these two expeditions, see the Abbé Faillon's *Histoire de la Colonie Française en Canada*, iii. 130–158 ; Parkman, *The Old Régime*, pp. 236–256.]

such profusion over that portion of the United States known as the Old Northwest preserve
Contrasts between New France and New England
for us an eloquent record of the travels and toils of the old explorers. The New England colonies were more than twenty times as populous as Canada, yet their furthest inland reach was to the shores of the Connecticut River at Deerfield and Hadley, while the French outposts were more than a thousand miles from the Atlantic. This difference was partly due to the fact that the primary object of the English was to found homes, and reproduce in the wilderness the self-supporting and self-governing rural communities of the Old Country; whereas the primary object of the French was either to convert the heathen, or to trade for peltries, or to settle geographical questions, and all this was a more migratory kind of work than founding villages. In particular, the effects of Champlain's policy in becoming a leader of the alliance against the Long House are conspicuously visible.[1] It will be observed that for more than half a century after Champlain's attack upon the Onondaga fort, the route taken by Frenchmen toward the great West was up the Ottawa River and across the northern portion of Lake Huron. The French acquaintance with Lake Ontario was as yet but slight, while of Lake Erie they knew

[1] [See above, p. 70.]

nothing save by hearsay. It was impossible for them to use those southerly routes because of the Iroquois. But inasmuch as the The French
trading route
to the north-
west Iroquois by sudden raids to the northward could cut off the current of the northwestern fur-trade at almost any point between Lake Ontario and the Sault Ste. Marie, it became very important for the French to maintain friendly relations with all the Algonquin tribes about the great lakes, from the Ottawas to the Ojibways and Pottawattamies. These were among the prime necessities which carried their activity so far to the west, and it so happened that side by side with the devoted missionaries a peculiar kind of population was developed in adaptation to the wild and lawless life of these woodland regions. Among the picturesque figures of New France are those of the *coureurs de bois*, which, literally rendered, would be "runners of the woods." Many of these men were ne'er-do-weels The cou-
reurs de bois brought over from France by a legislation which insisted rather upon quantity than quality for the settlers of the New World. Their ranks were reinforced by those who for whatever purpose were dissatisfied with steady work in a steady-going community. The paternal legislation of Louis XIV. would have had them marry French women of their own station, cultivate their small farm, and comport themselves with sober dignity. In point of fact, they tramped off to the woods, took to themselves Indian wives, and hunted the moose, or speared the salmon, or set traps for every four-footed creature with fur on its back. We are told, with much probability, by Charlevoix, that these men did not do nearly so much to civilize the Indians as the Indians did to barbarize them.

It was certainly felt by Father Allouez that these wood rangers were as much in need of a missionary as the red men themselves, for early *Father Allouez on the Wisconsin* in 1670 he busied himself in preaching to them. At this time he reached the head of the Wisconsin River, and was told that six days' journey from there it flowed into the Mississippi or "Great Water." The "Jesuit Relation" for 1670 speaks of this "great water" as a very wide river, of which none of the Indians had ever seen the end, and it was not clear whether it emptied into the Gulf of Mexico or that of California.

The politic Frenchmen at the north of Lake Michigan had their hands quite full with the relations, peaceful or hostile, of the Indian tribes. Thither had retreated the Hurons and Ottawas to get out of the reach of the dreaded Long House, and by coming hither they had given umbrage to the ferocious Dacotahs or Sioux, whom Father Marquette not inaptly termed the Iroquois of the West. But the chastisement wrought by Tracy in the Mohawk country was reported with savage exultation from red man to red man along the chain of lakes, until it encouraged the Ottawas with the remnant of Hurons to move backward as far as Mackinaw and the great Manitoulin Island.

In 1670, in accordance with the injunctions of the king, Talon despatched St. Lusson to take possession of the Northwest, and in the spring of 1671 the heights looking upon the Sault Ste. Marie witnessed a pageant such as none knew so well as Frenchmen how to prepare. Besides the tribes just mentioned, there were representatives from not less than a dozen others, Pottawattamies, Winnebagoes, Illinois, Shawnees, Ojibways, Nipissings, and others, a vast assemblage of grunting warriors hideous with every variety of lurid paint, and bedizened with feathers and wampum. Here were games of ball, mock fights, and whatever peaceful diversion the barbaric mind was capable of finding pleasure in. These festivities continued for some weeks, interspersed with feasts at which were served the wild fowl of the season and abundance of fish, with that pride of the red man's menu, boiled dog. On the 14th of June, a great concourse

The French take possession of the Northwest

of people assembled in the bright sunshine at the top of a lofty hill, and there all the magnates present, white and red, affixed their signatures or made their marks to a document which practically claimed for Louis XIV. all the continent there was, from the Arctic Ocean to the Gulf of Mexico, and from the coast of Labrador as far west as land might go, which some bold spirits thought might be two or three hundred miles west of the Wisconsin River. These signatures were supposed to commit the Indian tribes as well as the Frenchmen to this extensive French claim. After the signing was over, an immense wooden cross was reared aloft and planted in the hole which had been dug to receive it, while the Frenchmen present, with uncovered heads, chanted an ancient Latin hymn. A post with the lilies of France was planted close by, while the French commander, Sieur de St. Lusson, held up a sod as symbolic of taking seizin of the land. It was felt, however, that all this pageant would be incomplete without a speech that would stir the hearts of the Indians, and Father Allouez, the orator of the day, knew how to tell them what they could appreciate. He informed the gaping red men that when it came to the business of massacre, their bloodiest chiefs were mere tyros compared with the most Christian king of France. He depicted

Father Allouez depicts the greatness of Louis XIV.

that monarch as wet with the blood of his enemies, and declared that he did not keep scalps
as a record of the number slain simply because
the carnage to which he was accustomed was so
wholesale, that no such petty method of reck-
oning would be of any use. Having listened to
this ensanguined rhetoric, the assemblage broke
up, and with the usual choruses of yelps and
grunts, the tawny audience separated into count-
less little groups and disappeared in the recesses
of the forest.[1]

At the time of this wild ceremony there had
already entered upon the scene the man who in
some respects must be counted the most remarkable among all these pioneers of France.
In the city of Rouen there had dwelt for several generations a family by the name of Cavelier, wealthy and highly respected, whose members were often chosen as diplomats and judges,
or for other positions entailing large responsibility. Although these people did not strictly
belong to the noblesse, they were nevertheless
lords of small landed estates, and the estate belonging to the Caveliers was known as La Salle.
In the year 1643, Rouen witnessed the birth of
René Robert Cavelier, Sieur de La   Early life of
Salle. This boy seems to have been   La Salle
educated at a Jesuit school, but as he grew up,

---

[1] [For the text of this speech, see *Jesuit Relations*, lv.
109–113, and Parkman, *La Salle*, pp. 44–46.]

feeling no inclination for the priesthood, he parted from his old friends and teachers with a reputation for excellent scholarship and unimpeachable character. He had shown unusual precocity in mathematics, and a strong love for such study of physical science as could be compassed in those days of small things. He was noted at an early age for a reserved and somewhat haughty demeanour, a Puritanic seriousness in his views of life, and a power of determination which nothing could shake. It so happened that his elder brother, Jean Cavelier, a priest of St. Sulpice, was in Canada, and that circumstance may perhaps have drawn him thither. His entrance into a religious order had cut him off from his inheritance, so that his resources were then and always extremely meagre.

La Salle comes to Canada

On arriving in Montreal, La Salle accepted the feudal grant of a tract of land at the place now called La Chine, above the rapids known by that name. That La Salle must have entertained some purpose of exploring the wilderness before his coming to America is highly probable, for the first two or three years at La Chine were spent by him in the diligent study of Indian languages ; and he was not long in acquiring high proficiency both in Iroquois and in several dialects of Algonquin. One day he was visited by a party of Senecas, who spent some weeks at his house and had much to tell him about a river that they called the Ohio, which had its sources in their country and reached the ocean at a distance so great that many months would be required to traverse it. By the Ohio River, these Indians meant the Allegheny with the Ohio and the lower Mississippi, in which grouping their error was just as natural and no greater than we make in calling the upper and lower Mississippi by the same name; whereas in fact, the Missouri with the lower Mississippi is the main river, and the upper Mississippi is the tributary. From the Senecas' account of the immense length of their Ohio River, La Salle concluded that it must fall into the Gulf of California, and hence afford the much-coveted passage to China.

La Salle hears of the Ohio and resolves to explore it

La Salle therefore decided that he would visit the Seneca country and ascertain for himself the truth of what he had been told. He found no difficulty in obtaining the requisite authorization from Courcelles and Talon, but as he had no ready money he was obliged to sell his estate of La Chine in order to raise the necessary funds. Just at that moment the seminary of St. Sulpice was meditating a similar enterprise, but with a very different destination and purpose. They wished to go northwesterly to convert some Indians whom they had been told

His expedition combined with a mission exploration of the Sulpicians surpassed all others for heathenish ignorance. To combine two such diverse expeditions into one was not an augury of success.

In July, 1669, seven canoes carrying twenty-four men started up the river from La Chine, and after a voyage of thirty-five days they reached Irondequoit Bay on the south side of Lake Ontario, from which a march of twenty miles brought them to one of the principal Seneca villages. There they found the people in great excitement because of the return of a small war party with one young captive warrior. One of the French priests tried to buy him from his captors, but the village found the season dull and was determined not to be deprived of its night's pleasure. So the Frenchmen were obliged to look on for six weary hours while the young man was subjected to every torture that the red man's ingenuity could devise. After the life had quite left his charred and writhing form, and after the body had been cut into fragments and passed about to be eaten as dainty morsels, the savage hosts were ready to inquire what service they could do to their guests. But when they heard what was wanted they became profuse in their warnings against the wicked Indians who dwelt on the banks of the Ohio. They would furnish no guides nor be in any way instrumental in leading their

The way blocked by the Senecas

beloved friends into such unseemly dangers. Our Frenchmen had long since learned the true meaning of such ironical expressions of solicitude on the part of the red men. Practically, they often amounted to a threat, as if to say, If you go down there we will kill you and lay the blame upon the Indians of that part. Why the Senecas did not wish the Frenchmen to pass through their country at that moment, unless it may have been the general Iroquois feeling toward Frenchmen, is not clear. At this juncture one of the Indians offered to guide the party by an entirely different route, from which they could reach the Ohio at a point lower down than originally contemplated. La Salle and the Sulpicians concluded to accept this offer, and were led back to the shore of Lake Ontario. They crossed the Niagara River just below the bluffs at Queenston and distinctly heard the magnificent sub-bass monotone of the great cataract, to which, perhaps, they were the first of Europeans to approach so near. At a village on the present site of Hamilton, La Salle was presented with a Shawnee prisoner who promised to take him across Lake Erie to the Ohio; but a new turn to events was suddenly given by the unexpected arrival of a couple of Frenchmen from the north- Meeting with west. One of these was Louis Joliet, Joliet a man of about the same age as La Salle, who had, like him, been educated by the Jesuits and taken orders, but had afterward come to devote himself to mercantile pursuits. Talon, the Intendant, had heard much of the copper mines on the shore of Lake Superior, the fame of which was very widespread in aboriginal America, and he had sent Joliet to discover and inspect them. In this quest the young Frenchman had not been successful, but he brought with him such a desperate account of the sinful condition of the Pottawattamies that the Sulpician priests decided to go at once and convert them, in spite of all that La Salle could say. So the exploring party was broken up, the Sulpicians went to Sault Ste. Marie, where they met with a rather cold reception from the Jesuits, and after a while concluded to return to Montreal without anything to show for their pains.

La Salle parts from the Sulpicians

As for La Salle at that disappointing moment, he showed a quality for which he was ever afterward distinguished. When he had started to do a thing he never relinquished his purpose, although men and fortune forsook him. If he had been one of a Balaklava Six Hundred and the only survivor among them, he would have attacked the enemy, single-handed, with unabated courage. Unfortunately, our sources of information partially fail us at this point, so that

some uncertainty remains as to the route which
La Salle took after the Sulpicians had left him.
One account of his route — perhaps as probable
as any — takes him by way of Lake
Chautauqua into the Allegheny valley, and thence down the Ohio River
as far as Louisville. In the following year he
seems to have crossed Lake Erie from south to
north, and ascended the Detroit River to Lake
Huron ; thence to have passed into Lake Michigan and ascended the Chicago River, from which
he found his way across the brief portage to
the river of the Illinois. According to some
accounts, he reached the Mississippi River on
both these trips, first from the Ohio, and afterward from the Illinois. But these conclusions
are not well supported and have generally been
pronounced improbable.

La Salle ex-
plores the
Ohio

An interest in this remote "great water"
continued strongly to agitate many minds, and
Talon had already settled upon Louis Joliet
as a fit man to undertake its discovery, when
circumstances led to a change of governorship
for New France. Courcelles and Talon were
both recalled, and in place of them the affairs
of Canada were managed by one of
the most remarkable Frenchmen of
his time, Louis de Buade, Count of
Frontenac. This man was of the bluest blood

Frontenac
succeeds
Courcelles

of France, a veteran soldier of no mean ability, and for executive capacity excelled by few. His talents for dealing with Indians were simply marvellous. He could almost direct the policy of an Indian tribe by a wave of the hand. If need be, he could smear his face with war paint and lead off the demon dance with a vigour and abandon that no chieftain could hope to rival. He could out-yell any warrior in the Long House, and when he put on a frown and spoke sternly, the boldest warriors shivered with fear. Among white men he was domineering and apt to be irascible. A man of very clear ideas, he well knew how to re-
Character of alize them, and cared little for the
Frontenac advice of those who seemed to him frivolous or stupid. It was hinted that sometimes in his management of money he was not above sundry slight peccadilloes, with which his enemies were fond of twitting him, but this was not always a safe game, since he was liable to retort upon his accusers with an utterly overwhelming *tu quoque*. On the whole, however, he must be called a man of public spirit, devoted to the interests of his country, and with fewer serious failings than most of the public men of his age. In his general view of things he was far-sighted and not petty. If Talon had remained in Canada, Frontenac would probably

have quarrelled with him, but as it was, he adopted most of that official's intelligent plans; among other things he warmly espoused the ideas of La Salle, and he confirmed the choice of Joliet for the proposed expedition to the Mississippi. The mention of Joliet reminds us that New France was coming of age as a colony, for this explorer was a native of the country, having been born at Quebec in 1645, ten years after the death of Champlain. It appears that Joliet was a well-educated man and showed considerable proficiency in the higher mathematics. It was said, Joliet chosen to explore the Mississippi too, that he was rather a formidable debater on questions of logic and metaphysics. There is nothing in his career that shows qualities of a lofty or transcendent order, but we get the impression of a prudent and painstaking man of. sober judgment.

At Mackinaw Joliet was joined by a Jesuit priest named Jacques Marquette, a native of the old Carlovingian capital, Laon, born in 1637. He was distinguished for Marquette linguistic talents and for the deeply spiritual quality of his mind. He seems to have had a poetic temperament profoundly sensitive to the beauties of nature and of art, while his religion exercised upon him a transfiguring influence, so that all who met him became aware of a heavenly presence. This gentle and exquisite creature was as brave as a paladin and capable of enduring the fiercest extremes of hardship.

It was on the 17th of May, 1673, that Joliet and Marquette started with five companions in two birch canoes well supplied with dried corn and smoked buffalo meat. From Green Bay

Joliet and Marquette reach the Mississippi

they ascended the Fox River to Lake Winnebago, and after various adventures reached the portage from which they launched their canoes on the Wisconsin River. One month from the day of starting they passed the bluffs at Prairie du Chien and glided out upon the placid blue waters of the upper Mississippi. Their joy, as Marquette informs us, was too great for words. A fortnight passed while they floated down-stream without disclosing any trace of human beings, but at length they came to a village called Peoria, where they were treated with great civility and regaled with the usual Indian dishes, while the chief, in a more than usually florid speech, assured them that their visit to his village added serenity to the sky and new beauty to the landscape and a fresh zest to his tobacco, but he really, as a friend, could not advise them to pursue their course, as it abounded with dangerous enemies. Disregarding this caution, however, they kept on their way without any ill consequences. They did not fail to note the striking spectacle below the cliffs at Alton where the furious Missouri, with its load of yellow mud accumulated during its 3000 miles' course through the mountains, rushes through, swallows up and defiles the quiet blue waves of the Mississippi. Down the turbid and surging yellow river they kept on for hundreds of miles, until they encountered parties of Arkansas and narrowly escaped without a fight. Presently they stopped at an Arkansas village where they were feasted as usual, but after the hilarity was over the principal chief informed them that a foul conspiracy was on foot to murder them, — an infringement of the laws of hospitality which he felt himself unable to sanction. This incident seems to have had its effect in deciding them to retrace their course. They had gone so far southward as to convince themselves that the river must empty into the Gulf of Mexico and not into the Vermilion Sea, as the Gulf of California was then commonly called. This was the most important of the points which they had it in mind to establish, and it seemed to them better to return with the information already acquired than to run the risk of perishing and sending back no word. For such reasons they turned back on the 17th of July, just two months from their date of starting. After ascending to the mouth of the Illinois they went up to the head of that

They pass the mouth of the Missouri

stream, and there met some Indians who guided them to Lake Michigan. It was about the

The return   end of September when they reached Green Bay, after having wielded the paddles for more than 2500 miles. There the two friends parted. While Joliet made his way to Montreal with a report of what had been accomplished, Marquette lay ill at Green Bay for more than a year. A partial recovery of health led him to attempt the founding of a new mission at the principal town of the Illinois, to be called the Immaculate Conception, but his strength again gave out, and on the way to Mackinaw in the spring of 1675 this beautiful spirit passed away from the earth.[1]

The immediate effect of the voyage of Marquette and Joliet was to revive in La Salle the spirit which had led him down the Ohio River some years before. The conception of New France as a great empire in the wilderness was

La Salle's   taking a distinct shape in his mind.
great designs Among its comprehensive features were the extension of the fur-trade, the building up of French colonies with an extensive agriculture, the conversion of the Indians to Christianity, and the playing a controlling part in forest politics. Marquette and Joliet had

---

[1] [A translation of Marquette's own narrative may be found in J. G. Shea's *History and Exploration of the Mississippi Valley*, pp. 6–50.]

well-nigh demonstrated that the Mississippi River flows into the Gulf of Mexico. One might, perhaps, suppose that a reference to the expedition of Soto more than a century before would have sufficed to establish the identity of the river descended by Marquette and Joliet with the river where the great Spanish knight was buried. But the Frenchmen of the seventeenth century seem to have known nothing about Soto or his explorations. To them the problem was a new one. After once completely solving it, La Salle would be in a position to establish a town at the mouth of the great river. Such a town might become a commercial rival of the Spanish seaports in Mexico and the West Indies, while it would be a formidable menace to them in time of war. A chain of military posts might connect the town at the mouth of the Mississippi with the spot where the Illinois empties into that river, and similar chains might connect the Illinois on the one hand with the Sault Ste. Marie, and on the other hand with Lakes Erie and Ontario. It was the generally accepted French doctrine that the discovery of a great river gave an inchoate title to all the territory drained by the river, and this inchoate title could be completed by occupation. La Salle's plan was to effect a military occupation of the whole Missis-

The Mississippi valley to be occupied

sippi valley as far eastward as the summit of
the Appalachian range by means of military
posts which should control the communications
and sway the policy of the Indian tribes. Thus,
the Alleghanies would become an impassable
barrier to the English colonists slowly pressing
westward from the Atlantic coast. This became
the abiding policy of the French in North
America. This was the policy in attempting to
carry out which they fought and lost the Seven
Years' War. Of this policy such men as Talon,
Frontenac, and La Salle were the originators,
and in La Salle it found its most brilliant
representative.

An obvious criticism upon such a scheme is
its mere vastness. In a colony recruited so
slowly as Canada there were not
enough people to carry it into operation. Under the most favourable
circumstances it could scarcely remain more
than a sketch; but La Salle believed that
the inducements held out by an increasing fur-
trade and enlarged opportunities of agriculture
and commerce in general would bring settlers
to New France and greatly accelerate its rate
of growth. There was perhaps nothing necessa-
rily wild in his calculations, except that he entirely failed to understand the inherent weakness of colonization that was dependent upon
government support.

When it came to performing his own part of the great scheme, the essential point of weakness was want of money, — a kind of weakness which has proved fatal to many a great scheme. In order to cure this want La Salle was inclined to resort to the agency which was chiefly in vogue in the seventeenth century, namely, that of monopoly. This at once enlisted against him the fur-traders as a class. His friendly relations with Frontenac made it seem probable that he could get whatever he wanted, and in whatsoever quarter he turned his attention the monopoly scare was excited and every possible device was adopted for hindering his success, — devices which went all the way from attaching his property to hiring desperadoes to murder him. Besides this, La Salle was regarded with coldness, if not hostility, by the Jesuits, whose service he had abandoned and whose schemes for civilizing the wilderness were often at variance with his. Moreover, with all his admirable qualities, La Salle was not exactly a lovable person. He was too deeply absorbed in his arduous work to be genial, and he was a stern disciplinarian against whom lawless spirits, familiar with the loose freedom of the wilderness, were liable to rebel. The history of his brief career of eight years after he had finally given himself up to his life work is a singular record of almost unintermitted disaster leading

La Salle's privileges arouse opposition

to a tragic end, yet relieved by one glorious, though momentary, gleam of triumph.

One of Frontenac's first steps for the protection of the fur-trade between Montreal and the northwestern wilderness was the erection of a strong wooden blockhouse at the outlet of Lake Ontario. Its site was about that of the present town of Kingston, and it was long known as Fort Frontenac. It served as a wholesome menace to the men of the Long House over across the lake. La Salle went to France and had an interview with Louis XIV., in which he obtained that monarch's authority to conduct an exploring expedition, and he was placed in command of Fort Frontenac on his promise to rebuild and greatly strengthen it. This promise was amply fulfilled. The fortress was rebuilt of stone according to sound military principles, and was strong enough to defy the attempt of any force that was likely to be brought against it.

The next reach of La Salle's arm was from the outlet of Ontario to the Niagara River above the Falls. For the prosecution of his enterprise canoe navigation seemed hardly to suffice, and on the Niagara River La Salle built and launched a schooner of some forty-five tons burden, armed with five small cannon, and carrying on her prow a grotesque griffin, the name that was given to her in honour of Count Frontenac's family arms. While these preparations were going on La Salle received a treacherous dose of poison, the effects of which his iron constitution threw off with rather surprising ease. He started out on his enterprise with about forty men, two of whom deserve especial mention for various reasons. Henri de Tonty was a native of Naples, son of the gentleman who invented the kind of life insurance for a long time popular Henri de as the Tontine. In his youthful days Tonty Tonty had one hand blown off in battle ; he had it replaced by an iron hand over which he always wore a glove, and he was commonly known among the Indians as Iron Hand. He was a man of direct and simple nature, brave and resourceful, and in every emergency was absolutely faithful to La Salle.

A very different sort of person was Louis Hennepin, a native of Flanders, about thirty-seven years of age. He had early joined the Franciscan friars, and an irrepressible love for adventure brought him to Canada, Louis where he found the wild solitudes Hennepin about Fort Frontenac quite in harmony with his tastes. He was a capable man with many excellent qualities, and on most occasions truthful, although his reputation has greatly suffered

from one gigantic act of mendacity.[1]   We shall
have occasion to note his characteristics as we go
on.   He was one of the advance party sent by
La Salle to the Niagara River, and was probably
the first of Europeans to look at the Falls.   It
is certain that he was the first to make a sketch
of them for publication.   Such a sketch is en-
graved in his account of his journeys published
in Utrecht in 1697, and is extremely interesting and valuable as enabling us to realize the
changes which have since occurred in the con-
tour of the Falls.[2]

It was in the autumn of 1678 that La Salle
set sail in the Griffin. His departure was clouded
The voyage   by the news that impatient creditors
of the Griffin had laid hands upon his Canadian
estates, but nothing daunted, he pushed on
through Lakes Erie and Huron, and after many
disasters reached the southern extremity of Lake
Michigan.   The Griffin was now sent back with
half the party to the Niagara River with a cargo
of furs to appease the creditors and purchase

[1] [Hennepin, in his *Nouvelle Découverte d'un grand Pays
situé dans l'Amérique,* Utrecht, 1697, affirmed that he himself had explored the Mississippi to its mouth, in 1680, thus
anticipating the great exploit of La Salle, and he gave an account of the voyage.   This account Hennepin based on the
journal that Father Membré kept of his voyage down the
river in company with La Salle.]

[2] [Hennepin's sketch of the Falls is reproduced in Winsor's *Narr. and Crit. Hist.,* iv. 248.]

additional supplies for the remainder of the journey, while La Salle, with his diminished company, pushed on to the Illinois, where a fort was built and appropriately named Fort Crève-cœur. It was indeed at a heart-breaking moment that it was finished, for so much time had elapsed since the departure of their little ship that all had come to despair of her return. No word ever came from her. In that time of universal suspicion there were not wanting whispers that her crew had deserted and scuttled her, carrying off her goods to trade with on their own account. But perhaps she may simply have foundered in some violent gale on the lakes.

After a winter of misery it was evident that nothing could make up for the loss of the Griffin, except a journey on foot to Montreal. Accordingly, in March, 1680, La Salle started on this terrible walk of 1000 miles, leaving Fort Crèvecœur under command of the faithful Tonty. La Salle had with him a long-tried Indian guide, a Mohegan from Connecticut, who for many years had roamed over the country. He took with him also four Frenchmen ; and these six fought their way eastward through the wilderness, now floundering through melting snow, now bivouacking in clothes stiff with frost, now stopping to make a bark canoe, now leaping across streams on floating ice-cakes, like the runaway

La Salle's terrible winter journey

slave girl in " Uncle Tom's Cabin ; " in such
plight did they make their way across Michigan
and along the north shore of Lake Erie to the little blockhouse above Niagara Falls.   All but La
Salle had given out on reaching Lake Erie, and
the five sick men were ferried across by him in
a bark canoe to the blockhouse.   We may see
here how the sustaining power of wide-ranging
thoughts and a lofty purpose enabled the scholar
reared in luxury to surpass in endurance the
Indian guide and the hunters inured to the
hardships of the forest.   He had need of all this
sustaining power, for at Niagara he learned that
a ship from France, freighted for him with a
cargo worth about $30,000 in our modern
money, had been wrecked in the St. Lawrence,
and everything lost.   He received this stagger-
ing news with his wonted iron composure, and
taking three fresh men in place of his invalids,
completed his march of 1000 miles to Montreal.   There he collected supplies and reinforcements, and, returning as far as Fort Fron-
Fresh disas- tenac, was taking a moment's rest preters   paratory to a fresh start when further
ill tidings arrived.   In July there came a message from the fort so well named Heart-break.
The garrison had mutinied, and after driving
away Tonty with such men as were faithful,
they had pulled the blockhouse to pieces and

made their way eastward through Michigan. Recruiting their ranks with divers wood rangers of ill repute, they had plundered the station at Niagara, and their canoes were now cruising on Lake Ontario in the hope of crowning their work with the murder of La Salle. These wretches, however, fell into their own pit. Between hearing and acting, the interval with La Salle was not a long one. That indomitable commander's canoes were soon upon the lake, and in a few days he had waylaid and captured the mutineers and sent them in chains to be dealt with by the viceroy. La Salle now kept on his way to the Illinois River, intending to rebuild his fort and hoping to rescue Tonty with the few faithful followers who had survived the mutiny. That

La Salle goes to rescue Tonty

little party had found shelter among the Illinois Indians ; but during the summer of 1680 the great village of the Illinois was sacked by the Iroquois, and the hard-pressed Frenchman retreated up the western shore of Lake Michigan as far as Green Bay. When La Salle reached the Illinois village he found nothing but the horrible vestiges of fiery torments and cannibal feasts. The only thing to be done was without delay to utilize the situation by cementing a firmer alliance than before with the western Algonquins on the basis of their common enmity to the Iroquois. After thus spending the winter to good purpose, he set out again for Canada in May, 1681, to arrange his affairs and once more obtain fresh resources. At Mackinaw his heart was rejoiced at meeting his friend Tonty, after all these wild vicissitudes, and together they paddled their canoes a thousand miles and came to Fort Frontenac.

Destruction of the Illinois village by the Iroquois

La Salle's enemies had begun to grow quite merry over his repeated discomfitures, but at length his stubborn courage for a time vanquished the adverse fates. On the next venture things went smoothly and according to the programme. In the autumn he started with a fleet of canoes, passed up the lakes from Ontario to the head of Michigan, crossed the narrow portage from the Chicago River to the Illinois, and thence coming out upon the Mississippi, glided down to its mouth. On the 9th of April, 1682, the fleurs-de-lis were duly planted, and all the country drained by the great river and its tributaries, a country far vaster than La Salle ever imagined, was solemnly declared to be the property of the king of France, and named for him Louisiana.[1]

La Salle's winter voyage down the Mississippi

Returning up the Mississippi after this

---

[1] [Father Membré's narrative of this voyage is given in translation in J. G. Shea's *Discovery and Exploration of the Mississippi Valley*, pp. 165–184.]

triumph, La Salle established a small fortified post on the Illinois River which he called St. Louis of the Illinois. Leaving Tonty in command there, he lost no time in returning to France for means to complete his scheme. The time had arrived for founding a town at the mouth of the Mississippi and connecting it with Canada by a line of military posts. La Salle was well received by the king, and a fine expedition was fitted out, but once more the fates began to frown and everything was ruined by the ill fortune of the naval commander, Beaujeu, whom it was formerly customary to blame more than he seems really to have deserved. The intention was to sail directly to the mouth of the Mississippi, but the pilots missed it and passed beyond; some of the ships were wrecked on the coast of Texas; the captain, beset by foul weather and pirates, disappeared with the rest, and was seen no more. Two years of misery followed, and with the misery such quarrelling and mutual hatred as had scarcely been equalled since the days of the early Spanish explorers in South America. At last, in March, 1687, La Salle started on foot in search of the Mississippi, hoping to ascend it and find succour at Tonty's fort; but he had scarcely set out with this forlorn hope when

La Salle returns to France

Failure of the Mississippi expedition

two or three mutineers skulked in ambush and shot him dead.   Thus was cut short at the early

La Salle's   age of forty-two the career of the man
death   whose personality is impressed in some respects more strongly than that of any other upon the history of New France. His schemes were too far-reaching to succeed. They required the strength and resources of half a dozen nations like the France of Louis XIV. Nevertheless, the lines upon which New France continued to develop were substantially those which La Salle had in mind, and the fabric of a wilderness-empire, of which he laid the foundations, grew with the general growth of colonization, and in the next century became truly formidable. It was not until Wolfe climbed the Heights of Abraham that the great ideal of La Salle was finally overthrown.

V

WITCHCRAFT IN SALEM VILLAGE

IN the year 1670 the provincial parliament of Normandy condemned a dozen women, young and old, to be burned at the stake. Their crime was attendance upon the Witches' Sabbath. An appeal was taken to the Crown, and Louis XIV. was persuaded to spare their lives on condition that they should leave the kingdom and never return. Astonishment and indignation greeted this exercise of royal clemency, and the provincial parliament sent a petition to the king containing a grave remonstrance : "Your parliament have thought it their duty on occasion of these crimes, the greatest which men can commit, to make you acquainted with the general and uniform feeling of the people of this province with regard to them ; it being moreover a question in which are concerned the glory of God and the relief of your suffering subjects, who groan under their fears from the threats and menaces of this sort of persons. . . . We humbly supplicate

Louis XIV. commutes the sentence of death imposed upon alleged witches

your Majesty to reflect once more upon the
extraordinary results which proceed from the
The parliament of Normandy protests malevolence of these people; on
the loss of goods and chattels, and
the deaths from unknown diseases,
which are often the consequence of their menaces ; . . . all of which may easily be proved
to your Majesty's satisfaction by the records of
various trials before your parliaments." It is
pleasant to be able to add that Louis XIV. was
too well versed in the professional etiquette of
royalty to withdraw a pardon which he had
once granted, and so the poor women were
saved from the flames. What we have especially to note is that the highest court of Normandy, representing the best legal knowledge
of that province, in defining witchcraft as the
infliction of disease or the destruction of property by unknown and mysterious means, describes it as the greatest of all crimes, and has
no more doubt of its reality than of burglary
or highway robbery.[1]

This unquestioning belief in the reality of
witchcraft has been shared by the whole human

---

[1] [For the original text and further particulars in regard to
this petition Lecky refers to Garinet, *Histoire de la Magie
en France*, p. 337. Cf. also Rambaud, *Hist. de la Civilisa-
tion Française*, ii. 154. "In 1672, Colbert directed the
magistrates to receive no accusations of sorcery." Lecky,
Hist. of Rationalism, i. 118.]

race, civilized and uncivilized alike, from pre-
historic ages to the end of the seven- The belief in
teenth century.[1] There are tribes of witchcraft
men with minds so little developed universal
that travellers have doubted the existence of
religious ideas among them; but none have
been found so low as not to have some notion
of witchcraft. Indeed, one of the most primi-

[1] [For a comprehensive survey of the history of witchcraft
and allied occult phenomena, from the standpoint of modern
psychology, see Alfr. Lehman, *Aberglaube und Zauberei*,
Stuttgart, 1898. Mr. Lecky's opening chapter on Magic
and Witchcraft, in his *History of Rationalism*, still remains
for the English reader the most convenient sketch of witchcraft in modern times. On the rise of modern witchcraft,
the most scholarly investigation in English is that of H. C.
Lea, in his *Inquisition in the Middle Ages*, vol. iii. chaps. vi.
and vii.

Recently there has appeared an investigation into the beginnings of the witchcraft delusion that surpasses all previous
works in scientific thoroughness. It is Joseph Hansen's
*Quellen und Untersuchungen zur Geschichte der Hexenwahns
und der Hexenverfolgung im Mittelalter*, Bonn, 1901.
Hansen has presented his results in popular form in his *Zau-
berwahn, Inquisition und die Entstehung der Grossen Hexenverfolgung*, Munich, 1901. In the *Report of the American
Hist. Assoc.* for 1890 will be found an admirably compact
and learned sketch of "The Literature of Witchcraft," by
Professor George L. Burr. An excellent selection of extracts
illustrating the belief in witchcraft, the methods of trial, and
the growth of the opposition is given in Professor Burr's *The
Witch-Persecutions*, a pamphlet published by the University
of Pennsylvania.]

tive and fundamental shapes which the relation of cause and effect takes in the savage mind is the assumed connection between disease or death and some malevolent personal agency. The conceptions of natural disease and natural death are attainable only by civilized minds. To the savage, who has scarcely an inkling of such a thing as laws of nature, all death is regarded as murder, either at the hands of a superhuman power that must be propitiated, or at the hands of some human being upon whom vengeance may be wreaked. The interpretation of disease is the same, and hence one of the chief occupations of medicine-men and priests among barbarous races is the detection and punishment of witches.[1] Hence among all the superstitions, — or things that have " stood over " from primeval ages, — the belief in witchcraft Vitality of has been the most deeply rooted and the belief the most tenacious of life. In all times and places, until quite lately among the most advanced communities, the reality of witchcraft has been accepted without question, and scarcely any human belief is supported by so vast a quantity of recorded testimony.

At the present day, among communities like

[1] [On the stubborn resistance made in modern times to the displacement of the Satanic theory of disease and disaster by scientific theories, see A. D. White, *History of the Warfare of Science with Theology,* chaps. xi.-xvi.]

our own, we may observe a wonderful change. Among educated people the belief in witchcraft is practically extinct. It has not simply ceased to be taken seriously, but it has vanished from people's minds. We recognize it as one of the grotesque features in an Indian's theory of things, or perhaps we find it cropping out among the odds and ends of diabolism that the negro mind retains from the old stock of African folk-lore, but we no longer associate such a belief with civilized men, and a good deal of historical study is needed to enable us to realize adequately its omnipresence only two centuries ago.

What has caused this remarkable change in our mental attitude toward witchcraft? Surely not argument. Nobody has ever re- *Cause of the* futed the evidence that once seemed *final decay of* so conclusive in favour of the belief. *the belief* For the most part we should now regard that evidence as not worth the trouble of refuting. Some powerful cause has made our minds insuperably inhospitable to such sort of evidence. That cause is the gigantic development of physical science since the days of Newton and Descartes. The minds of civilized people have become familiar with the conception of natural law, and that conception has simply stifled the old superstition as clover chokes out weeds. It

has been observed that the existence of evidence
in favour of witchcraft closely depends
upon the disposition to believe it, so
that when the latter ceases the former disappears. Accordingly we find no difficulty in understanding the universality of the belief until quite modern times. The disposition to believe was one of the oldest inheritances of the human mind, while the capacity for estimating evidence in cases of physical causation is one of its very latest and most laborious acquisitions.

Rise of physical science

In 1664 there was a witch trial at Bury St. Edmunds in Suffolk. The presiding justice was Sir Matthew Hale, one of the most eminent and learned of English judges. Two aged widows, Amy Duny and Rose Cullender, were indicted for bewitching six young girls and one baby boy. This infant was seized with fainting turns, and his mother, suspecting witchcraft, took counsel of a country doctor, who told her to hang the child's crib blanket all day in the chimney corner, and if on taking it down at nightfall she should see anything strange there, she was not to be afraid of it, but to throw it into the fire. Well, when she was putting the baby to bed she took down the blanket, and a big toad fell out and hopped about the hearth. " Oh, put it in the fire, quick," said she to a boy

An English witch trial before Sir Matthew Hale

present, who forthwith seized the poor toad with a pair of tongs and held it in the blaze. There was a flashing as of powder, and a strange noise, and then the toad vanished ; but that Grotesque same evening Amy Duny sitting by evidence her own fireside had her face all smirched and scorched. Of course Amy was the toad, and it was natural that she should be vexed at such treatment, so that when the baby's sister suddenly sickened and died, and its mother grew lame enough to use crutches, it was all clearly due to Amy's diabolical arts. Absolute demonstration was reached when Amy was sentenced to death, for then her witch-power ceased, and the lame woman forthwith threw away her crutches and walked as briskly as anybody.

The other afflicted children complained of griping pains, and vomited crooked pins and twopenny nails. In the court-room when Amy Duny or Rose Cullender came near to them, they threw their aprons over their heads and writhed in agony. It happened that among the magistrates present were some hard-headed Sadducees. Lord Cornwallis and Sir Edmund Bacon suspected these fits and torments of being a wicked sham. They blindfolded the Indications of girls, and had other old women ap- shamming proach and touch them. The girls ignored went off into fits every time without discrimi-

nating between Rose or Amy and the other women. But this trifling flaw in the case was
nothing when set off against the weighty evidence of a witness who declared that Rose Cullender had given him hard words, and shortly
afterwards his hay-cart was stuck in passing
through a gate. Another deposed that Amy
Duny had said, "That chimney of yours will be
falling down one of these days," and so sure
enough it did. After this there could be no
doubt in any reasonable mind that Rose had bewitched the cart and Amy the chimney. The
learned justice in his charge aimed a rebuke at
the scepticism exhibited by some of the magis-
Sir Matthew trates; he declared that the reality of
Hale affirms
the reality of witchcraft was not open to question,
witchcraft since it was expressly affirmed in Holy
Writ, and provided for in the criminal codes of
all nations. The jury took less than half an hour
to agree upon their verdict of guilty ; and next
week the two old dames were hanged at Cambridge, protesting their innocence with their last
breath.[1]

Upon just such so-called " evidence " more
thousands of innocent persons than it will ever

[1] Linton's *Witch Stories*, p. 395. [Cotton Mather
printed an account of this trial in his *Wonders of the Invisible
World*, London reprint, 1862, pp. 111–120. He says it
" was a Tryal much considered by the Judges of New England." Ibid. p. 111.]

be possible to enumerate have been put to death under the forms of law. It is difficult to accept all the wholesale figures mentioned by old historians, yet the figures for which we have good authority are sufficiently dreadful. In general we may regard it as probable that during the Middle Ages executions for witchcraft occurred with much the same monotonous regularity as executions for murder and other felonies, but from time to time there were epidemics of terror when the number of victims was fearfully swelled. Now the famous bull of Pope Innocent VIII. against witchcraft, published in 1484, marks the beginning of a new era in the history of the superstition.[1] As literature and art have had their Golden Ages, so the sixteenth and seventeenth centuries were especially the Sulphurous Age of the witchcraft delusion. It was the period when the Church of Rome was engaged in a life and death struggle with heresy, and obnoxious persons suspected of heresy could sometimes be destroyed by a charge of witchcraft when there was no other method of reaching them. Thus the universal superstition was enlisted in the service of a militant and unscrupulous ecclesiastical organization with effects that were frightful. As it was understood that the diabolical crime of

Revival of witchcraft superstition

[1] [This bull is given in an English translation by Burr, *The Witch-Persecutions*, pp. 7–10.]

witchcraft was now to be stamped out once for all, the evidences of it were naturally found in plenty. The "Malleus Maleficarum," or Hammer of Witches,[1] published in 1489, became the great text-book of the subject, and at no time since history began have the fires of hell been so often lighted upon earth as in the course of the next two centuries.

The Ham-
mer of
Witches

We are told by Martin del Rio that in 1515 not less than 500 witches were executed in the single city of Geneva; and a certain inquisitor named Remigio boasted that in his district, in the north of Italy, within fifteen years he had personally superintended the burning of more than 900 such criminals.[2] In Scotland, from 1560 to 1600, the average annual number of victims was 200, making a grim and ghastly total of 8000 for the forty years. Or, to put it in another form, the executions averaged four each week in a population about equal to that of Massachusetts at the present day. In 1597 that grotesque royal author, James VI., published at Edinburgh his treatise on "Dæmono-

---

[1] [An extract from this book is given by Burr, *The Witch-Persecutions*, and an analysis of it in Roskoff's *Geschichte des Teufels*, ii. 226–292. Cf. also Hansen, as above.]

[2] [Williams, *The Superstitions of Witchcraft*, p. 107. See also White, *Warfare of Science and Theology*, i. 358, 359.]

logie," in which he maintained that against so foul a crime as witchcraft any sort of evidence is good enough, and the testimony of very young children, or of persons of the vilest character, ought on no account to be omitted. In the course of our story we shall see that James was by no means singular in this absurd style of reasoning. In 1604, scarcely more than a year after he had become King of England, Parliament passed the famous "Witch Act," which remained on the statute-book until the reign of George II.

King James on the reality of witchcraft

It was in the reign of Charles I. that trials and executions under the Witch Act were most frequent. While the Long Parliament was in session the affair attained almost the proportions of an epidemic, but under the rule of Cromwell there was a sudden halt, and thereafter the delusion never fully recovered its hold upon the community. Cases like those of Amy Duny and Rose Cullender were sporadic. In that age of Newton and Locke, the whole baleful troop of demons were spreading their wings for their final flight from this world.

The delusion increases with the rise of the Puritan party to power

The last executions for witchcraft, however, occurred in England in 1712 and in Scotland in 1722.[1] We may observe in passing that in

---

[1] [Cf. Lecky, i. 139.]

Germany the case of Maria Renata, a nun be-
headed for witchcraft, occurred as late
as 1749, the year in which Goethe
was born.[1]

Considering the fact that the exodus of
Puritans to New England occurred during the
reign of Charles I., while the prosecutions for
witchcraft were increasing toward a maximum
in the mother country, it is rather strange that
so few cases occurred in the New World. It
was already noted in Cromwell's time that Independency in ecclesiastical matters seemed to
be attended by a diminution of activity in the
world of witches, but on the other hand the
Independents who came over to New England voluntarily thrust themselves
into a country which was supposed
to be in a special sense under the
direct control and administration of
the Devil. It was believed that Pagan countries generally were ruled by Satan, and that
here in the American wilderness that old foe of
mankind had taken his stand to annoy and dis-
hearten the Lord's elect. As for the red men,
it was easy to see that they were his veritable
imps ; their tricks and manners proclaimed them

---

1 [On this case see White, *Warfare of Science*, ii. 121 and
156. He refers in particular to an essay on Maria (or Anna)
Renata by Johannes Scherr in his *Hammerschläge und Histo-
rien*.]

as such. There could be little doubt that the heathen New World was Satan's Kingdom ;[1] and in view of this very common belief it is strange that the instances of witchcraft or diabolism were so rare in the early history of New England.

During the sixty years following the first settlement of Boston, a dozen or more cases can be enumerated. The first victim in the New World was Margaret Jones, of Charlestown, who had some sensible ideas about medicine. She disapproved of wholesale bleeding and violent emetics, and used to work cures by means of herb tonics and other simple prescriptions. This offended the doctors, and in 1648 the poor woman was tried for witchcraft, convicted, and hanged. Governor Winthrop, who tells the story, adds that at the very hour of her execution there was a great gale in Connecticut, which blew down trees, and this he considers an absolute demonstration of her guilt.[2] When Winthrop wrote this, Isaac Newton was a child playing in the nursery. When we see a mind so broad and cultivated as Winthrop's enter-

The first victim of the witchcraft delusion in New England

[1] [See Cotton Mather, *The Wonders of the Invisible World*, London, 1693, London reprint, 1862, p. 74.]

[2] [See Winthrop, ii. 326 (rev. ed., ii. 397); W. F. Poole, *No. Am. Rev.*, April, 1869, pp. 343, 344.]

taining such notions of cause and effect, is it not obvious that the mainstay and support of the frightful superstition was ignorance of physical science?

About the same time, according to Thomas Hutchinson, a woman was hanged at Dorchester, and another at Cambridge, for the crime of witchcraft. The next case was a startling one, on account of the victim's social position. A woman like Margaret Jones, though perhaps educated, and such as would to-day be classed as a lady, was in those times not called Mrs. Jones, but simply Goodwife or Goody Jones. To be Mrs., or Mistress, one must be the wife of an esquire, and the rank of esquire was as carefully guarded in common forms of speech as the rank of knight or baronet. The next victim of the witch-delusion was Mistress The case of Ann Hibbins. Her husband, Wil-Mrs. Hibbins liam Hibbins, who died in 1654, had been for twelve years a member of the council of assistants, and at one time was the colony's diplomatic agent in England. Her brother, Richard Bellingham, was deputy-governor of Massachusetts. In 1656 this lady was tried for witchcraft before Governor Endicott and the General Court. She was found guilty, and was hanged on Boston Common on the 19th of June of that year. The verdict and death-warrant are in the Colonial Records,[1] but we have no report of the case, and do not know how the accusation was originated. Hutchinson, whose great-grandfather Edward was one of the lady's friends, believed it to be a case of outrageous persecution, and so some of her contemporaries regarded it. The Rev. John Norton, persecutor of Quakers, was by temperament quick to see marks of Satan's presence, but he tried his best to save Mrs. Hibbins, and afterward spoke of her accusers with his customary sarcasm. Mrs. Hibbins was A victim of malice acting through superstition hanged, he said, "only for having more wit than her neighbours."[2] One day she saw two persons whom she knew to be unfriendly to her talking together in the street, whereupon she exclaimed that she knew they were talking about her. Her guess being correct was forthwith cited against her as an instance of supernatural insight which must have been imparted to her by the Devil. According to Norton this argument had great weight with the Court. It is a pity, and it is strange too, that we know so little of this case, for there must have been something extraordinary in the circumstances that could thus send to the gallows one of the foremost persons in that colonial society. There

[1] [*Mass. Records*, iv. pt. i. 269. The record is quoted in Winsor's *Memorial Hist. of Boston*, ii. 139.]

[2] [Hutchinson's *Hist. of Mass.*, i. 173.]

is evidence that the affair created fierce excitement and left much bitterness behind. There were many in Boston who insisted that a saint had been wickedly done to death by slanderous tongues.

Out of a dozen cases in the course of the next thirty years we find several acquittals, and once in a while we encounter a gleam of genuine common sense, as in the case of John Bradstreet of Rowley, who was accused of familiarity with the Devil; forasmuch as the said Bradstreet confessed that he had " read in a book of magic, and that he heard a voice asking him what work he had for him. He answered, ' Go make a

A sensible bridge of sand over the sea; go make
jury   a ladder of sand up to heaven, and go
to God, and come down no more.' " When the case was tried at Ipswich, the jury found that the said Bradstreet lied, whereupon the court sentenced him to pay twenty shillings fine or else to be whipped.[1]

More disastrous was the case of the Goodwin children in Boston in 1688. An Irish Catholic woman named Glover was laundress for John Goodwin's family, in which there were four children. One day the eldest child, Martha, aged thirteen, accused the Glover woman of purloining some pieces of linen. Glover an-

[1] [Nevins, *Witchcraft in Salem Village*, p. 34. This case occurred in 1652.]

swered with threats and curses, and Martha presently fell down in a fit. The other children — aged eleven, seven, and five — soon followed her example. Then they went through with all sorts of pranks : they would pretend The Good-win children to be deaf and dumb ; they would complain of being pricked with pins or cut with knives ; they would bark like dogs and purr like cats ; they even performed feats of what modern spirit-rappers call "levitation," skimming over the ground without appearing to touch it, seeming, as Cotton Mather said, to "fly like geese." This sort of thing went on for several weeks. Doctors and ministers agreed that the children must have been bewitched by the Glover woman, and she was accordingly hanged.

The chief interest in this case arises from Cotton Mather's connection with it. That famous divine, son of Increase Mather Cotton Mather and grandson of John Cotton, was then five and twenty years of age. He had been graduated at Harvard ten years before, his career as an author had already begun, and he was already regarded as the most learned man of his time. The range of his reading was enormous. Theology, philosophy, history, literature, physical science, in all these he was omnivorous, and he could write and speak at least seven languages (one of them the Iroquois) with fluency and precision.[1] In the course of his life he published nearly four hundred books and tracts, most of which bring a high price now, while some are indispensable to the student of history. He was an earnest and severely conscientious man. His chief foible was vanity, which was perhaps not strange in view of the wholesale homage and adulation to which he was accustomed. He was not a profound or original thinker, nor was he free from the errors and superstitions characteristic of his time; but in most matters his face was set toward the future and his work was helpful to mankind. In 1721, in spite of furious opposition and some personal peril, he succeeded in introducing into America inoculation for small-pox,[2] the most conspicuous among many instances in which he showed himself wiser than his contemporaries. With his other fine qualities he was a man of loving heart and gracious sympathies. But in the disputes and conflicts of his time he took too prominent a part to get along without making enemies; and so it happened that after the witchcraft delusion had become thoroughly discredited, a malicious writer saw fit to distort and misrepresent his relations to it. The slanders of Robert Calef

His character

His courage in advocating inoculation

[1] [Samuel Mather, *Life of Cotton Mather*, p. 49.]
[2] [See Peabody's *Life of Cotton Mather*, pp. 311–326.]

became the commonplaces of historical writers in a later generation, and the memory Views of Calef and Upham of Cotton Mather has been held up to scorn as that of the man who did more than any one else to stimulate and foster the witchcraft delusion in Massachusetts. This view is maintained by Charles Wentworth Upham, in his history of "Salem Witchcraft," published in 1867 in two volumes, the most learned and elaborate work on the subject.[1] It was repeated at second hand from older writers and embellished with cheap rhetoric by George Bancroft, and has usually been copied by the makers of compendiums and school-books, so that it has obtained a firm lodgement in the popular mind. The correct view of Cotton Mather's relations to witchcraft was first set forth in Longfellow's "New England Tragedies," published in 1868. The poet had studied the original documents with profound attention, and his fine critical insight had detected the truth where Upham, the Dryasdust specialist, had missed it. But the first full and adequate statement of the case was made in Mr. W. F. Poole 1869 by the late William Frederick Poole, who was at that time librarian of the

---

[1] [For the literature of this subject, see G. H. Moore, *Bibliographical Notes on Witchcraft in Massachusetts*, Worcester, 1888, and Justin Winsor, "The Literature of Witchcraft

Boston Athenæum.[1] Cultivation of the critical faculty and the exercise of it upon original sources of information are perpetually obliging us to modify, and sometimes to reverse, long-accepted judgments upon historical characters and events. In the present brief narrative I shall simply indicate, without controversy, the true position of Cotton Mather.

His connection with the Goodwin case began late. He was the last minister invited to attend. He had nothing to do with the accusation or prosecution of the poor laundress, but after her

Cotton Mather and the Goodwin case

death sentence he visited her twice in prison to pray for her. She confessed to him that she had made a covenant with Satan, and was in the habit of going to meetings at which that personage was present. She was utterly impenitent and wanted none of his prayers. "However," as he says so sweetly in his account of the matter, "against her will I prayed with her, which, if it were a fault, it was in excess of pity." In her confession she implicated several other persons by name, but Mather never divulged any of these names, for, as he said, "we should be very tender in such

in New England," *Proceedings of the Am. Antiquarian Soc.,* 1895.]

1 [Mr. Poole's paper was published in the *No. Am. Review* in April, 1869. Mr. Upham replied to it in *The Historical Magazine* in September, 1869.]

relation, lest we wrong the reputation of the innocent by stories not enough inquired into." About the time of this woman's execution Mather took the little accuser, Martha Goodwin, into his own home and kept her there for several months, partly as a subject for investigation, partly a patient to be cured by prayer and judicious treatment,[1] for this brilliant young clergyman was also a doctor in medicine of no mean attainments, besides knowing more law, and knowing it to better purpose, than half the jurists of his time. The girl showed herself an actress of elf-like precocity and shrewdness. She wished to prove that she was bewitched, and she seems to have known Mather's prejudices against Quakers, Papists, and the Church of England; for she could read Quaker books and Catholic books fluently, and seemed quite in love with the Book of Common Prayer, but she could not read a word in the Bible or any book of Puritan theology, and even in her favourite Prayer Book, whenever she came to the Lord's Prayer, she faltered and

Cotton Mather and the Goodwin girl

Tests of bewitchment

---

[1] [" I took her home to my own family, partly out of compassion to her parents, but chiefly that I might be a critical eye-witness of things that would enable me to confute the *Sadducism* of this debauch'd age." Mather's *Magnalia*, ii. 460 (Hartford ed., 1853). The *Magnalia* was first published in 1700.]

failed. Gradually the young minister's firm
good sense and kindness prevailed in calming
her and making her discard such nonsense, but
during the cure her symptoms showed the
actress. She would refuse to go into the study,
lined with its goodly tomes of Greek and
Hebrew, because her devils forbade it ; then she
would go into hysterics of six-young-lady-power
until it occurred to some one of the family to
drag her, all screams and kicks, into the sacred
room; then she would instantly grow quiet
and say that the accursed thing had just gone
from her in the form of a mouse, — which was
of course a bit of ancient Teutonic folk-lore,
a remnant of the doctrine of changelings, im-
plicitly believed by our ancestors when they
lived in what Freeman used to call Oldest England, before ever Hengist and Horsa sailed for
Kent. After a while the little minx was cured ;
her distemper gave way to kind patience and
common sense, and the affair went no further.

Cotton Mather was a firm believer in the
reality of witchcraft. He published
an account of this case and its cure.[1]
His object in the publication was two-

Mather
publishes an
account of
this case

---

[1] [Mather's account of this case was included in his *Memorable Providences, relating to Witchcrafts and Possessions,*
etc., Boston, 1689. Reprinted in London in 1691 as *Late
Memorable Providences,* etc. He also gave a full account in
his *Magnalia,* Hartford ed., ii. 456–465.]

fold: first, to prove the reality of witchcraft against a few bold sceptics who were lately beginning to doubt it, in spite of the teachings of Holy Writ; secondly, to show the best method of effecting a cure. In this second point he was in advance of his age, and had others been as discreet and self-contained as he, there need have been no such tragedy as was soon to be enacted in Salem. All personal and local references, whatever could give the mania a concrete hold and a chance to work bodily mischief, he had kept, and ever after kept, locked up within his own breast. He had evidence enough, perhaps, to have hung half the old women in Boston, but his strong common sense taught him that the Devil is too tricksome a rascal to be worthy of much credit as an accuser. His rules of evidence were far in advance of those upon which the great lawyer, Sir Matthew Hale, had condemned people to death only four and twenty years before. Mather's rules would not have allowed a verdict of guilty simply upon the drivelling testimony of the afflicted persons, and if this wholesome caution had been observed, not a witch would ever have been hung at Salem.

Some writers have thought that the mere publication of Mather's book must have led to the outbreak of the delusion in Salem, since it must have helped put such ideas into the heads of Salem people. But this is forgetting that the superstitious ideas were in everybody's head already. Not a man, woman, or child in Massachusetts, or elsewhere in the civilized world, but knew exactly how a witch should behave. Tracts and chap-books on the wretched subject abounded, and poisoned young minds as dime novels do in our time. Even if Mather had written nothing, the execution of the Irish laundress and the pranks of her little accusers were familiar topics at every fireside in New England.

Cotton Mather's book and the Salem troubles

But in 1692, quite apart from any personal influence, there were circumstances which favoured the outbreak of an epidemic of witchcraft. In this ancient domain of Satan there were indications that Satan was beginning again to claim his own. War had broken out with that Papist champion, Louis XIV., and it had so far been going badly with God's people in America. The shrieks of the victims at Schenectady and Salmon Falls and Fort Loyal still made men's blood run cold in their veins; and the great expedition against Quebec had come home crestfallen with defeat. Evidently the Devil was bestirring himself; it was a witching time; the fuel for an explosion was laid, and it needed but a spark to fire it.

Gloomy outlook in 1692

That spark was provided by servants and

children in the household of Samuel Parris, minister of the church at Salem Village, a group of outlying farms from three to five miles out from the town of Salem. The place was sometimes called Salem Farms, and in later times was set off as a separate township under the name of Danvers. Any one who has ever visited a small New England village can _{Salem} form some idea of the looks of the _{Village} place, for the type is strongly characteristic, and from the days of Cotton Mather to the introduction of railroads the changes were not great. On almost any country roadside in Massachusetts you may see to-day just such wooden houses as that in which Samuel Parris dwelt. This clergyman seems to have lived for some years in the West Indies, engaged in commercial pursuits, before he turned his attention to theology. Some special mercantile connection between Salem and Barbadoes seems to have brought him to Salem Village, where he was installed as pastor in 1689. An entry _{Samuel} in the church records, dated June 18 _{Parris,} of that year, informs us that " it was _{the pastor} agreed and voted by general concurrence, that for Mr. Parris his encouragement and settlement in the work of the ministry amongst us, we will give him sixty-six pounds for his yearly salary, — one third paid in money, the other two third parts for provisions, etc. ; and Mr.

Parris to find himself firewood, and Mr. Parris
to keep the ministry-house in good repair ; and
that Mr. Parris shall also have the use of the
ministry-pasture, and the inhabitants to keep
the fence in repair ; and that we will keep up our
contributions . . . so long as Mr. Parris con-
tinues in the work of the ministry amongst us,
and all productions to be good and merchant-
able.   And if it please God to bless the inhabitants, we shall be willing to give more ; and to
expect that, if God shall diminish the estates of
the people, that then Mr. Parris do abate of his
salary according to proportion." [1]

This arrangement was far from satisfying the
new minister, for it only gave him the use of
the parsonage and its pasture lands, whereas
he was determined to get a fee simple of both.

Parish trou-
bles in Salem
Village

Another entry in the parish book
says that it was voted to make over
to him that real estate, but this entry
is not duly signed by the clerk, and at the time
there were parishioners who declared that it
must have been put into the book by fraudu-
lent means.   Out of these circumstances there
grew a quarrel which for utterly ruthless and
truculent bitterness has scarcely been equalled
even in the envenomed annals of New England
parishes.   Many people refused to pay their
church-rates till the meeting-house began to

[1] [C. W. Upham, *Salem Witchcraft*, i. 291.]

suffer for want of repairs, and complaints were made to the county court. Matters were made worse by Parris's coarse and arrogant manners, and his excessive severity in inflicting church discipline for trivial offences. By 1691 the factions into which the village was divided were ready to fly at each other's throats. Christian charity and loving-kindness were well-nigh forgotten. It was a spectacle such as Old Nick must have contemplated with grim satisfaction.

In the household at the parsonage were two coloured servants whom Parris had brought with him from the West Indies. The man was known as John Indian; the hag Tituba, who passed for his wife, was half-Indian and half-negro. Their intelligence was of a low grade, but it sufficed to make them experts in palmistry, fortune-telling, magic, second-sight, and incantations. Such lore is always attractive to children, and in the winter of 1691–92 quite a little circle of young girls got into the habit of meeting at the parsonage to try their hands at the Black Art. Under the tuition of the Indian servants they soon learned how to go into trances, talk gibberish, and behave like pythonesses of the most approved sort. These girls were Parris's daughter Elizabeth, aged nine, and his niece Abigail Williams, aged eleven; Mary Walcott and Eliza-

Mr. Parris's coloured servants

The "afflicted children"

beth Hubbard, each aged seventeen; Elizabeth Booth and Susannah Sheldon, each aged
eighteen; Mary Warren and Sarah Churchill,
each aged twenty. Conspicuous above all
in the mischief that followed were two girls
of wonderful adroitness and hardihood, Ann
Putnam, aged twelve, daughter of Sergeant
Thomas Putnam, and Mercy Lewis, aged
seventeen, a servant in his family. This
Thomas Putnam, who had taken part in the
great Narragansett fight, was parish clerk and
belonged to an aristocratic family. One of his
nephews was Israel Putnam, of Revolutionary
fame. Mistress Ann Putnam, the sergeant's
wife, was a beautiful and well-educated woman
of thirty, but so passionate and high-strung
Mistress Ann that in her best moments she was
Putnam scarcely quite sane. She was deeply
engaged in the village quarrels; she also played
an important part in supporting her daughter
Ann and her servant Mercy Lewis in some of
the most shocking work of that year. Beside
Mrs. Putnam, two other grown women, one
Sarah Vibber and a certain Goody Pope, appeared among the sufferers, but were of no
great account. The minister withdrew his own
daughter early in the proceedings and sent her
to stay with some friends in Salem town. The
chief managers of the witchcraft business, then,
were two barbarous Indians steeped to the

marrow in demonolatry, the half-crazed and vindictive Mrs. Putnam, and nine girls between the ages of eleven and twenty.

These girls came to be known as the "Afflicted Children." Their proceedings began at the parsonage about Christmas time, 1691. They would get down on all fours, crawl under chairs and tables, go off into fits, and speak an unintelligible jargon. All this may have been begun in sport. It would doubtless tickle them to find how well they could imitate Indian medicine, and the temptation to show off their accomplishments would be too great to be resisted. Then if they found their elders taking the affair too seriously, if they suddenly saw themselves in danger of getting whipped for meddling with such uncanny matters, what could be more natural than for them to seek an avenue of escape by declaring that they were bewitched and could not help doing as they did? As to these first steps the records leave us in the dark, but somewhat such, I suspect, they must have been. The next thing would be to ask them who bewitched them; and here the road to mischief was thrown open by Mr. Parris taking the affair into his own hands with a great flourish of trumpets, and making it as public as possible. Such was this man's way, as different as possible from Cotton Mather's.

Beginnings of the troubles

Physicians and clergymen, who came from all quarters to see the girls, agreed that they must be suffering from witchcraft. When commanded to point out their tormentors, they first named the Indian hag Tituba, and then Sarah Good and Sarah Osburn, two forlorn old women of the village, who were not held in high esteem. On the last day of February, 1692, these three were arrested, and the examinations began next day. The chief accusations against Sarah Good were that after she had spoken angrily to some neighbours their cattle sickened and died; that she threw Mary Walcott and other children into convulsions; and that she tried to persuade Ann Putnam to sign her name in a book. It was supposed that such signatures were equivalent to a quitclaim deed surrendering the signer's soul to the Devil; and his agents, the witches, were supposed to go about with that infernal autograph book soliciting signatures. Similar charges were brought against the other prisoners. In their presence the afflicted children raved and screamed. At the indignant denials of the two old white women the violence of these paroxysms became frightful, but when Tituba confessed that she was an adept in witchcraft and had enchanted the girls, their symptoms vanished and perfect calm ensued. As the result of the examination

Physicians and clergymen called in

The trial of Sarah Good

the three prisoners were sent to the jail in Boston to await their trial.[1]

The country was now getting alarmed, and the girls began to feel their power. Their next blow was aimed at victims of far higher sort. The wretched Tituba knew human nature well enough to consult her own safety by acting as king's evidence,[2] and in her examination she testified that four women of the village tormented the girls ; two of them were Good and Osburn, but the faces of the other two she said she could not see. After Tituba had gone to prison, the girls were urged to give up the names of these other two tormentors. At first they refused, but shortly it began to be whispered in bated breath that some of the most respected and godly persons in the village were leagued with Satan in this horrible conspiracy. About the middle of March the whole community was thunderstruck by the arrest of Martha Corey and Rebecca Nurse. Of these two ladies the for-

---

[1] [For the details of these examinations, see W. E. Woodward, *Records of Salem Witchcraft*, Roxbury, Mass., 1864, i. 1–49 ; Upham, ii. 4–32 ; Nevins, *Witchcraft in Salem Village*, pp. 57–69.]

[2] [" The account she since gives of it is, that her master did beat her, and otherways abuse her, to make her confess and accuse (such as he called) her sister-witches ; and that whatsoever she said by way of confessing, or accusing others, was the effect of such usage." Robert Calef, *More Wonders of the Invisible World*, Salem reprint, 1823, p. 189.]

mer was about sixty years of age, the latter
more than seventy. As they were addressed not
as " Mrs.," but as " Goodwife," their
position was not exactly aristocratic.
It was nevertheless most respectable.
They were thoroughly well-bred and
well-educated ladies, full of sweet courtesy and
simple-hearted kindliness, like the best of
farmers' wives in New England villages of to-
day. Martha Corey was third wife of Giles
Corey, a farmer eighty years old, a man of herculean stature and strength, proud, self-willed,
and contentious, but frank and noble, with a
rash, unruly tongue. He had been in many a
quarrel, and had made enemies. His wife, so far
as we know, had not. She was a wo-
man of deep and sincere piety, with as
clear and sound a head as could be
found anywhere between Cape Cod and Cape
Ann. She disbelieved in witchcraft, was inclined
to regard it as a mere delusion, and had no sympathy with the excitement which was beginning
to turn the village topsy-turvy. She did not
flock with the multitude to see the accusing
girls, but she reproved her more credulous husband for giving heed to such tomfoolery, and
he, with that uncurbed tongue of his, was heard
to utter indiscreet jests about his good wife's
scepticism. It was probably this that caused
her to be selected as a victim. Sceptics must

be made to feel the danger of impugning the authority of the accusers and the truth of their tales. Accordingly Martha Corey, accused by little Ann Putnam, was soon in jail awaiting trial.

The next was Rebecca Nurse. She was one of three sisters, daughters of William Towne of Yarmouth, in England. Her two Rebecca sisters, who were arrested soon after Nurse her, were Mary Easty and Sarah Cloyse. With their husbands they were all persons held in highest esteem, but an ancient village feud had left a grudge against them in some revengeful bosoms. Half a century before there had been a fierce dispute between parties from Salem and from Topsfield who had settled in the border region between the two townships. The dispute related to the possession of certain lots of land ; it had grown more and more complicated, and it had engendered hard feelings between A village the Putnams on one side and the feud Eastys and Townes on the other. Besides this, Rebecca Nurse and her husband had become obnoxious to the Putnams and to the Rev. Mr. Parris from reasons connected with the church dispute. There was evidently a method in the madness of the accusing girls. Rebecca Nurse was arrested two days after the committal of Martha Corey. The appearance of this venerable and venerated lady before the magistrates caused most profound sensation. Her numerous children and grandchildren stood high in public esteem, her husband was one of the most honoured persons in the community, herself a model of every virtue. As she stood there, delicate and fragile in figure, with those honest eyes that looked one full in the face, that soft gray hair and dainty white muslin kerchief, one marvels what fiend can have possessed those young girls that they did not shamefastly hold their peace. In the intervals of question and answer they went into fits as usual. When the magistrate Hathorne became visibly affected by the lady's clear and straightforward answers, the relentless Mrs. Putnam broke out with a violence dreadful to behold : "Did you not bring the black man with you ? Did you not bid me tempt God and die ? How oft have you eaten and drunk your own damnation ?" At this outburst, like the horrible snarl of a lioness, the poor old lady raised her hands toward heaven and cried, "O Lord, help me ! " Whereupon all the afflicted girls "were grievously vexed." Hathorne thought that their spasms were caused by a mysterious influence emanating from Goodwife Nurse's lifted hands, and so his heart was hardened toward her. Mary Walcott cried out that the prisoner was biting her, and then showed marks of teeth upon her wrist. Thus the abominable scene went on till

The examination of Rebecca Nurse

Rebecca Nurse was remanded to jail to await her trial.

That was on a Thursday morning. The Rev. Deodat Lawson, a fine scholar and powerful preacher, had arrived in the village a few days before, and it was known that he was to preach the afternoon sermon familiar in those days as the Thursday lecture. He had scarcely arrived when two or three of the girls called upon him and drove him nearly out of his wits with their performances. Their victory over him was complete, and the result was seen in that Thursday lecture, which was afterwards printed, and is a literary production of great intensity and power. The arrests of Martha Corey and Rebecca Nurse had destroyed all confidence, everybody distrusted his neighbour, and that impassioned sermon goaded the whole community to madness. If the Devil could use such " gospel women " for his instruments, what safety was there for anybody ? Arrests went on with increasing rapidity during the spring and summer, until at least 126 persons, of whom we know the names and something of the family history, were lodged in jail ; and these names do not exhaust the number. Among them — to mention only such as were executed — we may note that John Procter and the venerable George Jacobs had each had one of the accusing girls in his family

Deodat Lawson

The spread of the delusion

as a domestic servant, and in both cases personal malice was visibly at work. In the case Cases of personal malice of George Jacobs it may also be observed that his own granddaughter, to save her own life, confessed herself a witch, and testified against him ; afterward she confessed this horrible wickedness. Sarah Wildes, Elizabeth How, and Mary Easty were connected with the Topsfield affair already mentioned. Some, such as Susannah Martin, seem to have owed their fate to mere superstition of the lowest sort. On a rainy day she walked over a good bit of country road without getting her hose or skirts muddy, and it was sagely concluded that such neatness could only have been attained through the aid of the Devil. She was mother of the Mabel Martin about whom Whittier wrote his beautiful poem, " The Witch's Daughter." John Willard incurred his doom for having said that it was the accusing girls who were the real witches worthy of the gallows, and John Procter in a similar spirit had said that by the judicious application of a cudgel he could effect a prompt and thorough cure for all the little hussies. People who ventured such remarks took their lives in their hands.

The boldest and most remarkable of all these arrests was that of the Rev. George Burroughs, and it was one of the cases in which malice was most clearly concerned. This gentleman was graduated at Harvard College in 1670, and had been pastor over the church in Salem Village from 1680 to 1682. He had left there because of church feuds, in which he had the misfortune to belong to the party hostile to Mrs. Ann Putnam and her friends. He was afterwards settled over a church in Wells, Maine, and was living there quietly in 1692, when about the first of May he was arrested and taken to Salem to answer a charge of witchcraft. His physical strength was alleged against him. Though small in frame he could carry a barrel of cider and hold out a heavy musket at arm's length, which without infernal aid was not likely. On accusations brought by the afflicted girls he was thrown into prison.[1]

The Rev. George Burroughs

All the events thus far recounted happened under the provisional government of Massachusetts that followed the overthrow of Andros. Now in the middle of May the first royal governor, Sir William Phips, arrived in Boston with the new charter. Military duties soon called him far down East, and he did not return till October. Before his departure he appointed a special court of Oyer and Terminer to try the witchcraft cases. William Stoughton was presiding justice, and among his colleagues it may suffice to mention John Hathorne for his connection with one of the

The special court erected

[1] [Cf. Nevins, *Witchcraft in Salem Village*, pp. 131 ff.]

most illustrious names in modern literature, and Samuel Sewall, in whose voluminous diary we have such a wonderful picture of that old Puritan society.

Early in the proceedings this court requested the opinion of the ministers in Boston and neighbouring towns concerning the subject then uppermost in all minds. The opinion, written by Cotton Mather, one of the youngest of the ministers, and subscribed by all the most eminent, was calm and judicial. It ran as follows : —

BOSTON, June 15, 1692.

1. "The afflicted state of our poor neighbours that are now suffering by molestations *The advice of* from the Invisible World we appre-*the ministers* hend so deplorable, that we think their condition calls for the utmost help of all persons in their several capacities.

2. "We cannot but with all thankfulness acknowledge the success which the merciful God has given unto the sedulous and assiduous endeavours of our honourable rulers to detect the abominable witchcrafts which have been committed in the country ; humbly praying that the discovery of these mysterious and mischievous wickednesses may be perfected.

3. "We judge that, in the prosecution of these and all such witchcrafts there is need of a very critical and exquisite caution, lest by too

much credulity for things received only upon the devil's authority, there be a door opened for a long train of miserable consequences, and Satan get an advantage over us ; for we should not be ignorant of his devices.

4. " As in complaints upon witchcraft there may be matters of inquiry which do not amount unto matters of presumption, and there may be matters of presumption which yet may not be matters of conviction, so it is necessary that all proceedings thereabout be managed with an exceeding tenderness toward those that may be complained of, especially if they have been persons formerly of an unblemished reputation.

5. " When the first inquiry is made into the circumstances of such as may lie under the just suspicion of witchcrafts, we could wish that there may be admitted as little as possible of such noise, company and openness as may too hastily expose them that are examined, and that there may be nothing used as a test for the trial of the suspected, the lawfulness whereof may be doubted by the people of God, but that the directions given by such judicious writers as Perkins and Barnard may be observed.

6. " Presumptions whereupon persons may be committed, and much more, convictions whereupon persons may be condemned as guilty of witchcrafts, ought certainly to be more considerable than barely the accused persons being

represented by a spectre unto the afflicted, inasmuch as it is an undoubted and notorious thing, that a demon may by God's permission appear, even to ill purposes, in the shape of an innocent, yea, and a virtuous man. Nor can we esteem alterations made in the sufferers, by a look or touch of the accused, to be an infallible evidence of guilt, but frequently liable to be abused by the devil's legerdemains.

7. "We know not whether some remarkable affronts given the devils, by our disbelieving these testimonies whose whole force and strength is from them alone, may not put a period unto the progress of the dreadful calamity begun upon us, in the accusation of so many persons, whereof some, we hope, are yet clear from the great transgression laid to their charge.

8. "Nevertheless, we cannot but humbly recommend unto the government, the speedy and vigorous prosecutions of such as have rendered themselves obnoxious, according to the directions given in the laws of God and the wholesome statutes of the English nation for the detection of witchcrafts."

Had these recommendations been followed, not a single capital conviction could have been secured. Note the warning to the judges against relying upon "spectral evidence" or upon the physical effects apparently wrought upon the accusers by the presence of the accused persons, since evidence of that sort is "frequently liable to be abused by the devil's legerdemains." Now every one of the victims was convicted and hung upon the strength of "spectral evidence" or the tantrums of the afflicted children, or both combined. And what, pray, was "spectral evidence"? Little Ann Putnam's testimony against Mr. Burroughs was an instance of it. She said that one evening the apparition of a minister came to her and asked her to write her name in the devil's book; then came the forms of two women in winding sheets, and looked angrily Spectral evidence upon the minister and scolded him till he was fain to vanish away; then the women told little Ann that they were the ghosts of Mr. Burroughs's first and second wives whom he had murdered, and one of them showed the very place under the left arm where he had stabbed her. At another time three other persons who had recently died appeared to Ann and accused Mr. Burroughs of murdering them, and commanded her to tell these things to the magistrates before Mr. Burroughs's face. On such evidence was a gentleman and scholar condemned to death.[1] So when Mercy Lewis was found sobbing and screaming, "Dear Lord, receive my soul," "O Lord, let them not kill

[1] [See Cotton Mather's account of Burroughs's case, *Wonders of the Invisible World*, pp. 120 ff.]

me quite," the same Ann Putnam and Abigail Williams were sent for to see what was the matter, and both declared that they saw the apparitions of Mary Easty and John Willard pinching and biting and strangling poor Mercy Lewis. On such evidence Mary Easty and John Willard were sent to the gallows. With such ghost stories did Mary Walcott and Elizabeth Hubbard convict Rebecca Nurse of three hideous murders, naming persons who had died within a few years. When the astounded old lady called upon God to witness her innocence, the girls all went into fits. Nevertheless it was hard to obtain a verdict against her.

An ancestor of mine (my great-grandfather's great-great-grandfather), Dr. John Fisk, one of the most eminent physicians in the colony, then lived in Wenham, within four miles of Mr. Parris's meeting-house. The family tradition has it that he was sceptical about witchcraft. His uncle, Thomas Fisk, was a firm believer in witchcraft, but disapproved of spectral evidence. He was foreman of the jury in the trial of Rebecca Nurse, and the verdict was Not Guilty, whereat the girls began screaming and rolling about as if all Bedlam were let loose. The judges then told the jury that they must have overlooked one fact, — that in an unguarded moment the prisoner had really confessed her guilt! It seems

The jury acquit Rebecca Nurse

that one of the prisoners, Deliverance Hobbs, had gone clean daft with fright, confessed herself a witch, and joined the accusing girls as a sort of king's evidence. When she was brought in to testify against Rebecca Nurse, the old lady exclaimed: " What! do you bring *her*? She is one of us." Of course she meant *one of us prisoners*, but the atrabilious chief justice was sure she meant *one of us witches*, and he insisted that the jury should go out again. They were not convinced, but presently returning to the court-room asked the accused to explain what she meant. She made no reply, and the jury at length reluctantly accepted this silence as a confession of guilt. Afterwards she explained that, being somewhat " hard of hearing and full of grief," she did not realize what was asked of her. She was sentenced none the less, and after being excommunicated from the church with elaborate ceremony was taken to the gallows. Thomas Fisk, the juryman who held out longest, made a written statement afterward in which he declared that what finally overcame him was her sudden silence at the critical moment. The whole incident is a pretty clear case of judges browbeating jury.[1]

The court sends them back

---

[1] [See Calef, *New Wonders of the Invisible World*, pp. 209–211 ; Nevins, *Witchcraft in Salem Village*, pp. 125–130.]

The case of Mary Easty, sister of Rebecca Nurse, still further illustrates the fierce persistency of the accusing girls and the completeness of the influence which they exercised over a large portion of the community. Mary Easty had been arrested soon after her sister, but had borne herself so well upon examination that after two months' imprisonment she was set free on May 18. Evidently, the accusing girls made up their minds that it would not do to allow this sort of thing. One day elapsed, during which they had plenty of time to interchange messages with one another and with Mrs. Putnam. On the 20th, at about nine o'clock in the morning, Mercy Lewis, being at John Putnam's house, was suddenly seized with the paroxysms above mentioned. Let us observe the rapidity with which the desired effects were produced. A neighbour named Samuel Abbey was sent in all haste to Thomas Putnam's house, to bring little Ann to see what was the matter. The distance was about a mile. He found Abigail Williams with Ann, and brought the two girls back with him. On the way, they both exclaimed that they saw the apparition of Goody Easty afflicting Mercy Lewis. When they arrived upon the scene, they found Mercy in convulsions, apparently choked and strangled, and catching for each breath as if it were the last. The two

The case of Mary Easty

girls exclaimed, "There are Goody Easty and John Willard and Mary Whittredge afflicting poor Mercy Lewis!" After this had continued for some time, a messenger was sent up to Captain Jonathan Walcott's to get his daughter Mary. The distance was a mile and a half. She arrived about one o'clock, and immediately cried out that she saw the spectre of Mary Easty standing over the patient and tightening a chain about her neck. Presently a messenger was sent to the house of Dr. Griggs, three and a half miles distant, to get Elizabeth Hubbard, who upon her arrival immediately saw Goody Easty, as she said, torturing Mercy in a most dreadful manner. Occasionally Mercy would grow tired, but as her convulsions ceased, Elizabeth Hubbard would be seized with fits and would ask the spectre why she had brought with her a coffin and winding-sheet. By eight o'clock in the evening the room was full of neighbours, who were so impressed by the acting of the girl that some of them were afterward ready to testify that they saw the winding-sheet, the coffin, and the devil's autograph book, and heard words uttered by the spectre as well as by the girls. About eight o'clock two messengers went to Salem town to apply to Justice Hathorne for a warrant for the arrest of Mary Easty. The distance was seven miles. Hathorne at once issued the warrant, which bears the date, May 20. The constable went with it to the house of Isaac Easty, nine miles distant, which he seems to have reached about midnight.   For two days poor Mary had enjoyed her freedom, the comforts of home, and the pleasure of being once more with her husband and children. Now at midnight she was aroused from sleep, carried off to prison, and put in irons, after which the constable returned seven miles to John Putnam's house to witness the performances of Mercy Lewis until dawn. Mercy kept screaming, "What! Have you brought me the winding-sheet, Goodwife Easty? Well, I had rather go into the winding-sheet than set my hand to the book." About daybreak she fell asleep, but only for a short time; her paroxysms were not finished until Mary Easty had been examined before Hathorne and finally committed to prison early the next morning. Nothing could show more forcibly than the events of that 20th of May the extent to which the community was dominated by the accusing girls. There is no hint that among all the bystanders who watched Mercy Lewis in the course of that day and night there was one who ventured to express any doubt as to the reality of the pretended apparitions. Indeed, the slightest expression of any such doubt would have been fraught with peril to the doubter, and it is most likely that none but willing believers made

Mary Easty torn from her home at midnight

Doubt perilous

bold to attend the scene. It only need be added that after Mary Easty was finally committed for trial and the news of it reached John Putnam's house, the wretched Mercy Lewis at once recovered, thus sealing the belief in the truth of her story. From that moment it was a foregone conclusion that Goody Easty must die, slain by the same degrading methods which had achieved the destruction of her sister.

Further details of the trials seem unnecessary; it was but the same old story repeated. In all, nineteen persons were hanged, one died of ill-treatment in prison, and the old wretch Tituba was sold into slavery to pay for her board in prison. One often hears people allude to the burning of witches in New England; no persons were ever burned there by white people for witchcraft. One cruel punishment, however, was inflicted on this occasion for the only time in American history. In old English law, in cases working corruption of blood, the refusal to plead either guilty or not guilty to *Peine forte* an indictment would prevent confisca- *et dure* tion of estates. Hence a prisoner would sometimes refuse to plead, and in order to overcome his obstinacy the law would stretch him on the floor and pile weights upon his chest until the breath was gradually squeezed from his body. This was appropriately called the *peine forte et dure*. Now Giles Corey was arrested for witchcraft in April. His wife, who had been in jail since March, was sentenced to death on September 10, and his own trial came two or three days later. The knowledge that thoughtless words of his, uttered in jest, had been used against his wife had broken his heart, but not his will of iron. This man, who in all his eighty years had never known the meaning of fear, expected nothing but death, and probably wished for nothing better, but he had made up his mind to leave his property where he pleased, and baulk his enemies of at least one gratification. So he stood mute before the court until he was taken out and pressed to death. Nothing could quell that indomitable spirit. Three days later, on September 22, his good wife and seven companions were taken to the gallows. One of the most busy witch-hunters, ever since the The Rev. affair began, had been Rev. Nicholas Mr. Noyes Noyes, pastor of the First Church in Salem town. Such meagre pity as his soul found room for was expressed when he pointed to the swinging bodies and exclaimed, " What a sad thing it is to see eight firebrands of hell hanging there ! " [1] Some weeks before, this truculent Mr. Noyes had been present at the execution of Sarah Good, and just before she was turned off he said to her, " You are a witch, and you know you are ! " The spirited answer of the

[1] [Calef, p. 221.]

dying woman is refreshing to read : " You are a liar ! I am no more a witch than you are a wizard, and if you take away my life, God will give you blood to drink ! " [1]

In strong contrast with this were the dying words of that noble Christian woman, Mary Easty : —

" The humble petition of Mary Easty unto his Excellency, Sir William Phips, and to the Honoured Judge and Bench now sitting in Judicature in Salem, and the Reverend Ministers, humbly showeth, that, whereas your poor and humble petitioner, being condemned to die, do humbly beg of you to take it in your judicious and pious consideration, that your poor and humble petitioner, knowing my own innocency, blessed be the Lord for it! and seeing plainly the wiles and subtilty of my accusers by myself, cannot but judge charitably of others that are going the same way of myself, if the Lord steps not mightily in. I was confined a whole month upon the same account that I am condemned now for, and then cleared by the afflicted persons, as some of Your Honours know. And in two days' time I was cried out upon [by] them, and have been confined, and now am condemned to die. The Lord above knows my innocency then, and likewise does now, as at the great day

The petition of Mary Easty

[1] [Calef, p. 209.]

will be known to men and angels. I petition not
to Your Honours for my own life, for I know I
must die, and my appointed time is set; but the
Lord he knows it is that, if it be possible, no
more innocent blood may be shed, which un-
doubtedly cannot be avoided in the
way and course you go in. I question
Her warning
not but Your Honours do to the utmost of your
powers in the discovery and detecting of witchcraft and witches, and would not be guilty of
innocent blood for the world. But, by my own
innocency, I know you are in the wrong way.
The Lord in his infinite mercy direct you in this
great work, if it be his blessed will that no more
innocent blood be shed! I would humbly beg
of you, that Your Honours would be pleased
to examine these afflicted persons strictly, and
keep them apart some time, and likewise to try
some of these confessing witches; I being con-
fident there is several of them has belied themselves and others, as will appear, if not in this
world, I am sure in the world to come, whither
I am now agoing. I question not but you will
see an alteration of these things. They say myself and others having made a league with the
Devil, we cannot confess. I know, and the
Lord knows, as will [shortly] appear, they belie
me, and so I question not but they do others.
The Lord above, who is the Searcher of all
hearts, knows, as I shall answer it at the tri-

bunal seat, that I know not the least thing of witchcraft ; therefore I cannot, I dare not, belie my own soul. I beg Your Honours not to deny this my humble petition from a poor, dying, innocent person. And I question not but the Lord will give a blessing to your endeavours." [1]

The execution of Mary Easty, Martha Corey, and their six companions was the last scene in the tragedy. Further trials were held, but there were no more executions, and early in 1693 all the prisoners were set free. As to the cause of this sudden collapse in the frenzy we may say that it came, as such collapses always come, when humanity has been outraged more than it will bear. Why did the guillotine stop its work in 1794 just after the fall of Robespierre? The men who overthrew him were not much better than himself, but the state of things had come to be unendurable. Such periods of furious excitement inevitably lead up to a moment of reaction, and the suddenness and completeness of the reaction is apt to be proportionate to the intensity and ferocity of the excitement. The reign of terror in Salem Village was due to a temporary destruction of confidence; everybody became afraid of his neighbours, and there is nothing so pitiless as

Sudden collapse of the trials

[1] [Upham, ii. 328, 329 ; Calef, pp. 219, 220. There are slight differences in the two texts. The two insertions in brackets are from Calef's text.]

fear. But many long ages of social discipline based upon mutual confidence, without which human society could not exist, have made that sentiment so strong and tough that it cannot be suppressed for more than a short time. The feeling with which people endured the sight of Rebecca Nurse and George Burroughs and Martha Corey hanged like common felons was a feeling of tension that must soon give way. The accusing girls did not appreciate this point; they became overweeningly bold and aimed too high. Increase Mather, President of Harvard College, had expressed his disapproval of the methods of the court, and a member of his family was accused. Then the girls cried out against Rev. Samuel Willard, pastor of the Old South Church in Boston, a man of as much eminence in his day as the late Phillips Brooks. They even assailed Lady Phips, the governor's wife, who condemned their proceedings and expressed sympathy with the victims. In these instances the girls struck too high. The same Stoughton and Hathorne, who could take for granted the guilt of Martha Corey, could entertain no such thoughts about Mr. Willard, and when some of the girls mentioned his name they were sharply rebuked and told to hold their tongues. Their final and most fatal mistake was made in October, when they accused Mrs. Hale, wife of

Reaction follows the intense strain

The accusers aim too high

the minister in Beverly, a lady known throughout the colony for her noble Christian character.
The vile accusation opened the eyes of her husband, who had been active in the pursuit of the
witches. He instantly faced about, began to op-
pose the whole prosecution, and confessed that
he had been deceived. This was a fatal blow to
the witch-hunters, and the effect was presently
enhanced when some high-spirited persons in
Andover, on being accused of witch- Accusers
craft, retorted by bringing an action threatened
with a suit
for defamation of character with heavy for damages
damages. This marked the end of the panic,
and from that time people began to be quick in
throwing off the whole witchcraft delusion.

Another circumstance is worthy of notice in
this connection. About three weeks after the
execution of Martha Corey and her companions
the General Court of Massachusetts was assembled at Boston. It was different from any General Court that had sat before, for it was the
first Court elected under the new charter. Under the old charter none but church members
could either serve as representatives or vote for
representatives.[1] Under the new charter such
restrictions were abolished and a property qualification was substituted for them. The effect

[1] [This was modified in 1664, in response to the king's
command, so as to extend the suffrage to all respectable citizens of orthodox opinions.]

was not only greatly to widen the suffrage, but
also to secularize it.   One of the first
acts of the new legislature was to abolish the special court of Oyer and Terminer under which the witchcraft trials had been
held, and to establish a superior court.   When
the new court met in January, the change was
visible. The grand jury began by throwing out
more than half of the indictments.[1] In the mean-
time a tract published by Increase Mather, entitled " Cases of Conscience," [2] had done much
to cast discredit upon spectral evidence. As for
Cotton Mather, he had not been pre-
sent at any of the witch trials, nor
do we know of any comment which he made
upon them at the time, except that Calef tells
us that at the execution of Mr. Burroughs young
Mather was present on horseback, having, perhaps, ridden down from Boston for the occasion.
Calef says the spectators were so impressed with
Burroughs's innocence of demeanour that Cotton Mather felt it necessary to tell them that the
devil might take on the semblance of a saint or
an angel ; and that thereupon, the people being
appeased, the executions went on.   Now Calef
has so often been convicted of inaccuracy that

The Court of Oyer and Terminer abolished

Cotton Mather

---

[1] [See Sir William Phips's report to the home government
of his policy in regard to the troubles, Palfrey, iv. 112, 113.]

[2] [This occupies pp. 220–291 of the London reprint of
the *Wonders of the Invisible World.*]

his statement here is open to suspicion. The argument that Satan might assume the appearance of some person of known innocence or excellence was a favourite one with Cotton Mather when he was inveighing against spectral evidence. As applied to the alleged testimony of the two deceased wives of Mr. Burroughs, it had a peculiarly Matherian meaning ; it meant that instead of the first and second Mrs. Burroughs, it was the devil who was talking to little Ann Putnam, so that therefore the unfortunate minister was condemned upon the devil's evidence. As ordinarily understood, in the sense that Mr. Burroughs himself was an impersonation of the devil, the remark ascribed by Calef to Mather does not fit in with his habits of expression and has no point. Apart from this misconstruction, there is nothing in the records to set off against the weighty evidence of Mather's own rules of procedure, which were in themselves the strongest condemnation the court could have had. Longfellow's picture of Mather in his tragedy of Giles Corey seems absolutely justified, except in one trifling particular, when he makes him say to Mary Walcott, " Accept an old man's blessing," which from a spruce young minister of twenty-nine is, no doubt, a slight anachronism.

Explanation of Mather's speech

The reign of terror we have been describing was the expiring paroxysm of the witchcraft

delusion. In the energy of the reaction sceptics declared themselves in all quarters. How
Judge Sewall, only five years afterward, got up in the Old South
Church and publicly acknowledged
his shame and repentance is known
to every one. Not all the court were so open
to conviction. Stoughton, who was at best
a narrow-minded and cross-grained creature,
maintained to his dying day that he had done
nothing to be sorry for. Of the wretched children, one of the most active, Ann
Putnam, fourteen years afterward,
humbled herself before the village
church at Salem and declared that she had
been instrumental, with others, in bringing
upon the land the guilt of innocent blood;
" though what was said or done by me against
any person, I can truly and uprightly say before God and man, I did it not out of any
anger, malice, or ill-will to any person, for I
had no such thing against one of them, but
what I did was ignorantly, being deluded of
Satan. And particularly as I was a chief in-
strument of accusing Goodwife Nurse and her
two sisters, I desire to lie in the dust and to
be humbled for it, in that I was a cause, with
others, of so sad a calamity to them and their
families." [1]

Judge Sewall's public acknowledgment of wrong

Ann Putnam's confession

[1] [Nevins, *Witchcraft in Salem Village,* p. 250.]

I think we should accept this solemn dis-
claimer of malice as sufficient evidence that in
1706 the poor girl did not believe herself to
have been actuated by unworthy motives in
1692. By declaring herself to have been deluded by Satan she meant that when she accused
Rebecca Nurse and George Burroughs and
others she said what she believed to be true at
the time, but had since learned to reject as false.
In other words, when a little girl of twelve, she
believed that she had seen the ghosts of Mr.
Burroughs's wives and other persons who said
that they had been murdered, but as a young
woman of six and twenty she looked back upon
this as a delusion, and charged it to Satan. This
brings us to the question, Are we justified in
accepting this explanation of Ann Put- Were the
nam as to her own conduct, and shall accusers
misled or
we suppose the case to have been sub- shamming?
stantially the same with the other girls? Did
they really have visions of ghosts and black
men and yellow birds and devil's autograph
books, or was it all a lie? Did they really fall
into convulsions, and fancy themselves pricked
with pins, and cut and bitten, or was all that put
on for effect? In his elaborate history Mr. Upham seems to incline toward the latter view.
Certainly the fits came and went, and the ghost
stories were told, as if to order, and certainly
there was methodical coöperation of some sort,

if not collusion, between most if not all the Evidences of collusion girls, and Ann Putnam's mother and the minister Parris. There can be no doubt as to such coöperation. They all worked together as harmoniously and relentlessly as the cog-wheels in a machine. Of the victims from Salem Village and the towns near by, a large majority were persons against whom either the Putnam family, or the minister, or some of the afflicted girls, are known to have entertained a grudge; others were sceptics whose scoffing remarks were liable to weaken the authority of the accusers. When we have eliminated these two classes, very few names are left. Like the tracks of various beasts which Master Reynard saw, all pointing toward the lion's cave and none coming out from it, the traces of evidence here all point in the same direction, — all point toward methodical coöperation between the accusers.

The question remains, however, was this coöperation a case of conscious and deliberate conspiracy, or must we seek some other explanation? The theory of conspiracy, toward which Mr. Upham seems inclined, offers us a spectacle of astounding wickedness. We are asked to believe that a minister of the gospel and a lady of high position in the community make up their minds to destroy their enemies, and for that purpose employ young girls in their families to pretend illness and bring false accusations conceived and supported with all the skill of trained actresses! Such a conspiracy is much too diabolical and altogether too elaborate for belief. Moreover, it leaves out of account the most important fact in the whole case, — the fact that the accusers, like nearly all the rest of the community, unquestionably believed in the reality of witchcraft. It will not do to invest those poor girls with a nineteenth century consciousness. The same delusion that conquered learned magistrates led them also astray. Still more, they were doubtless in a morbid mental condition. A large part of Indian medicine consists of convulsive muscular movements, twitching, capering, and groaning, accompanied by an awestruck belief in the presence of some supernatural agency. Such convulsive movements tend to prolong themselves, to recur with spasmodic violence, and they are in a high degree contagious. Abundant instances may be found among the experiences of revival meetings, where multitudes of ignorant minds are at work after much the same fashion as the Indian's, though in connection with different religious symbols. This kind of hysterical excitement selects for its victims impressionable people with sensitive nerves; it attacks children more frequently than adults, and women more

Was there a deliberate conspiracy?

Contagion of hysterical emotion

frequently than men; vivacious and quickly

Psychology
of hallucina-
tions

responsive temperaments are more subject to it than those that are phlegmatic and slow. Under suitable circumstances it easily develops into a thoroughly morbid mental state, in which convulsive movements are attended by partial and temporary hallucinations; the nervous impressions become so vivid that ideas are clothed with externality and mistaken for realities. Such are the characteristics of hysteria and allied forms of mental disturbance, which differ from true insanity in being merely temporary and functional, and not connected with any organic lesion. They are very striking phenomena, and often very shocking, but not more mysterious than many other phases of abnormal mental life. It was not strange that an ignorant age should have called them the result of witchcraft; that same age, we must remember, regarded ordinary insanity as the direct work of the devil.

Applying these considerations to the case of the Salem girls, we may suppose that the minister's West Indian servants began by talking Indian medicine and teaching its tricks to his daughter and niece; then the girls of their acquaintance would naturally become interested, and would seek to relieve the monotony of the winter evenings by taking part in the performances. Their first motives are most likely to have been playful, but there was prob- Playing with fire ably a half-shuddering sense of wickedness, a slight aroma of brimstone, about the affair, which may have made it the more attractive. I feel sure that sooner or later some of those girls would find themselves losing control over their spasms, and thus, getting more than they had bargained for, would deem themselves bewitched by Tituba and John Indian. But, especially if they found themselves taken to task by their parents, the dread of punishment — perhaps of church discipline, wherein Parris was notably severe — would be sure to make them blame the Indians in order to screen themselves. If Cotton Mather's methods had now been followed, the affair would have been hushed, and the girls isolated from each other would have been subjected to quiet and sooth- The evils of publicity in the examinations ing treatment; and thus no doubt it would all have ended. But when Parris made the affair as public as possible, when learned doctors of divinity and medicine came and watched those girls, and declared them bewitched, what more was needed to convince their young minds that they were really in that dreadful plight? Such a belief must of course have added to their hysterical condition. Naturally they accused Tituba, and as for the two old women, Good and Osburn, very likely some of the girls may really have been afraid of them as evil-eyed or otherwise uncanny.

For the rest of the story a guiding influence is needed, and I think we may find it in Mrs. Putnam. She was one of the Carrs of Salisbury, a family which for several generations had been known as extremely nervous and excitable. There had been cases of insanity among her near relatives. The deaths of some of her own children and of a beloved sister, with other distressing events, had clouded her mind. She had once been the most sparkling and brilliant of women, but was sinking into melancholia at the time when the first stories of witchcraft came from the parsonage and she learned that her little daughter Ann, a precocious and imaginative child, was one of the afflicted. Mrs. Putnam and her husband were both firm believers in witchcraft. I do not think it strange that her diseased mind should have conjured up horrible fancies about Goodwife Nurse, member of a family which she probably hated all the more bitterly for the high esteem in which it was generally held. Mrs. Putnam fell into violent hysterical fits like her daughter, and their bright and active servant Mercy Lewis was afflicted likewise. These three, with the minister's niece Abigail Williams and her friend Mary Walcott, were the most aggressive and

Explanation of Mrs. Putnam's part

driving agents in the whole tragedy. I presume
Mrs. Putnam may have exercised *She exercised*
something like what it is now fashion- *hypnotic con-*
trol over the
able to call hypnotic influence over the *children*
young girls. She honestly believed that witches
were hurting them all, and she naturally suspected foes rather than friends. I see no good
reason for doubting that she fully believed her
own ghost stories, or that the children believed
theirs. In their exalted state of mind they could
not distinguish between what they really saw
and what they vividly fancied. It was analogous
to what often occurs in delirium.

Such an explanation of the witchcraft in
Salem Village accounts for the facts much better than any such violent supposition as that
of conscious conspiracy. Our fit attitude of
mind toward it is pity for all concerned, yet the
feelings of horror and disgust are quite legiti-
mate, for the course of the affair was practically
the same as if it had been shaped by deliberate
and conscious malice. It is on the whole the
most gruesome episode in American history,
and it sheds back a lurid light upon the long
tale of witchcraft in the past. Few instances of
the delusion have attracted so much attention
as this at Salem, and few have had the details
so fully and minutely preserved. It was the
last witch epidemic recorded in the history
of fully civilized nations. It occurred among

people of our own sort, and the sixth generation, born since it happened, has not yet passed away. It came just as the superstition which produced it was about to die out from the thoughts of educated men, and there is no monument more conspicuous than the Salem Witchcraft to mark the remote and fast receding side of the gulf which the human mind has traversed in these two centuries. For these reasons it looms up in our memory, and is sometimes alluded to as if it were in some way a singular or exceptional instance of superstition. Yet in Europe, only a few years earlier, the hanging of nineteen persons for witchcraft in a single village and in the course of a single summer would have called forth no special comment. The case of Salem Village may help us in the attempt to form some dim conception of the stupendous wickedness that must have been wrought by the terrible delusion in the days of its stalwart prime, when victims by the hundred were burned at the stake. We can but faintly imagine what must have been the destruction of confidence, the breaking of the dearest ties, the madness, the reign of savage terror; and we cannot be too grateful that the gaunt spectre which stalked so long over the fairest parts of earth has at length been exorcised forever!

The case of Salem Village helps one to realize the terrors of the witchcraft delusion in the past

VI

THE GREAT AWAKENING

ONE of the effects of the witchcraft epidemic at Salem was to cast discredit
upon the clergy, who still represented
the old theocratic ideal which had founded the
Commonwealth of Massachusetts. It is true,
that with regard to the prosecutions of witches,
the more eminent among the clergy had behaved
with much wisdom and discretion; nevertheless,
the new public opinion, receiving its The reaction
tone far more from laymen than for- from the
merly, was inclined to charge this whole witchcraft
delusion
business of diabolism to the account of the men
who represented an old and discredited state of
things. With regard to the reality of witchcraft,
Cotton Mather had been foremost among the
defenders of the belief, and now that there came
a sudden and violent reaction against the superstition, it made little difference to people that
he had been remarkably discreet and temperate
in his handling of the matter; it was enough
that he had been a believer and prominent advocate. To some extent Cotton Mather was
made the chief butt of popular resentment be-

cause he and his father especially typified the old theocratic state of things.

Now the old Puritan theocracy in the early days when Winthrop and Cotton led it had framed for itself an ideal of society that was at least lofty and noble, although from the first there were settlers who dissented from it. The defensive wall behind which the theocracy sought to shelter itself from all hostile attack was the restriction of the rights to vote and hold office to members of the Congregational churches in full communion. One of the first effects of this policy was to drive away from Massachusetts the men who founded Connecticut[1] and some of those who founded Rhode Island; but after such depletions there was a considerable number left in Massachusetts who were disfranchised, and who would have been glad in many respects to secularize the government. In the second period of the theo-

Rise of secular opposition to the theocracy

cracy, with Endicott, Bellingham, and Norton at the head, the opposition had become very strong; indeed, it numbered a majority of the population. When the Quakers arrived upon the scene, determined to stay in the Commonwealth at all hazards and thus destroy its character as a united body of believers, there is little doubt that a majority

[1] [Fiske, *The Beginnings of New England*, pp. 123, 249.]

of the people sympathized with them.[1] The violent policy pursued by magistrates and ministers soon failed because the force of a new and growing public opinion was arrayed against it. During the reign of Charles II. the course of the theocracy, in spite of its narrowness and arrogance, commands our admiration for the boldness with which it resisted all attempts of the British government to interfere with the local administration of the colony. There can be no doubt that the Massachusetts theocracy then made a splendid fight for the principles of political freedom, so far as they concerned the relation between a colonial and imperial government. At the same time, the theocracy at home was felt as more and more oppressive. By the time of the death of Charles II. it was reckoned that four fifths of the adult males in Massachusetts were disfranchised because of inability to participate in the Lord's Supper. It is not strange, therefore, that between the one fifth who ruled, and the four fifths who had no voice in ruling, there should have been marked differences of policy accompanied with a good deal of ill-feeling.

[1] [On the Quakers in Massachusetts, cf. Fiske, *The Beginnings of New England*, pp. 179 ff. ; Doyle, *The English in America, The Puritan Colonies*, ii. 126 ff. ; and R. P. Hallowell, *The Quaker Invasion of Massachusetts.*]

In view of such difficulties which began to be foreseen soon after 1650, an opinion grew up that all baptized persons of upright and decorous lives ought to be considered, for practical purposes, as members of the church, and therefore entitled to the exercise of political rights, even though unqualified for participation in the Lord's Supper. This theory, according to which a person might be a halfway member of the church, — member enough for political purposes, but not for religious, — was known at the time as the "Halfway Covenant."[1] It formed the occasion for prolonged and bitter controversy, in which prominent clergymen took opposite sides. It was contended by some that its natural tendency would be toward the spiritual demoralization of the church, while others denied that such would be its practical effect, and pointed to the lamentable severance between ecclesiastics and laymen as a much greater evil. In the

The Halfway Covenant

[1] [Cf. Dexter, *Congregationalism as seen in its Literature*, pp. 467 ff.; Walker, *History of Congregational Churches*, pp. 170 ff.; Trumbull, *History of Connecticut*, i. 296 ff.; Palfrey, *History of New England*, ii. 487 ff.; Doyle, *The English in America, The Puritan Colonies*, ii. 96; Bancroft, *History of the United States* (author's last revision), i. 360; *Massachusetts Colonial Records*, vol. iv. pt. ii. pp. 117 and 164. Dr. Dexter, p. 476, gives two specimen "Halfway Covenants."]

First Church of Boston, the Halfway Covenant was decisively condemned, and the Rev. John Davenport, a theocrat of extreme type, was called from New Haven to be its pastor. Then the minority in the church, who approved of the Halfway Covenant, seceded in 1669 and formed themselves into a new society known as the South Church, further defined in later days as the " Old South." The wooden meeting-house of this society, which occupied the spot of land upon which its brick successor still stands to-day, was a favourite place for meetings which dealt with political questions, and in a certain sense its founding may be regarded as a kind of political safety valve for the agitation in Massachusetts.[1]

The South Church

In spite of such palliatives, however, the opposition grew, and it was apt to take the form of political Toryism, or a disposition to uphold the British government in its contests with the theocracy. From this point of view, we may regard Joseph Dudley and his friends as the founders of New England Toryism. Boston was becoming a place of some commercial note, sustaining business relations with various parts of the world. Among its residents were

The opposition to the theocracy lays the foundation of Toryism

[1] [Mr. Fiske writes a little more fully of this movement in *The Beginnings of New England*, pp. 314 ff.]

members of the Church of England, who desired a place of worship for themselves, and
naturally felt indignant that nothing of the sort
was allowed to be provided.

Such was the state of affairs when the old
charter was rescinded, and Sir Edmund Andros
was sent by James II. to govern New England
according to his own sweet will, without any
constitutional checks or limitations. The rule
of Andros produced for the moment something
approaching to unanimity of opposition, for
there were few men in Massachusetts ready to
surrender the charter of their liberties, although
there were many who would be glad to see it
modified. After the well-planned and fortunate
insurrection which expelled Andros, the representatives of the theocracy, and in particular
Increase Mather, made every effort to obtain
from William III. a charter essentially similar
to the old one. In this they were completely
defeated. The new charter, with its
substitution of a royal governor for a
governor elected by church members,
dealt a serious blow at the independence of the
Commonwealth. At the same time the wide
extension of the suffrage, and its limitation only
by a property qualification, was equivalent to the
death-blow of the old theocracy. It was a revolution, the severity of which for the clergy was
but slightly disguised by the appointment of

The new
charter of
Massachu-
setts

Mather's candidate, Sir William Phips, to be the first royal governor.[1]

Five years after the new charter had gone into operation, an event occurred which illustrated most strikingly the decline in the power of the clergy. Increase Mather had been for many years minister of the North Church in Boston, and in 1685 was appointed president of Harvard, but continued to live in Boston. During the Andros interval he was occupied in protecting the interests of the colony in London. Thus the management of affairs at Harvard was left chiefly in the hands of William Brattle and John Leverett, who both belonged to the extreme liberal wing of the clergy ; for the influences which were raising up a crop of freethinkers for the eighteenth century in England were not entirely without effect in the English colonies. Under the influence of Brattle and Leverett, grew up Benjamin Colman, who took his master's degree at Harvard in 1695, and then went to England, where he was settled over a congregation at Bath. The group of liberals in Boston was steadily increasing in number, and one of their leaders was Thomas Brattle, treasurer of Harvard, a wealthy merchant whose leisure hours were more or less devoted to astronomy and physics. He was the author of several papers on lunar eclipses and of an able

[1] [On the new charter, see Palfrey, iv. 76.]

criticism of the witchcraft delusion. In 1698 Thomas Brattle conveyed to a body of trustees the land upon which a new meeting-house was to be built, and in the following year an invitation was sent to Benjamin Colman to become the pastor of the new Brattle Church. Upon Colman's arrival in Boston, his church issued a manifesto in which two startling novelties were announced. It had been the custom to require from all candidates for admission to the Lord's Supper not only a general subscription to the Westminster creed, but also a relation of personal experiences, which in order to insure their admission must be satisfactory to the presiding clergy. The new church announced that it would dispense with such personal experiences, requiring merely a formal subscription to the Westminster creed. It had also been customary to confine the choice of a minister to the male communicants alone ; the new church proposed to allow all members of the congregation who contributed money toward the support of the church to have votes in the election of ministers. It is hardly necessary to point out the far-reaching character of these provisions in allowing a wholesome opportunity for variations in individual opinion to creep into the church. A body of ministers elected only by communicants, and able to exclude all communicants save

The Brattle Church founded 1698

Relaxation of conditions of membership

such as could satisfy them in a relation of personal experiences, was naturally able to exert a very powerful influence in repressing individual divergences. The Mathers were quite right in thinking that the Brattles and their friends aimed a blow at the vitals of the church. On the 5th of January, $\frac{1699}{1700}$, Cotton Mather writes in his diary : " I see Satan beginning a terrible shake in the churches of New England, and the innovators that have set up a new church in Boston (a new one, indeed !) have made a day of temptation among us. The men are ignorant, arrogant, obstinate, and full of malice and slander, and they fill the land with lies. . . . Wherefore I set apart this day again for prayer in my study, to cry mightily unto God."[1]

Cotton Mather's alarm

It was indeed probable that should the new Brattle Church succeed in obtaining recognition as a Congregational church in good standing, it would create a precedent for latitudinarianism which might be pushed to almost any extent, and yet there was no available method of preventing it. Under the old theocracy, that clause of the Cambridge Platform would have been sufficient which enjoined it upon the magistrates to suppress heresy. Had the old state of things continued in 1699, there can be little doubt that Leverett, Colman, and the two Brattles

[1] [See Quincy's *Hist. of Harvard University*, i. 487.]

would either have been expelled from the
Commonwealth or heavily fined, as had been
The theo-   the case with William Vassall, Robert
cracy helpless   Child, and their companions. But the
under the
new charter   Cambridge Platform had fallen with
the fall of the old charter; and although Increase
Mather had endeavoured to obtain a provision
substantially replacing it, King William, who was
no friend to theocracies, would not hear of such
a thing. The Mathers were therefore reduced to
the expedient of declining to exchange pulpits
with the new pastor; this refusal of ecclesiasti-
The new   cal courtesies was all that was left for
church finally   them, and from the theocratic point
recognized
of view one cannot wonder if they
thought that in some essential respects the world
was coming to an end. In the course of the
following year a kind of peace was patched up
between the party of the Brattles and that of
the Mathers, and blessings were interchanged;
but as we look back upon the affair we can see
that the theocracy had received a fatal blow.

The increasing power of the liberals was displayed about the same time in what went on
at Harvard College. The charter of 1650, by
which the Company of Massachusetts Bay had
incorporated that institution, was generally regarded as having lost its validity when the charter of the company was repealed; and although
things went on about as usual at the college, it

was felt that things stood upon a precarious footing. But to obtain a new charter which would be satisfactory to the theocrats was no The effort to get a new charter for Harvard easy matter, for any such charter must either exclude or allow the exclusion from the teaching body of all persons not in communion with the Congregational church, and King William would never consent to the exclusion of Episcopalians. It will be remembered that one of the chief sources of contention between Charles II. and the government of Boston had been the repressive policy pursued by the latter toward members of the Church of England. King William felt, both as an advocate of liberalism and as the representative of imperial authority, that no concessions could be allowed to the theocracy on this point. In 1699 the party of the Mathers introduced a bill into the General Court, providing for a religious test in Harvard College, the substance of which was, " that in the charter for the college, our holy religion may be secured to us and unto our posterity, by a provision that no person shall be chosen president or fellow of the college, but such as declare their adherence unto the principles of reformation which were espoused and intended by those who first settled the country . . . and have hitherto been the general professions of New England." This bill passed both houses, but, fortunately, was

vetoed by the royal governor, Lord Bellomont.
Meanwhile, the discontent in Cambridge aris-

Governor
Bellomont
vetoes a test
act for col-
lege officers

ing from President Mather's non-residence had been increasing. That
worthy divine seems to have felt
more attachment to his church in Bos-

ton than toward the college.[1] After a while the
Rev. Samuel Willard of the Old South was appointed vice-president of the college, but he,
too, seems to have preferred the duties of pastor
to those of administering a college, and his ab-
senteeism attracted comment as well as Mather's.
I think, however, that the true explanation of
Mather's difficulty with the college lies deeper.

Rise of liber-
alism in the
college

There can be no doubt that between
1685 and 1700 the intellectual atmosphere of the college was rapidly be-

coming more and more liberal. Leverett and
the Brattles were the ruling spirits, and the
events of each passing year made Mather more
and more uncongenial to them; whereas, Willard was both in character and in turn of thought
more to their mind. It is not strange, therefore, that we find Mather's non-residence complained of, while the same fault in Willard is
but lightly noticed. After a while Mather sig-
nified that if the General Court were not satisfied with his conduct, it might perhaps be well
for them to choose another president. To his

[1] [Sewall's *Diary*, i. 493.]

intense chagrin, he was taken at his word, and in September, 1701, the dignity and duties of the president were trans- ferred to Willard, who, however, re- tained the title of vice-president, thus somewhat President
Increase
Mather
displaced softening the blow. A couple of entries in Judge Sewall's diary are rather amusing in this connection. Sewall was a member of the court which had just wrought this change in the presidency. The first entry is: " Mr. Cotton Mather came to Mr. Wilkins's shop, and there talked very sharply against me as if I had used his father worse than a neger; spake so loud that people in the street might hear him. . . . I had read in the morning Mr. Dod's saying: Sanctified afflictions are good promotions. I found it now a cordial." Then follows a memorandum: " Octr 9. I sent Mr. Increase Mather a hanch of very good venison; I hope in that I did not treat him as a negro." [1] As for Cotton Mather, he hoped to be chosen president of Harvard when Willard should die or resign, but he did not read correctly Cotton
Mather's
indignation the signs of the times, nor did he play his part with skill; for he chose the part of sulking, and went so long without attending the meetings of the corporation, of which he was a member, that people spoke of his having abdicated his office. [2]

---

[1] [Sewall's *Diary*, ii. 43, October 20, 1701.]

[2] [See Quincy's *Hist. of Harvard University*, i. 151.]

In 1702 Joseph Dudley, who had been in England ever since the Andros days and had just been appointed to succeed Lord Bellomont as governor of Massachusetts, arrived in Boston.

Governor
Dudley The enmity between Dudley and the Mathers was of long standing, and may be said to have had its origin in the very roots of things. Between the representatives of the old theocracy and the subtle founder of Toryism there could be no love lost at any time; on the other hand, by that very law of selection which was apt to bring together revolters against the theocracy, whether for religious or political reasons, a strong alliance grew up between Dudley and Leverett. When Willard died, in September, 1707, the corporation at once chose Leverett as his successor. At his instigation a resolution was introduced into the General

The new
charter for
Harvard a
substantial re-
enactment. of
that of 1650 Court declaring that the charter of 1650 was still in force; or rather, enacting a charter which in its essential provisions was identical with the old one. This charter was at once signed by Governor Dudley. The English Privy Council might still have overturned it, but they never did, so after the vicissitudes of the great revolution through which Massachusetts had passed, Harvard College started quietly upon a new chapter in her career, with her hands tied as little as possible by hampering statutes or traditions.

While these things were going on in Massachusetts, affairs were taking a somewhat different turn in Connecticut. The confederacy of river towns which gave birth to the state of Connecticut had represented a more liberal principle than that upon which Massachusetts was founded. The wholesale migration which carried the people of Dorchester, Cambridge, and Watertown to the Connecticut River was a migration of people for whom Massachusetts was too theocratic. In Connecticut there was no restriction of civil rights to church members ; the relative power of the representa- Conditions in tives as compared with the Council Connecticut of Assistants was much greater, and the local independence of the several towns was more complete. Connecticut was originally more democratic and more liberal in complexion than Massachusetts.

On the other hand, the federal republic of New Haven closely resembled the commonwealth of Massachusetts, but was even more theocratic and aristocratic.[1] But the union of

[1] [After the Restoration the people of Connecticut through their governor, the younger Winthrop, secured from the king a charter which included New Haven in the boundaries allotted to Connecticut, and in spite of the reluctance of the people of New Haven the absorption of their republic was

New Haven with Connecticut did not by a mixture of plus and minus make a commonwealth
quite like Massachusetts. The most theocratic elements in New Haven either migrated in large bodies to New Jersey, or came as individuals one by one back to Massachusetts. Of those who remained on the shores of Long Island Sound, the greater part were those who had protested against the New Haven theocracy with its exclusiveness. On the whole, the Connecticut of 1670 to 1690 seems to have been a more liberal-minded community than Massachusetts.

New Haven annexed to Connecticut

But if we come forward into the nineteenth century, it can hardly be denied that while both states have maintained a high intellectual level, Massachusetts has been the more liberal-minded community. Or, if a different phrase be preferred, Massachusetts has been somewhat more prompt in adopting new ideas or in following out new vistas of thought, especially in all matters where theology is concerned. Or, to put the case in yet another way, Massachusetts has shown less hesitation in departing from ancient standards. The history of Unitarianism is of itself a sufficient illustration of this. To some minds the rise of Unitarianism seems like a great step in advance ;

Comparison of Massachusetts and Connecticut

consummated in 1665. Doyle, *The Puritan Colonies*, ii. 154–162.]

to other minds it seems like a deplorable for-
saking of the highroad for byways that lead to
Doubting Castle; but all will agree that the
great development of Unitarianism in Massachusetts, as compared with its small development in Connecticut, shows in the former state
less hesitation in deviating from old standards.
Something of the same contrast in regard to
deviation is shown in the history of Yale College as contrasted with Harvard; no
one will deny that the temper of the Causes of Connecticut conservatism
former has been more conservative.
It becomes interesting, then, to inquire what
has produced this change. In what respects
have circumstances operated to render the career
of Connecticut more conservative than that of
the sister commonwealth? Such questions are
always difficult to answer with confidence, but
certain facts may be pointed out which have a
bearing upon the question.

It is a general tendency of organizations to
grow more rigid through increase of rules and
definitions, and to interfere more and
more with the free play of individu- The tendency in organizations to become rigid and mechanical
ality; so that often in the pursuit of
a given end, the organization will so
far hamper itself as to decrease its
fitness for attaining the ends desired; in other
words, the ends become a matter of secondary
importance, while the machinery of the organi-

zation absorbs the entire attention. Especially
has this been true in the case of ecclesiastical
organizations. The members of a priesthood
are apt to acquire an exaggerated idea of the importance of the body to which they belong and
which is invested by public opinion with a peculiar sanctity, and they are apt to feel justified in
making laws and regulations tending to coerce
all their members into conformity with some
prescribed set of rules. In Massachusetts an
The instance   early and baneful source of rigidity
of the Cam-
bridge Plat-   was the Cambridge Platform of 1648,
form, 1648   which enjoined it upon magistrates to
punish any infractions of ecclesiastical doctrine
or observance. Among the fruits of this Cambridge Platform were the odious proceedings
against Baptists and Quakers, which have left
such a stain upon the annals of Boston. But it
is worthy of note that owing to the very restrictions which confined the civil liberties of
Massachusetts to communing church members,
a large body of citizens grew up in opposition,
so that the Commonwealth was never deprived
of the healthful stimulus of competition and
struggle between opposing views in interest.
To such a point had this conflict come that
when, in 1699, an attempt was made to fasten
a religious test upon Harvard, it fell to the
ground, and that critical period of the history
of the Commonwealth saw Harvard falling more

and more completely under the guidance of the
party opposed to the old theocracy. Lack of a
On the other hand, Connecticut pur- party of op-
position in
sued the even tenor of her way from Connecticut
the first beginnings into the nineteenth century
with comparatively little severe internal commo-
tion. She had for a moment, of course, resented
the arrogance of Andros, but her constitution was
never wrenched out of shape by such violent
changes as those which Massachusetts witnessed
after 1685. I think we must attribute it to this
very fact of the slightness and gentleness of the
opposition, — to the comparative mildness of ecclesiastical life in Connecticut, — that at the beginning of the eighteenth century her clergymen
and people should have yielded so easily to the
natural impulse to improve, or, rather, to define
and limit their ecclesiastical organizations. By
that time it had come to seem to many worthy
people that the work of the church might be
greatly facilitated if its organization were made
a little more thorough in its working. The
result was the synod held at the town of Saybrook in May, 1708, which adopted the famous
constitution known as the Saybrook Platform.

This constitution provided that " the particular pastors and churches, within the respec-
tive counties in this government," should " be
one consociation, or more if they should judge
meet, for mutual affording to each other such

assistance as may be requisite, upon all occasions ecclesiastical." Hitherto ecclesiastical authority had been exercised by councils
The Saybrook Platform formed by voluntary election by individuals or by single churches. Such
authority was henceforth to be vested in permanent councils appointed by the consociation
of churches. Disobedience to the decree of one
of these permanent councils was punished by
excommunication of the too independent pastor
or church. The council of one consociation
might invite councils from one or more neighbouring consociations to take part in its proceedings, and it was further provided that a general
association consisting of representatives from all
the churches in the commonwealth should be
held every year at the time of the election of
governor and legislature.

This platform was adopted by the General
Court of Connecticut, with the proviso that a
church which conducted itself discreetly and
soberly might be allowed to carry on worship
and exercise discipline according to its own conscience, even though it should not be able to
enter into the consociation of churches. This
was a prudent and liberal provision, and was
intended to prevent injustice and persecution.
The general effect of the platform was to assimilate Congregationalism in Connecticut to Presbyterianism, and there can be little doubt that

this was an important change in the direction of conservatism. Manifestly, the power of any ecclesiastical organization in checking individual variations depends upon the coercive power which the whole can bring to bear upon any one of its parts. Manifestly, the conservative power of a Mussulman caliph, being absolutely unchecked, was greater than that of the mediæval Pope, who might be limited by a council or thwarted by an emperor. Still less coercive power could be exercised by a sovereign head of a church, like Elizabeth or Charles II. Still less could be exercised by a Presbyterian synod, and from this again down to an independent congregation the step in diminution of coercive power was a long one. It is therefore interesting and significant that just at the moment when Massachusetts by the founding of Brattle Church took a long step in the direction of further independency, Connecticut should have taken a decided conservative step in the direction of Presbyterianism. The effect exerted by the mere possession of coercive power does not always need to be exhibited by overt actions; it is a subtle effect consisting largely in the colouring which it gives to that indefinable thing known as public opinion, but I suspect that in the circumstances here narrated we have at least a partial explanation

The Platform tends to assimilate Congregationalism to Presbyterianism

Massachusetts and Connecticut change places

of the fact that a century later, when so many churches in Massachusetts adopted Unitarian theology while still remaining Congregational churches, on the other hand, in Connecticut a step so extreme was very difficult to take, and that while there were churches in which dissent from time-honoured doctrines was rife, nevertheless it was seldom that Unitarian doctrines were avowed.

One effect of the Saybrook Platform was to make it easy in later times for the Congregational churches in Connecticut to fraternize with the Presbyterian churches. To such an extent has this fraternization been carried in modern times, that persons in Connecticut and states to the west of it are very apt to use the word " Presbyterian " in a loose sense when they really mean " Congregational," — a use of language which would have made the hair of one of Cromwell's Ironsides stand on end with horror.

The beginning of the eighteenth century in Connecticut was also memorable for the founding of Yale College. The journey from the Connecticut towns to Cambridge was much longer than it is now, and it was felt that there ought to be a college nearer home. The movement was begun by a meeting at Branford of ten ministers, nine of whom were graduates of Harvard. These gentlemen con-

The founding of Yale College

tributed from their libraries about forty gigantic folios for the founding of a college library. Other gifts began to come in, and an act of incorporation in 1701 created a body of trustees, all of whom were to be clergymen and not less than forty years of age. The college was at first situated in Saybrook, though in the first years the classes were taught at Killingworth, where the first rector of the college, Abraham Pierson, was pastor. At length the college was settled in New Haven in 1716, and two years later it received the name of Yale College in recognition of a donation from Elihu Yale, a merchant of London, whose father had been one of the original settlers of New Haven. Now this founding of Yale College exerted a conservative effect upon the mind of Connecticut. While on the one hand it brought a classical education within the reach of many persons who would not have gone to Cambridge to get it, on the other hand it tended to cut off the clergy of Connecticut from the liberalizing influences which were so plainly beginning to be powerful at Harvard. From the outset something like a segregation began. Many persons in Massachusetts who were disinclined to the liberalism of Leverett and the Brattles transferred their affections to Yale College, making gifts to it and sending their sons there, and in this way the

The conservative tendencies of Connecticut reinforced by the college conservatism of the university that was controlled entirely by ministers holding under the Saybrook Platform was increased. When to all these circumstances we add that the royal governor in Boston, although an abiding cause of irritation, nevertheless kept bringing in ideas and fashions from Europe, we can see how the stormier life of Massachusetts Bay was more favourable to change than the delicious quiet of the land of steady habits.

The general state of the church in New England in the first decades of the eighteenth century was one which may be best characterized by saying that spirituality was at a low ebb. Pretty much the same might be said of the church in England, and if we were to extend the observation to France, we should have to make it still more emphatic. The causes of this state of things were complicated. Among other things, the scientific reaction against supernaturalism, which was so rapidly destroying the belief in witchcraft, was leading the great mass of superficial thinkers in the direction of materialism. In France the church had discredited itself through an alliance with despotism, until nearly all the best minds had turned against it. In England the epoch of intense mental exaltation which characterized the seventeenth century had provoked a reaction in which worldly-mindedness

State of religion early in the eighteenth century

prevailed and sanctity was derided. There can be little doubt, I think, that the political uses to which religion had been put during the terrible struggle of the counter-reformation had done much to loosen its spiritual hold upon men's minds. Something may be said, too, of the rapidly expanding effects of commerce. Men's interests were multiplying so that something must suffer for a time, and religion, for the causes already mentioned, was the weak spot in the social fabric.

Rise of commercial interests

But whatever the explanation may be, the fact is generally accepted that the early years of the eighteenth century were a period of coldness in religious matters. This coldness was quite generally perceived and lamented by clergymen and laymen throughout New England, and speculations were rife as to the probable cause and the best cure. It is not unlikely that among other things the Halfway Covenant may have exerted a baneful influence. If there could be anything serious and solemn in life it would seem to be the ascertainment of the state of mind which would qualify a person for participation in the Lord's Supper, yet the Halfway Covenant practically admitted to this sacrament all persons of decorous lives who had been baptized in infancy. One effect of this was to endow infant baptism with the character of a

magical ceremony and to make of the communion a mere lifeless form. At first, indeed, the
supporters of the Halfway Covenant simply
allowed baptized members of the congregation
" Stoddard- to vote and hold office, without allow-
eanism" ing them to participate in the communion until they could make some statement
of their internal experience which proved them
qualified for such participation; but a crisis
seemed to be reached when the Rev. Solomon
Stoddard of Northampton admitted people to
communion without any other credentials than
proof of baptism in infancy.[1]

This work was to be undone and this whole
state of things put an end to by the writings
and the preaching of Solomon Stoddard's grandson, a man who was one of the wonders of the
world, probably the greatest intelligence that
Jonathan the western hemisphere has yet seen.
Edwards Jonathan Edwards was born at East
Windsor, Conn., in 1703, inheriting extraordinary abilities both from his father, Rev. Timo-
thy Edwards, and from his mother, Esther
Stoddard. From early childhood Edwards was
a personage manifestly set apart for some high
calling. His " Notes on Nature," written at the

[1] [On this outgrowth of the Halfway Covenant, see
Walker, *Hist. of the Congregational Churches in the U. S.*,
pp. 180–182. Stoddard advocated this practice as early as
1679. It was adopted in his church in 1706.]

age of sixteen, show a precocity as remarkable as that of Pascal; his Treatise on the Will and other works of his maturity show a metaphysical power comparable with that of Kant or Berkeley; while in many of his speculations his mind moves through the loftiest regions of thought with a sustained strength of flight that comes near reminding one of the mighty Spinoza. There can be no doubt that the more one considers Edwards, the more colossal and astonishing he seems. Among writers of Christian theology his place is by the side of Augustine, Aquinas, and Calvin. At the same time, there was more in Edwards than sheer power of intellect. His character was as great as his genius. The highest attributes of manliness were united in him. He was a man of deep affection, abounding in sympathy, so that without resorting to the ordinary devices of rhetoric he became a preacher of the first order. Now in the mind of Jonathan Edwards there was a vein of mysticism as unmistakable as that in the mind of William Penn. Such mysticism may be found in minds of medium capacity, but in minds of the highest type I believe it is rarely absent. A mind which has plunged deeply into the secrets of nature without exhibiting such a vein of mysticism is, I believe, a mind sterilized and cut off in one direction from access to the truth. Along with

Edwards's vein of mysticism

Edwards's abstruse reasoning there was a spiritual consciousness as deep as that of Spinoza or Novalis. From his mystic point of view, the change whereby a worldly, unregenerate man or woman became fitted for divine life was a conversion of the soul, an alteration of its innermost purposes, a change of heart from evil to goodness. Perhaps this way of conceiving the case was not new with Edwards. From the earliest ages of Christianity a turning of the soul from the things of this world to Christ has been the essential, but the importance of what has since come to be known as conversion, or change of heart, assumed dimensions never known before. As Calvinism enhanced the value of the individual soul by representing it as the subject of a mighty struggle between the powers of heaven and those of hell, so Edwards, while setting forth this notion in all its grimness, gave it a touch of infinite tragedy and pathos through the power with which he conceived the situation of the soul whose salvation trembled in the balance. The distinction between the converted and the unconverted became in his hands more vitally important than the older distinction between the elect and the non-elect. There was great difficulty in working the two distinctions together, and a large portion of the eighteenth century was consumed by New England theologians in grappling with

His emphasis on conversion

this difficulty. It was due to Edwards that the prime question with every anxious mind was not so much, Am I one of the elect? as this other question, Have I surrendered my heart to Christ? It is obvious that this new point of view in itself, and even more in the mood in which it was set forth, soon worked a vivifying change in the religious consciousness of New England. The effect was presently shown in those so-called revivals which are in the strict sense a product of the Revivals New England mind. Phenomena of religious excitement, sometimes reaching epidemic proportions, are of course to be found among heathen savages, but religious emotion of an intense sort, coupled with a high general level of education, such as we see it in modern revivals, is something that had its beginnings in New England. The essential features of a revival are the aroused consciousness of sin, overwhelming fears associated therewith, and a condition of doubt as to whether one has really satisfied the conditions of salvation. One can see that when such a state of things has been generally reached in a community, there is no longer any room for such mechanical devices as the Halfway Covenant. Before such a state of things can be reached, the ecclesiastical atmosphere must be spiritualized. To this end the whole tenor of Edwards's preaching contributed, for he insisted, with as much emphasis as William Penn, upon the insignificance of the form as compared with the spirit.

Sometimes the religious revival seemed a mere survival of barbaric superstition, — as when the earthquake of 1727 brought people in The Revival crowds into the Boston churches. But of 1734 in 1734 there began at Northampton, where Edwards, who had succeeded his grandfather, had been preaching for eight years, a revival of a much higher kind. This wave of religious excitement spread through the whole Connecticut valley and lasted for six months. It attracted some notice in England, and presently George Whitefield accepted an invitation from Dr. Benjamin Colman to come to New England and preach. Whitefield was twenty-six George years of age, and had just been or-Whitefield invited to dained as a minister of the Church of New England England. He was a man of mediocre intelligence, without distinction either as a scholar or as a thinker, but his gifts as an orator were very extraordinary. In 1740 Whitefield preached in various parts of New England, sometimes in churches, sometimes in the open air, to audiences which on occasion reached 15,000 in number. He made a pilgrimage to Northampton in order to visit the preacher of the late revival there, and thought he had never seen such a man as Edwards, while, on the other hand, under the influence of Whitefield's musical voice, Edwards sat weeping during the entire sermon.

The example set by Whitefield was followed after his departure by a Presbyterian minister from New Jersey named Gilbert Ten- Gilbert nent. This preacher came to Boston Tennent and spent some three months in the neighbourhood, preaching to enormous audiences with most startling effect. Tennent was followed by James Davenport of Southold, Long Island, a great-grandson of the famous Davenport of the old New Haven colony. This James Davenport was highly esteemed by Whitefield and other revivalist preachers, but his ill-balanced enthusiasm led him to very strange lengths. On one occasion he is said to have preached a sermon nearly twenty-four hours in length, with such violence of intonation and gesture that he brought on a brain fever. He was constitutionally intemperate in speech, eccentric in action, and inspired by that peculiar self-conceit which is one of the marks of mental derangement. If he came to a town where James little excitement was manifested on Davenport the subject of religion he would revile the ministers of the town, accusing them of being unconverted, blind leaders of the blind, and he warned the people that by listening to such preaching they were imperilling their souls. At

Boston he grew so abusive that the ministers held a conference and decided that they would not allow him the use of their pulpits. Nothing daunted, however, this Boanerges hurled forth his thunderbolts on such places as Copp's Hill and Boston Common, where he spoke his mind with great freedom to thousands of listeners. For example, in one of his prayers, he said, "Good Lord, I will not mince the matter any longer with Thee, for Thou knowest that I know that most of the ministers of Boston and of the country are unconverted, and are leading their people blindfold to hell." For these words Davenport was indicted for slander, but was acquitted on the ground of insanity.

A situation had now arisen in some respects not unlike that when Mrs. Hutchinson and her Antinomian friends had been preaching in Boston a century earlier. One of the chief objections to the Antinomians was that they professed to have their minds illumined by a divine light which enabled them to see truths hidden from the generality of Christians, and in this belief they confidently assailed even the highest of the clergy as creatures acting under a covenant of works. It was now held by many clergymen that the conduct of Tennent and Davenport and other followers of Whitefield resembled that of the Antinomians, and tended to intro-

Comparison with the Antinomians

duce dissensions into the churches. There can be no doubt that such was its immediate effect. Emotional extravagances on the part of revivalists were so marked as to lead many persons to question whether, in view of this and of the intemperate criticism that had been indulged in, the revival had not really been productive of more harm than good. Such questions were agitated until in almost every church there came to be a party who approved of the revival and a party which condemned it. Under these circumstances it is not strange that the power of the revival should have declined, or that we should find the Rev. Thomas Prince writing in 1744 that "The Sovereign Spirit, in His awakening influence, has seemed these two last years in a gradual and awful manner to withdraw. For a twelvemonth I have rarely heard the cry of any new ones, What shall I do to be saved? But few are now added to our churches and the heavenly shower in Boston seems to be over." About the time that Prince expressed himself so despondingly Whitefield returned to New England, but he was not so much a novelty as before and made less sensation. The Brattle Church showed its liberality by inviting him, an Episcopal priest, to administer its Communion. On the other hand, President Holyoke and the Faculty of Harvard passed a resolution condemning his

Whitefield's return to New England

itinerant methods, and the clergymen of Cambridge refused to allow him in their pulpits; so that his preaching was done to a large audience on Cambridge Common.

In Massachusetts the opposition to the revivalists showed itself only in such protests by professors and clergymen, but in Connecticut the matter went further. Whitefield, Tennent, and Davenport travelled about in that commonwealth, making converts by hundreds, and Davenport, at least, made no scruple of attacking the settled ministers. These proceedings called forth interference from the government. Davenport arrested for public disturbance At Stratford Davenport was arrested for disturbing the peace by gathering great crowds of people, filling their heads with pernicious doctrines, and inciting them to a noisy and disorderly demeanour. During their examination a mob of their converts undertook to rescue them from the sheriff's custody, and in order to quiet the disturbance it proved necessary to call out the militia. For revivalist practices similar to Davenport's the Rev. Benjamin Pomeroy was turned out of office and deprived of his salary.

It thus appears that one result of the Great Awakening was to stir up dissension in the churches between the more aristocratic ministry of the old type and the more democratic preachers like Whitefield and his friends. Our ac-

count would be far from complete if we were to
omit the conclusion of the story at Northampton, the home of Jonathan Edwards, from whose
preaching this Great Awakening had Last days of
emanated. We have seen that the Edwards
Edwards doctrine of conversion was flatly opposed to the Halfway Covenant to which Edwards's grandfather in Northampton had given
its most extreme form. In 1749, after Edwards
had been settled twenty-two years over that parish and regarded with extreme reverence by his
parishioners, he suddenly lost favour with them
by insisting upon more rigorous requirements
in admitting communicants to the church.
This gave rise to a quarrel of such bitterness
that Edwards's parish not only dismissed him,
but obtained a vote in town meeting to the
effect that he should not be allowed any more
to enter a pulpit in that town. The result was
the removal of Edwards to Berkshire for missionary work among the Stockbridge Indians,
and thence after six years to the presidency of
Princeton College. He died in Princeton at the
early age of fifty-five.

One result of the breaking down of the Halfway Covenant was to discredit infant baptism, so
that the majority of the revivalists of the more
democratic type went over to the Baptist church
and greatly swelled its numbers in New England. With regard to the general effect of the

Awakening, in spite of the extravagances with which it was here and there attended, it certainly did much to heighten and deepen the religious life in New England. As compared with the old days of the Halfway Covenant, the new doctrine of conversion was like an uplifting of the soul to better things. The religious thought of the seventeenth century was in danger of losing its life among dry logical formulas. It needed to be touched with emotion, and that Results of the was what the Great Awakening accomplished. It may be said to have exerted a stimulating influence similar to that which attended the preaching of the Wesleys in England, and it should not be forgotten that John Wesley in the early part of his career received a powerful stimulus from news which reached him from New England. If we were able thoroughly to sift all relevant facts I think we should conclude that in producing the tenderness of soul in which the nineteenth century so far surpassed the eighteenth, a considerable share must be assigned to the preaching and self-searchings, the prayers and tears, the jubilation and praise, of the Great Awakening.

VII

NORRIDGEWOCK AND LOUISBURG

WHEN Mr. Seward, about forty years ago, spoke of the "irrepressible conflict" between slavery and freedom, it was generally felt that he had invented a happy and telling phrase. It was a conflict equally irrepressible that was carried on for seventy years between France and England for the possession of North America. It was the strife between absolutism and individualism, between paternal government carried to the last extreme, and the spontaneous life of communities that governed themselves in town meeting. Alike in Europe and in America each party was aggressive and uncompromising. Particularly in America the proximity of the Indians made it next to impossible to avoid bloodshed even when the governments of France and England were nominally at peace with one another. There is no better illustration of this than is afforded by the story of Norridgewock.

The treaty of Utrecht, by which the long war

The "irrepressible conflict" between France and England in America of the Spanish succession was brought to an end in 1713, transferred the province of Acadia from France to England. After many changes of ownership backward and forward it was de-

Acadia finally passes to England

cided that Acadia was finally to become English. But what was Acadia?

As customarily applied, the name included Nova Scotia, New Brunswick, and a part of Maine; and the English maintained that all this territory was ceded to them by the treaty; but the French, on the other hand, maintained that they had only given away Nova Scotia, and woe to the Englishman who should dare to meddle with the rest! It was intended that this question should be settled by a special commission, but the question was such a ticklish one that neither country was in haste to appoint a commission, and so things remained until the matter was settled forever by the mighty Seven Years' War.

According to the French view, the boundary between their territory and that of New England was the river Kennebec. This line they felt it important to defend for two reasons.

The French view of the limits of Acadia

First, the New England settlements were rapidly extending northeastwardly along the coast; secondly, the sources of the Kennebec were connected by an intricate network of streams, marshes, and lakelets, with those of the Chaudière, which falls into the St. Lawrence just opposite Quebec. It was an excessively difficult route by which to invade Canada, as Benedict Arnold found half a century later. Nevertheless, it was a possible route which the French felt it necessary to bar. In this they proceeded according to their usual manner by establishing a hold upon their Algonquin friends along the Kennebec River.

These Algonquins were commonly known as Abenakis, or Eastern Men. Their grade of culture was quite similar to that of the tribes in Massachusetts and considerably more advanced than that of the Micmacs of Nova Scotia. They were divided into numerous tribes and subtribes, the names of which, such as Kennebec, Penobscot, etc., have in many cases remained as local names upon the map, while the most important of these Abenaki tribes was that of the Norridgewocks, inasmuch as their position guarded the approaches to the upper waters of the Kennebec. The stockaded Norridgewock village was situated close by the river, about seventy-five miles from its mouth, and a journey to it from Portsmouth or Boston seemed like plunging into the innermost depths of the wilderness. These Indians were no longer heathen, for they had all been converted and baptized by the devoted efforts of Father Sebastian Rale. This interesting man was a native of that part of Burgundy known as Franche-

Comté, and when thirty-two years of age came over to Canada with Frontenac in 1689. After a more or less migratory service extending as far west as the Illinois River, Father Rale took charge of the Norridgewock Indians in 1693, and remained with them until his death. His attainments in American languages were very considerable, for he possessed a fluent knowledge of at least three dialects of Algonquin, besides the Huron dialect of Iroquois, and his knowledge of the Indian character was as thorough as his proficiency in their tongue. The Norridgewock village was a square enclosure 160 feet on each side, walled in with a palisade of stout logs about nine or ten feet in height. In the middle of each side was a gate, and the two streets connecting the gates crossed each other in an open square at the centre. Within the enclosure were twenty-six wigwams, and outside of it at a distance of a few yards stood the chapel. Altogether it was a much ruder village than the Iroquois Hochelaga which Cartier had visited nearly two centuries before, and very much ruder than the Onondaga village attacked by Champlain in 1615. Besides being the spiritual father of this little community, Father Rale was of necessity a jack-of-all-trades. He must be a bit of a carpenter, and more or less of a gardener, with a pennyweight

Sebastian Rale

The Norridgewock village

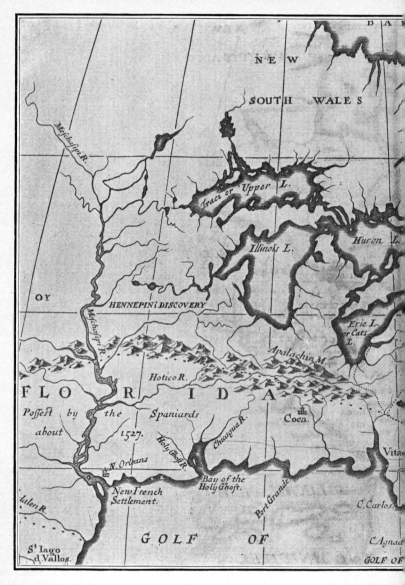

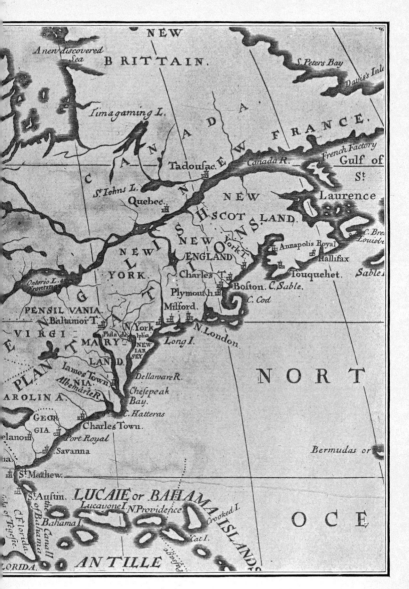

NEW

BRITTAIN.

A new discovered Sea

S. Peters Bay

Davis's Inle

Timagaming L.

C A N A D A

NEW FRANCE.

French Factory

Canada R.

Gulf of

Tadousac.

St

St Johns L.

NEW

Laurence

Quebec.

SCOT LAND.

C. Bre

Louisb

NEW IONS

York

Annapolis Royal

YORK

NEW

ENGLAND

Hallifax

Ontario L.

Frontenac

Charles T.

Touquehet.

Sable

C. Sable

Boston.

G

Plymouth

C. Cod

PENSILVANIA.

Milford.

Baltmor T.

N.York

N. London

VIRGI

MARY

Phila delphia

Long I.

NORT

NEW

LAND.

IAR

SEY

PLAN

James Town

Dellaware R.

Albemarle R.

NIA

AROLINA.

Chesepeak

Bay.

GEOR

C. Hatteras

GIA

Charles Town.

elanob

Port Royal

Savanna

Bermudas or

ha

St Matthew

OCE

St Austin.

LUCAIE or BAHAMA ISLANDS

Lucayone I. N. Providence

Crooked I.

of Bahama

C. Florida

Bahama I.

Cat I.

Gulf of Teneffe

LORIDA.

ANTILLE

of medicine to an intolerable deal of theology, and unlimited devotion to the spiritual needs of his flock. To these duties he added those of linguist and diplomat ; for his leisure hours were whiled away in making a vocabulary of the Abenaki tongue, while his own talent of speech was put to diligent use in instructing all the tribes of that region how to comport themselves in the presence of the much hated English.

At the time of the peace of Utrecht, the country between the Piscataqua and the Kennebec had been the scene of atrocious warfare for nearly forty years. First there was King Philip's War in which the French had no part, and then there were the two great wars between France and England from 1689 to 1697, and from 1702 to 1713. The result was that this border country had almost relapsed into a desert. But after 1713, a new wave of settlement advanced northeasterly, old villages were rebuilt and new ones founded, and in all directions might be seen clearings in the forest, where the smoke curled up from the log cabins of English pioneers. Now this advance of the white frontier incensed and alarmed the Indians, as it was natural that it should. They maintained that the English were encroaching upon their lands. The English retorted that these lands were their own, in-

The country between the Piscataqua and the Kennebec

asmuch as they had formerly been bought from Indian sachems, and prices had been paid for them which the Indians had deemed liberal and satisfactory. But the red man's notions of ownership and transfer of real estate were in a hopelessly different stage of evolution from those of the white man. To an Indian, the selling of a territory meant little more than granting permission to catch fish and game upon it, or to pass through it unhindered for whatever purpose. The Indian had not arrived at the point where the sale of an estate conveys to the vendee the right to exclude the vendor; but his mind was open to a suggestion of Father Rale, that no sale of land by a sachem could be other than void because the land was the property of the clan, and must be kept in trust for the children born to the clan. This was exactly in accordance with Indian ways of thinking, and it is not strange that Father Rale's doctrine suited the red men's temper better than the English notion that after once buying the land they had a right to fence the Indian out. As the English farmhouses came nearer and an occasional blockhouse was erected, the disgust of the Abenakis increased beyond all bounds, but they entertained a wholesome dread of attacking the English without assistance from the French, and this was difficult to obtain in time of peace.

While the French, however, prudently refrained from gross violations of international law, they were nevertheless quite willing to incite the Indians to attack the English. Vaudreuil, the governor of Canada, expressly declared that it was convenient to maintain a secret alliance with the Indians, since the latter might inflict much damage upon the English, while the French could disclaim all responsibility for their acts.

The Indians and the French

In 1717, when Colonel Shute was royal governor of Massachusetts, a conference was held on Arrowsick Island at the mouth of the Kennebec River. There the Indians showed themselves so eager for peace that even the insults of Governor Shute, who was an arrogant person utterly destitute of tact, failed to produce an outbreak. A Puritan minister from Medfield by the name of Joseph Baxter was left among the Indians to counteract by his preaching the influence of Father Rale ; and the twain indulged in a Latin correspondence, in which the writers not only attacked each other's politics and theology, but made game of each other's Latin style, — a kind of fierce banter in which the Puritan came off second best. This contest over the Kennebec River was typical of the whole struggle between the French and the

Conference between Governor Shute and the Indians

Baxter and Rale

English. On the one hand, there was the steadily advancing front of the self-governing and greatly thriving agricultural community ; on the other hand, there was the little group of French noblemen and priests governing a mere handful of settlers, and striving to keep back the advancing English by means of diplomatic control over barbarous Indians. It was a struggle which could really have but one issue. It was a struggle, moreover, that was conducted without pity or mercy, with scarcely a pretence of regard for the amenities of civilized warfare. Neither side was particularly scrupulous, while from that day to this, each side has kept up a terrible outcry against the other for doing the very same thing which it did itself. From that day to this English writers have held up their hands in holy horror at the atrocious conduct of the French in sending savages to burn villages and massacre women and children on the English border. Yet was it not an English governor of New York who in 1689 launched the Iroquois thunderbolt against Canada, one of the most frightful Indian incursions known to history? It does not appear that the conscience of either Puritan or Catholic was in the slightest degree disturbed by these horrors. Each felt sure that he was fighting the Devil, and thought it quite proper to fight him with his own weapons.

On the Kennebec frontier the problem for New France was to prevent English villages and fortresses from advancing in that direction, and the most obvious way of accomplishing the result was to instigate the Indians to acts of warfare. This was the avowed policy of Vaudreuil, and it was carried out by Father Rale to the best of his ability. When he found that his Norridgewock Indians were timid, and inclined to peace, he sent to Montreal and caused parties of warriors from divers tribes, Ottawas, Caughnawagas, Hurons, and others, to be sent to the Kennebec River, where all engaged in a frantic war dance, and quite carried away the Norridgewocks in a frenzy of bloodthirsty enthusiasm. This was in 1721. Then began the sickening tale so many times repeated in early American history, — the tale of burning homes, of youth and beauty struck down by the tomahawk, and of captives led away through the gloom of the forest to meet a fiery death. Thus, in turn, the English government at Boston was confronted with its problem : how to put a stop to these horrors without bringing on a new war with France. The practical New England mind saw that the principal hotbed of all the mischief must be destroyed, and if a Frenchman or two should come to grief in the process, it was his own fault for playing so recklessly with fire. It

The Indians instigated to attack the English

Border warfare

was easier, however, for Boston to know what ought to be done than to do it ; for there was the irreconcilable hostility between governor and legislature to be reckoned with. For example, when the Norridgewocks on one occasion complained to Governor Shute that they were cheated and shamefully used by irresponsible traders, the governor undertook to set up certain trading stations on the frontier which should be controlled by trustworthy persons, and where Indians might rest assured of fair

Conflicts between the Governor and the Assembly

treatment, but when he proposed this plan to the Assembly, that body flatly refused to appropriate any money for the purpose. Finally, when the torches were lighted and the shrieks of the victims were heard, when the indignant governor was raising his arm to strike, what should this contumacious Assembly do but interpose obstacle after obstacle ! Not only was it unwilling to entrust the governor with the money for obtaining military supplies, but it even insisted upon carrying on the war through committees of its own. Its blundering conduct was not unlike that of the Continental Congress in the War for Independence. After a while the course of the legislature put the governor into such a rage that on New Year's day, 1723, he drove down to the water side, and embarked in a ship for London without so much as telling anybody what he was about to do. He left it for the town to rub its eyes in astonishment at finding its governor gone.

His place was filled by the lieutenant-governor, William Dummer, who fared no better at the hands of the Assembly, although he was a native of New England. The Assembly insisted that two competent but unpopular officers should be removed from command, and when Dummer refused, the many-headed king retorted by refusing to grant supplies until the officers in question should have been removed. When we read of such scenes as this, which were perpetually recurring during the seventy years' struggle with France, we can understand why the British government thought it necessary to raise money by stamps in order to protect the frontier against the Indians.

Shute succeeded by Dummer

After much tribulation an expedition under Colonel Westbrook sailed for the Penobscot River, ascended it for some distance above the site of Bangor, and destroyed a missionary village which the French had founded there. The next year, 1724, a force of about 200 men went up the Kennebec River, carried the Norridgewock village by storm, and slew many of its defenders,

Expeditions against the Indians

while the rest were scattered. In the course of the fight Father Rale was shot through the head. Puritan writers have sought to stigmatize this interesting man as a murderer, while Catholics have praised him as a martyr. In the impartial light of history, he was neither the one nor the other. He was true to his own sense of duty, and the worst that can be said about him is The death of that he was not exceptionally scrupu-
Father Rale lous in his choice of political and military means; while on the other hand, the title of " martyr" seems hardly to belong to a man who was killed in the ordinary course of battle, not because of his religious faith, but because he was fighting in the service of France.[1]

The fighting thus begun continued for nearly four years, and in the course of it the Norridge-
Extermina- wock tribe was practically extermi-
tion of the nated. The destruction of that mis-
Norridge-
wock tribe sion was a serious blow to the French hold upon the Maine frontier, and they never succeeded in making good the loss.

Our forefathers of that time had come to regard Indians very much in the light of wolves or panthers, to be hunted and slain wherever found. Parties of yeomanry were enlisted for the purpose of penetrating into the wilderness

---

[1] [On the manner of Rale's death, see Parkman, *Half Century of Conflict*, i. 237–239 ; and on the Norridgewock troubles as a whole, the same, pp. 205–240.]

and finding the enemy in his lair. The regular wages paid by the Commonwealth for such service were half a crown a day, paid in a currency so depreciated that the half-crown amounted to about twenty-five cents of our money; but, in addition, there was a liberal bounty of a hundred pounds for each Indian scalp. Even in that detestable rag money a hundred pounds was worth securing. Among the leaders in this rough service was Captain John Lovewell of Dunstable on the Merrimac River, a son of one of Cromwell's soldiers. In January, 1725, he earned his first hundred pounds by bringing a scalp from a remote point among the White Mountains. It was customary for the Massachusetts rangers to patrol those wild stretches of forest, through which Captain Lovewell Algonquins from Canada used to come on their murderous raids. Toward the end of February, 1725, Lovewell's party were passing the shores of a large pond in what is now the township of Fryeburg in Maine, just on the border of New Hampshire, and about sixty miles north of Dover. That sheet of water is still known as Lovewell's Pond. Near its shore his party suddenly came upon ten Indians sleeping around a fire, and immediately killed them all, for which they received a thousand pounds from the treasurer at Boston. The

Indians who were killed were on their way to
join an expedition for massacre in the frontier
villages, so that the bounty would seem to have
been well bestowed. A few weeks later Lovewell once more tried his fortune at the head of
forty-six men, but as they approached the pond
which had witnessed their winter performance,
one or two of their number fell sick, so that it
was necessary to build a rude fortification and
leave there a guard for the sick ones. This reduced the number to thirty-four. Early on a
bright May morning these men fell into an ambuscade of Pequawket Indians, and they kept
Lovewell's up a desperate fight all day against
fight overwhelming odds. Toward sunset
the Indians gave way and retired from the
scene, leaving a tremendous harvest of scalps
for the victors. But these children of the Ironsides had paid a high price for their victory.
Captain Lovewell and eleven others were slain,
being rather more than one third of the number.
One coward had run away and told so dismal a
story to the sick men and their guard that they
deemed it best to quit their rude fortification
and travel southward with all possible despatch.
The retreat from the battlefield began at midnight and was led by Ensign Wyman. One of
the party was the chaplain of the expedition,
Rev. Jonathan Frye of Andover, a youth of
twenty-one, recently graduated at Harvard, who

was as zealous an Indian killer as any of the party. He had been terribly wounded in the fight, and as he felt his strength giving out so that he must lie down upon the ground, he begged his comrades not to incur danger by waiting with him, but to keep on their The death way, and he said to one of them, of Frye "Tell my father that I expect in a few hours to be in eternity, and am not afraid to die." So they left him alone in the forest and nothing more was heard of him. The survivors of this expedition were rewarded with extensive grants of land on the mountain ridges between Lancaster and the Connecticut River, which down to that time were a howling wilderness, and it was in this way that Petersham and others of the hill towns in that region originated.

For half a century, until its memory was obscured by the incidents of the Revolutionary War, Lovewell's fight was a popular theme with the New England farmers. Ballads as long as "Chevy Chase" were written about it, and perhaps a few verses should be quoted in this connection.

"Then spake up Captain Lovewell, when first the fight began,
'Fight on, my valiant heroes, you see they fall like rain!'
For, as we are informéd, the Indians were so thick,
A man could scarcely fire a gun, and not some of them hit.

.   .   .   .

Our worthy Captain Lovewell among them there did die ;
They killed Lieutenant Robbins, and wounded good young
     Frye,
Who was our English chaplain : he many Indians slew,
And some of them he scalpéd, when bullets round him
     flew.'' [1]

As for this worthy young chaplain, he was
mourned by the fair Susanna Rogers, daughter
of the minister at Boxford, to whom he was betrothed. She afterward wrote a long monody
which thus begins : —

    '' Assist, ye Muses, help my quill
       While floods of tears does down distil,
       Not from mine eyes alone, but all
       That hears the sad and doleful fall
       Of that young student, Mr. Frye,
       Who in his blooming youth did die.''

Such incidents as the destruction of Norridgewock and Lovewell's fight occurred in
what was reckoned as an interval of peace between the second and third great intercolonial
wars.

We may now pass over twenty years and
make some mention of the most important
event that marked in America the war of the
Austrian Succession, which began with the seizure of Silesia by Frederick the Great in 1740,

[1] [The whole of this ballad is given in Hart's *American
History told by Contemporaries*, ii. 344–346.]

and ended with the peace of Aix-la-Chapelle in 1748.

On the southeast side of Cape Breton Island, in a very commanding position, was a small town which had been known as English Harbour, but which in the many vicissitudes of Acadia had passed into the hands of the French and had been by them christened Louisburg, after the king. After the treaty of Utrecht, the French refused to surrender Cape Breton Island on the ground that the name "Acadia" applied only to Nova Scotia in the strictest sense, excluding the adjacent islands. About 1720 the French began fortifying this place, and went on until they had spent a sum equivalent to more than $10,000,000 of our modern money, and had made it one of the strongest places in the world, scarcely surpassed by Quebec or Gibraltar. With reference to Canada, France, and the West Indies, this place occupied a central position. It blocked the way to any English ascent of the St. Lawrence, such as had been attempted in 1690 and 1711, and it afforded an admirable base of supplies from which a powerful French squadron might threaten Boston or any other English city upon the Atlantic coast.

It was in 1744 that France and England were dragged into the war between Austria and

Prussia, and no sooner had the news arrived in America than Duquesnel, the French commander of Louisburg, sent a squadron to surprise and capture such English ports in Nova Scotia as might be found insufficiently guarded. The little port of Canseau was at once taken, and an energetic, but fruitless attack was made upon Port Royal. A certain number of prisoners who had been taken from Canseau to Louisburg were returned in the autumn of 1744, and they sent such messages to Governor Shirley as

The project to capture Louisburg

led him to believe that a prompt attack upon Louisburg itself might prove successful. Perhaps the first person to entertain such a scheme seriously was William Vaughan, a graduate of Harvard in 1722, whose father had been lieutenant-governor of New Hampshire. Vaughan had an estate on the Damariscotta River, and did a brisk trade in lumber and fish. There was imminent danger that Louisburg might work the destruction of the English fisheries, and Vaughan, who was daring to the verge of foolhardiness, thought it a good plan to anticipate such a calamity by capturing the impregnable fortress. So bold was the project that Parkman gives to his chapter on this subject the simple heading, " A Mad Scheme." [1] Fortunately, Shirley was himself a man of courage and resource. After a conversation with

[1] [*Half Century of Conflict*, ii. 78–107.]

Vaughan, Shirley informed his legislature that he had a proposal to make of such great importance that he wished them before receiving it to take an oath of secrecy. Shirley had shown much tact in avoiding dissensions with his legislature, and this extraordinary request was granted, but when the Assembly came to consider the question of attacking Louisburg without assistance from British arms, the Assembly deemed the proposal chimerical, and voted to reject it. Nothing daunted, however, Shirley returned to the attack, and with the active co-operation of many merchants who felt that their business absolutely demanded the reduction of the French stronghold, he succeeded at last in obtaining a majority of one vote in the Assembly. The next step was to seek aid from the other colonies, but only New Hampshire, Rhode Island, and Connecticut gave favourable responses. *The New England colonies undertake the attack* Connecticut and New Hampshire furnished each 500 men, and Rhode Island furnished the sloop of war Tartar. Massachusetts supplied 3000 men, and Shirley selected William Pepperell to command the expedition. Pepperell was a very wealthy merchant of Kittery, who had served as justice of the peace and as a militia officer of various grades, ending with colonel. He was by no means a genius, but a man of energy, good sense, and tact. He was now raised to the rank of lieutenant-general, and Roger Wolcott of Connecticut was commissioned major-general and appointed second in command. Pepperell's good sense was sufficient to make him doubt the possibility of success; and the Rev. George Whitefield, when asked to furnish a motto for one of the flags, suggested *Nil desperandum Christo duce*, or, in other words, There is room for hope when Christ is leader, which, under the circumstances, does not seem to indicate a very exuberant confidence on the part of the great preacher.

As for a naval force, it was always possible to extemporize something of the sort in New England, where almost every seaport had citizens ready to venture money in privateering, or perhaps in equipping expeditions for capturing privateers from Frenchmen and Spaniards. The force collected for the Louisburg expedition consisted of one new 24-gun frigate and twelve smaller vessels, mostly sloops of from 8 to 20 guns. This was a ludicrous force for the purpose assigned; one French line-of-battle ship could easily have destroyed the whole of it. To put 4000 men upon Cape Breton Island without an adequate naval force to insure their retreat might easily entail their starvation or capture. More ships must be had, and Shirley sent a message to Commodore Peter Warren, at the island of Antigua, requesting

The naval force

assistance. Warren was inclined to give the aid
required, but a council of war overruled him,
and he declined; but Shirley had wisely provided another string to his bow, and had written some time before to the Duke of Newcastle,
Secretary of State, pointing out the great danger
to the fisheries and the Acadian ports from the
proximity of Louisburg. It was this Duke of
Newcastle who knew so little about American affairs that, one day when he was told that
Annapolis must be fortified, replied, " Annapolis, Annapolis! Oh, yes, Annapolis must be
defended; to be sure, Annapolis should be defended. Where is Annapolis?"[1] Fortunately,
this amiable secretary's zeal was better than his
knowledge, and he promptly wrote to Commodore Warren, ordering him to sail for Boston and do what he could to help the cause.
Warren accordingly sailed with one line-of-battle ship and two 44-gun frigates. While on the
way he met a Boston vessel which informed
him that Pepperell's force had already sailed,
so Warren changed his course and joined the
expedition at Canseau. Perhaps Pepperell had
been precipitate, but in point of fact   The French
this headlong speed was the salvation   surprised
of the enterprise. The French were practi-

[1] [Horace Walpole, *Memoirs of the Reign of King George
II.*, i. 396.]

cally taken unawares; for although rumours of the scheme had reached them, they had been inclined to laugh them to scorn. What likelihood was there of an enemy attacking them with any hope? Their batteries mounted at least 150 heavy guns, against which the provincial assailants brought a vastly inferior armament in size and strength. The British ships, however, constituted a powerful reinforcement. The French garrison consisted of 560 French regulars and Swiss mercenaries, with about 1400 Canadian militia, some 2000 in all.

The New Englanders effected a landing on the 1st of May, and immediately laid siege to the town. On the next day Vaughan led 400 men behind a line of hills to a point where there were large magazines of naval stores. These he set on fire; and what with the pitch and tar and other such combustibles, the smoke that came up and floated over the town was something quite tremendous. One effect upon the French was absurd. Near the burning stores was a large fortification known as the Grand Battery, mounting 30 heavy guns. As the thick clouds of smoke rolled up and enveloped this battery, the defenders were seized with panic and abandoned it without firing a shot; so that when Vaughan's men passed it, observing the profound quiet, they reconnoitred for a moment

The Grand Battery abandoned in panic

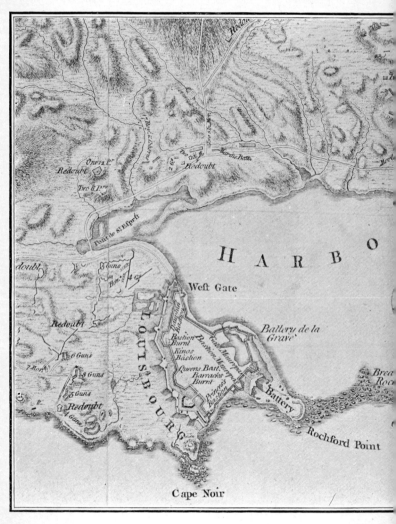

and then exultingly marched in. So hastily had the French departed that they left an immense quantity of ammunition as a present for Vaughan's men, while the cannon were so poorly spiked that the gunsmith, Seth Pomeroy, had them all ready for use the next morning. So that our New Englanders could now bombard the town with cannon and shot provided by the most Christian king.

This capture of the Grand Battery was something on which the besiegers had no right to count, for if it had been properly defended they probably could not have taken it. As it was, its loss by the French probably decided the issue of the whole conflict. The New England troops pressed matters with vigour, and at the end of a week demanded the surrender of the place, but the time had not yet come. On May 19 a French line-of-battle ship arrived upon the scene heavily laden with material of war, and on approaching the town she encountered one of the English ships of smaller calibre, which, retreating before her, lured her within reach of the whole British fleet. She was soon surrounded and captured, and all her material of war passed into the hands of the besiegers. Presently the latter received a great reinforcement by the arrival of eight British seventy-fours, under cover of which the troops were able to establish new

Capture of a French line-of-battle ship

batteries at various points. By the middle of June there was scarcely a house in the town that had not been more or less riddled by shot and shell. The British fleet held the harbour closely invested, and 1000 scaling ladders were made ready for a grand attack. This was too much for the Frenchmen, and on the 17th of June this famous fortress was surrendered. The mad scheme of Vaughan and Shirley had become a sober reality. When the news was disseminated abroad the civilized world was dumb with amazement. For the first time it waked up to the fact that a new military power had grown up in America. One of the strongest fortresses on the face of the earth had surrendered to a force of New England militia. Pepperell was at once created a baronet, being the only native American who ever attained that rank. Warren was promoted to the grade of admiral. Louisburg Square in Boston commemorates the victory. Some twenty-five years ago, when we were rebuilding the eastern transept of Harvard College Library, I discovered in a gloomy corner an iron cross about thirty inches in height, which had stood in the market-place at Louisburg and was brought to Cambridge as a trophy. I thought it a pity to hide such a thing, so I had it gilded and set up over the southern entrance to the library,

Louisburg surrendered June 17, 1745

A relic of Louisburg

where it remained several years, until one night some silly vandals, presumed to be students, succeeded in detaching this heavy mass of iron and carrying it away.[1]

[1] [Fortunately it has since been returned, and is now in the library.]

VIII

BEGINNINGS OF THE GREAT WAR

THE treaty of Aix-la-Chapelle did very little to set matters at rest in North America; it provided only a short breathing spell before the numerous unsettled questions gave rise to another and far greater war. The treaty did little or nothing toward marking out boundaries either at the east in Acadia, or at the west toward the Ohio valley, and it was in the latter region that the next great storm was to burst. By 1748 the schemes of La Salle had developed as far as they were ever destined to do. A thriving colony had been founded near the mouth of the Mississippi River, and that region was connected with Canada by a straggling series of fortified villages at great distances apart. Such places were Kaskaskia and Cahokia, as well as Fort Chartres in the Illinois country, and Detroit.

The treaty of Aix-la-Chapelle

But the French were now beginning to feel the disadvantage of scarcity of numbers distributed over long exterior lines. Every year that brought them closer to contact with the English made this disadvantage more apparent. Since La Salle's time a great change had come over the land. In his day, Pennsylvania was merely the banks of the Delaware River, while the Maryland and Virginia settlements were confined to the tidewater regions; but by 1748 not only had these English populations spread for many miles into the interior, but a fresh migration from Europe, conducted on a greater scale than any of its predecessors, had introduced into the middle Appalachian region an active and aggressive population. Of the 3,000,000 inhabitants of the United States in 1776, at least one sixth part were Presbyterians who had come from the north of Ireland since 1720.[1] Along with these there was a considerable population of Protestant Germans who had come at about the same time. By far the greater part of this population had passed through the old settled seaboard districts and made homes for itself on what was then the western frontier; that is to say, the Alleghany region of Pennsylvania,

The spread of the English westward

The Scotch-Irish

[1] [Cf. on the Scotch-Irish, Fiske, *Old Virginia and her Neighbours*, ii. 456–462 ; *The Dutch and Quaker Colonies*, ii. 410–414 ; and Mr. C. A. Hanna's elaborate work, *The Scotch-Irish, or the Scot in North Britain, North Ireland, and North America*, 2 vols., New York, 1902.]

Maryland, Virginia, and the Carolinas. From this population came some of the most hardy and enterprising pioneers of the old west, such men as Daniel Boone, James Robertson, and John Sevier the Huguenot; for in this movement we find the name of many a Protestant Frenchman enlisted under the banner of St. George. By 1748 the settled English population was fast approaching the Appalachian ranges, and the more mobile company of hunters, trap-

The pioneers pass the Alleghanies pers, fur-traders, and other pioneers were passing beyond them and fast making their mark upon the western country. A company had already been formed in Virginia for the improvement of lands on the Ohio River, and in this company were interested some of the most prominent men in the colony, including two brothers of George Washington. Some of the pioneers were pressing forward to make homes in the wilderness where afterward grew up the two great commonwealths of Kentucky and Tennessee; but that stage was only realized three years later. Meanwhile as the Indian trade was lucrative, and hunting had its charms, all the restless spirits who preferred life in the wilderness to life on plantations were finding their way through the picturesque defiles of the mountains down the broad grassy slopes through which flowed the western rivers.

Now this advance of the English frontier was an advance against the centre of the whole French position. In those days, as at present, there were two great routes, whether for military purposes or for trade, between the Atlantic seaboard and the Mississippi valley. One of these was from Albany to the Niagara River, and thence westward either to the north or to the south of Lake Erie. The other was from Philadelphia or Baltimore to Pittsburg, and thence down the Ohio River. It followed, therefore, that if the English could firmly hold both the Niagara River and the junction between the Allegheny and the Monongahela, where Pittsburg now stands, it would be in their power to strike at the centre of the long exterior line held by the French, and forever to cut Louisiana asunder from Canada. By degrees the more far-sighted Frenchmen who administered the affairs of Canada had been taking in the alarming character of the situation. Since the early part of the century the influence of the Frenchmen over the Indian tribes had relatively diminished. They held as firmly as ever the alliance of the northern Algonquins, from the Micmacs of Nova Scotia to the Ojibways of Lake Superior, and at one time in the early part of the eighteenth century their

[marginal note: This advance of the English a menace to the French]

[marginal note: The French influence with the Indians declines]

influence had waxed strong even among their ancient enemies of the Long House.   The persuasive tongues of the Jesuits had even won converts among the Mohawks, a small colony of whom they had established at Caughnawaga on the St. Lawrence River, a short distance above Montreal.   These Caughnawagas were useful as middle men in the trade between the remote northwest and the province of New York by way of Lake Champlain, and they were also of considerable service as spies to report in Canada the affairs of New York.   These circumstances led William Burnet, the able governor of New

The founding   York, to build a fortress at Oswego in
of Oswego   1722 upon land which he bought for
the purpose from the Six Nations.   As the New York Assembly was as froward and penny wise as usual, Burnet cut the Gordian knot by paying the expenses out of his own pocket.   This founding of Oswego was an event of prime importance in the history of the United States, inasmuch as it diverted the main current of the northwestern fur-trade from the valley of the St. Lawrence to the valley of the Mohawk, and thus greatly strengthened the hold of the English upon the Long House all the way from the Hudson River to Lake Erie.[1]   In 1738 this English influence was still further increased by

[1] [W. L. Stone, *Life and Times of Sir William Johnson*, i. 30–32.]

the arrival of that remarkable man, William Johnson, a native of Ireland, who waxed rich in the Indian trade, built for himself two strongholds in the Mohawk valley, and acquired such a reputation among the Mohawks that they revered him like one of their natural chiefs. The influence exerted upon the In- Sir William dians by Johnson and by the Schuy- Johnson lers of Albany, as well as through the trading station at Oswego, made it probable that in the event of a conflict with France the English could control the Niagara River.

Still more important, however, was the mountainous site of Pittsburg, the Gateway of the West, as it used to be called ; for it was in that neighbourhood that the English were already pressing westward and winning control over the numerous and powerful tribes of the Ohio valley. Among these should especially be mentioned the Delawares and Shawnees upon the upper Ohio ; and with them were associated the remnants of the Hurons, generally known as Wyandottes, and likewise a group which had migrated from the Long House, apparently consisting chiefly of Senecas, but called by the frontiersmen Mingos. Westward of all these came the Miamis, and then the Illinois. Late in the seventeenth century all these tribes had been invaded, tormented, and made more or less trib-

utary by the Long House. Whether they acknowledged the relationship or not, the Long
House asserted it whenever an occasion offered.
French influence over these tribes had never
been strong except among the Illinois. On the
English other hand, the English traders as
traders in they came into the Ohio valley were
the Ohio
valley careful to propitiate the natives, and
succeeded in establishing a strong influence over
them, especially the tribes of the upper Ohio.
Obviously, if this sort of thing were to go on,
it would not be long before the English would
hold the whole stretch of country from Oswego
south of Lake Erie to Cahokia as firmly as the
French held the country from Montreal to the
Sault Ste. Marie; in other words, the English
would hold both the great routes between east
and west, and New France would be severed in
twain.

This situation was distinctly realized by the
Marquis de la Galissonière, who governed Canada in 1749; and that year he sent a party of
about 250 men to inspect the country between
the Niagara and Ohio rivers, to take possession
of it in the name of the French king, and to ascertain the sentiments of the native tribes. The
command of this party was entrusted to a captain and chevalier named Céloron de Bienville.
They went up the St. Lawrence as far as Fort

Frontenac, crossed Lake Ontario in canoes which they carried up by the bank of the Niagara River, and launching them at a safe distance above the falls, made their way into Lake Erie. Then for seven days they forced their way through the dense forest to the placid waters of Chautauqua Lake, and after landing where Jamestown now stands, and struggling once more with the tangled woods, they reached the Allegheny River. At that point of their route on the 29th of July they took possession of the country in the name of Louis XV. This act of taking possession was performed as follows: The royal arms of France stamped upon a tin plate were nailed to a tree. At the foot of the tree a plate of lead was buried, upon which was an inscription stating that Monsieur Céloron had buried this plate " as a token of renewal of possession heretofore taken of the aforesaid river Ohio, of all streams that fall into it, and all lands on both sides to the source of the aforesaid streams, as the preceding kings of France have enjoyed or ought to have enjoyed it, and which they have upheld by force of arms and by treaties, notably by those of Ryswick, Utrecht, and Aix-la-Chapelle." [1]   It

Céloron takes possession of the Ohio valley for Louis XV., 1749

[1] [A facsimile of this plate is given in Winsor, *Narrative and Critical Hist. of America*, v. 9.]

will be observed that this is the usual style which France has maintained for some centuries. Whenever her borders have been extended it has always been officially declared to be simply taking possession of what was hers already. Upon various other spots as they descended the river our party of Frenchmen buried these leaden tablets, the last place being at the mouth of the Great Miami. Some of the plates have since then been dug up and preserved in museums. The general demeanour of the Indians through whose towns the Frenchmen passed was polite, but suspicious and unsatisfactory. It was evident that the English influence was strong throughout the upper country drained by the Ohio. When Céloron reached the Great Miami he turned his course up that river and presently came to a village of the Miamis, ruled by a chieftain who was a firm friend to the English, in so much that they commonly called him "Old Britain," but the French oddly called him "La Demoiselle," or "The Maiden." Whether he was faint-hearted, as such an epithet might seem to imply, or perhaps more delicate of feature than others of his race, we cannot say ; but as to his capacity for lying, we are not left in doubt. His home had formerly been upon the Maumee River, not far from the site of Fort Wayne, and

Céloron
among the
Miamis

he had now moved close down to the Ohio, apparently in order to be in the highway of English trade. Céloron heaped gifts upon him and urged him to take his men back to their old home on the Maumee. The astute Demoiselle accepted the presents and was profuse in promises, but so far was he from re- The Miamis tiring that he gathered into his new under English town as many recruits as he could influence summon.[1] The English called it Pickawillany. It became one of the principal Indian towns of the west, completely under English influence, and was a serious obstacle to all French schemes in that quarter. For some time Canadian officials intrigued and fulminated against Pickawillany, until at length in the summer of 1752 Charles de Langlade, a young French trader of Green Bay, led a large The French force of Ojibways and Ottawas against destroy the Miami trad- the obnoxious town. They took it ing village by surprise, slaughtered many of the defenders, and burned the town, crowning the work by a hilarious supper in which they feasted upon the boiled carcase of the Demoiselle himself.

Considering the vital importance of the Gate-

[1] [A facsimile of the map of Father Bonnecamp, the chaplain of the expedition, is given in Winsor, *Narr. and Crit. Hist. of Amer.*, v. 569.]

way of the West, it seems very strange that
the English, who were then in possession of it,
did not build and maintain a strong fortress
there, but in truth the spot was claimed at once
by Virginia and by Pennsylvania, and in neither
of these provinces did the legislature wish to
invest money in property that might be adjudged
to belong to another province. The swarm of
difficulties that surrounded this unsettled question sufficed to prevent all action. Meanwhile,
a new governor came to Canada, the Marquis
Duquesne, who saw clearly that New France
The Marquis must either control the Gateway of
Duquesne the West, or give up all hold upon
the Ohio valley and submit to see Canada
severed from Louisiana. Accordingly, in the
spring of 1753 Duquesne sent out a force of
1500 men commanded by an able veteran named
Marin. This little army crossed Lake Erie at
some distance to the west of Niagara River,
and landed at Presqu'Isle, where the town of
Erie now stands, and there they built a strong
The French blockhouse. From that point they
expedition cut a road through the forest to the
of 1753 stream since known as French Creek,
and there they erected a second blockhouse and
called it Fort Le Bœuf. Here they could re-
sume their canoes and easily float down French
Creek to the Allegheny River, and so on, if need

be, to the Gulf of Mexico. At this point the
French commander fell dangerously ill, and his
place was taken by another skilful veteran, Legardeur de Saint-Pierre.

By these active measures the French were
gaining strength daily. It is true that the Indians of the region they were entering were
friends of the English, but the red man's politics were apt to be of a vacillating sort, and
truckling to strength was one of their chief characteristics. They resembled
the politics of the famous Vicar of
Bray, whose conduct was always guided by one
unswerving principle, no matter what party
might be uppermost, always to remain Vicar
of Bray, sir. The red man was usually ready
to follow the advice of Mr. Pickwick and shout
with whichever mob shouted the loudest. This
was seen in the conduct of a feathered potentate
whom the English called the Half-King; he
came out from his village with a show of fight,
but soon made up his mind that discretion
was the better part of valour. Fifteen hundred
Frenchmen! truly the white father at Quebec
must be a mighty chief. Several tribes sent
messages seeking to curry favour with the invaders.

It was Duquesne's intention to have a third
fort built at Venango, where French Creek flows

The Indians between two fires

into the Allegheny, and an advance party, commanded by Joncaire, had arrived at that place and seized and fortified an English trading house there. Thus far had things proceeded in the early days of December, 1753, when one

A chance meeting

evening as Joncaire and his friends were sitting down to supper, some unbidden guests arrived upon the scene. The party consisted of Christopher Gist, a veteran trader who acted as guide, an Indian interpreter named Davison, a French interpreter named Vanbraam, and four wood rangers as servants. The person for whom this little party acted as escort was a tall and stately youth named George

Major George Washington sent to warn the French

Washington, a major in the Virginia militia. Governor Dinwiddie of Virginia, who was keeping as keen a watch upon the Ohio valley from Williamsburg as Duquesne was keeping from Montreal, had heard of the crossing of Lake Erie by the French and their approach toward the Gateway of the West. To warn them off was a delicate matter, while to counteract their intrigues with the Indians a wise head was called for. Washington had been in the employ of Lord Fairfax in surveying frontier land, and had made good use of the opportunities for studying Indians. Governor Dinwiddie, moreover, gave him credit for a clear-sightedness that nothing could hoodwink and a courage that nothing could daunt, and in this the wise old Scotchman was not deceived.

After the party had sat down to supper and the wine had begun to circulate, the Frenchmen grew somewhat confidential, and with their politest smiles assured Washington that they intended to drive the English out of all that country; and they felt sure that they could do it, for although inferior in force, they more than made up for this by their quickness of movement. The next day Washington proceeded to Fort Le Bœuf, where he met the French commander, and gave him a polite letter from Dinwiddie expressing his surprise that he should thus venture to encroach upon English territory in time of peace. The old Frenchman treated Washington with extreme politeness, but said that he should feel it necessary to remain where he was until he should have had time to transmit Dinwiddie's letter to Montreal and get a reply from Governor Duquesne. Washington's return to Virginia was marked with adventures and some hair-breadth escapes.[1] When Governor Dinwiddie heard the results of his journey, which were not very dif-

The French boast of their plans

---

[1] [Washington's Journal of this expedition is in Sparks's ed. of his works, ii. 432–447. For other reprints, see Winsor, *Narr. and Crit. Hist.*, v. 572. Gist's Journal is to be found in the *Mass. Hist. Soc. Coll.*, 3 ser. v. 101–108.]

ferent from what he had anticipated, he made up his mind that as large a force as possible must

Governor
Dinwiddie
resolves to
occupy the
Gateway of
the West

be collected from Virginia and other colonies, to advance, while there was yet time, and occupy the Gateway of the West; but the governor of a free English colony was at a great disadvantage as compared with a despotic governor of Canada. Dinwiddie must persuade his legislature, and he must notify other governors, who in turn must persuade their legislatures. We need not be surprised that the English were too late. Washington had selected the spot where Pittsburg now stands as the proper place for a commanding fortress, but scarcely had his men begun to work there when they were driven away by a superior force of Frenchmen, who proceeded to build a stout fortress and call it Fort Duquesne. Well might the indig-

Duquesne
anticipates
the English

nant Dinwiddie exclaim in a letter written at this time, "If our Assembly had voted the money in November which they did in February, it's more than probable the fort would have been built and garrisoned before the French had approached; but these things cannot be done without money. As there was none in our treasury, I have advanced my own to forward the expedition; and if the independent companies from New York come soon, I am in hopes the eyes of the other colonies will be opened; and if they grant a proper supply of men, I hope we shall be able to dislodge the French or build a fort on that river." [1] When we read such letters as this and realize that through the whole seventy years of struggle with New France the difficulty was always the same, we surely cannot much wonder that the British minister at the beginning of Pontiac's war should have deemed it necessary to resort to such a measure as the Stamp Act. Americans should not forget that while that measure was ill-considered, the evil which it was designed to relieve was most flagrant and dangerous.

In point of fact, in May, 1754, Dinwiddie's force on the frontier was only the Virginia regiment of about three hundred men under Colonel Joshua Fry, with Major Washington second in command. Fry was detained by sickness at Will's Creek, about one hundred and forty miles from Fort Duquesne. The advance was slow and difficult, as it was necessary to cut roads through the virgin forests and over the mountains in order to drag cannon and wagons. An advance of a mile in a day was sometimes all that could be accomplished. In spite of these obstacles,

The Virginia expedition to Fort Duquesne

[1] [Parkman, *Montcalm and Wolfe*, i. 144.]

Washington had crossed the mountains and encamped at a spot called Great Meadows with about one hundred and fifty men, when a message came to him from his friend the Half-King, saying that the French were upon the march to meet him. For two or three days Washington watched vigilantly for a surprise, and the reports that came in seemed to indicate that a French force was lurking in the neighbourhood. Presently the Half-King arrived

Washington surprises a French force

upon the scene, and as everything indicated that the enemy intended a surprise, it was decided to find them if possible and inflict a counter surprise. The result was that presently the French were discovered in a ravine, and there was a brief fight in which the French commander, an ensign named Jumonville, was killed, with nine others, and the remaining twenty-two were captured. After it was all over some of the prisoners informed Washington that they were a party sent from Fort Duquesne by its commander, Contrecœur, to carry a message to Washington. In point of fact, it was a scouting party intended to look out for any approaching party of English, and to warn them to withdraw from this portion of New France. A great outcry was afterward raised by the French at what they chose to call perfidy on Washington's part, and an absurd story was circulated to the intent that he had fired upon a flag of truce. The whole case may, however, be properly summed up as a chance encounter between two forces engaged in actual hostilities before any declaration of war. Each side professed to be unwilling to force on hostilities, while each side was eager to strike the other as soon as a proper occasion offered.

After this affray Washington built a rude entrenchment at Great Meadows which he called Fort Necessity. A few days after- Fort ward news came of Colonel Fry's Necessity death, and presently other troops arrived from Virginia and South Carolina, until Washington was in command of some three hundred men besides about one hundred and fifty Indians under the Half-King and others.

Meanwhile, the authorities in Canada had not been idle, and the garrison of Fort Duquesne now numbered fourteen hundred men. A force of about six hundred under Coulon de Villiers, brother of the slain Jumonville, marched up the Monongahela in quest of Washington. Villiers arrived at Great Meadows on a rainy day, and a lively firing was The battle kept up until dark. By that time the of Fort English found their powder nearly Necessity exhausted and their guns foul, while their food was gone and starvation faced them. Washington therefore accepted the terms offered by the French commander, that the English should march away with the honours of war, with drums beating and colours flying, and that they should be protected from insult, while on the other hand, they should surrender their prisoners of Jumonville's party. So the English marched away. It was not a very murderous affair, and Washington's friend, the red man Half-King, sarcastically gave it as his opinion that the Frenchmen had behaved like cowards and the English like fools. It was on the 4th of July that young Washington began his doleful retreat across the mountains into Virginia. The situation seemed to have nothing to retrieve it. At this first outbreak of the struggle with France the enemy seemed to be carrying everything before them. The Gateway of the West was in their possession, and the red flag of England waved nowhere within the limits of what they chose to call New France. Yet Washington even at that early age was already a marvel of fortitude and may have consoled himself with the thought that better days were coming.

The English retreat

Before he was permitted, however, to see such better days, the cup of disaster must be drained to its dregs. Nothing could be clearer than that

the possession of Fort Duquesne by the French
and their infliction of a slight defeat upon the
English would have an immediate and disastrous effect upon most of the Indian tribes in
the Ohio valley. Dinwiddie therefore at once
prepared to assume the offensive and carry the
war on a larger scale into the enemy's country.
But he found himself impeded at every step by
the Virginia House of Burgesses. Those
canny planters were loath to put much money
into the governor's hands lest he should make
an improper use of it. At one time they would
refuse the appropriation asked for, at Niggardli-
another time they would grant a sum ness of the Provincial
too small to be of much use, and yet Assemblies
again they would grant a sufficient sum, while
attaching to the bill a rider concerning some
long-disputed question which they knew would
elicit an angry veto from the governor. Simi-
larly in Pennsylvania the Assembly refused
money for military purposes in order to wring
from the governor some concession with regard
to the long-vexed question of taxing proprietary
lands. Moreover, the Assembly at Philadelphia was not quite sure that it was worth while
to raise troops for taking Fort Duquesne from
the French if it should thereby fall into the
possession of Virginia. It was with difficulty
that these representative bodies could be made
to see anything that required any breadth of

vision. Moreover, they were used to contending against their governors ; in the eyes of most
representatives that was the sole object for
which legislatures existed, but they were not
accustomed to devote much thought to the
French as enemies, nor had they as yet learned
very well what it meant to be invaded by Indians. On the other hand, New York and

The defence
of the colo-
nies depend-
ent on the
governors

Massachusetts were somewhat more
forward inasmuch as they had a keen
perception of what was involved in
warfare against Frenchmen and In-

dians. Here too, however, the zeal of the governors far outran the efficiency of the legislatures. Shirley, in particular, a veteran lawyer
of great sense and more than average insight,
appreciated the nature of the threatened struggle more keenly than any of the other governors except Dinwiddie.

In fact, something was happening of the sort
that people never quite see until they can look
backward. The English colonies had insensibly
drifted into a continental state of things. The
crisis had been hastened by the wholesale in-
coming of the Scotch-Irish and Germans. The
bulging of the centre of the English line toward
the Ohio valley had brought things to a pass
where it was no longer a conflict between New
France and New England in the narrower sense,

but between New France and the entire world
of English America. Under these circumstances
the next war that should break out must be a
continental affair; it would concern Louisiana
and Georgia as well as New York and The need of
Canada; and yet, here were the peo- a union of
ple of these colonies profoundly the colonies
ignorant and almost culpably careless of each
other's interests, ready to throw away all the
advantages of numerical strength and interior
lines and give away the victory to an inferior
enemy rather than coöperate with one another
in defeating him. Obviously, the crying need
of the time was some feasible plan for a federal
Union. In the event of a war, it was important
to insure the aid of the Six Nations, and to
this end it was necessary to let them know how
much support they might expect from the English colonies. For this purpose a congress was
called to assemble at Albany in the summer of
1754 in order to consider the situation. It was
the second congress that assembled on American soil, the first having been the one called by
Leisler at New York in 1690.[1] It is significant
that even on this verge of a mighty conflict only
the four New England colonies with New York,
Pennsylvania, and Maryland were represented

[1] [Cf. Fiske, *The Dutch and Quaker Colonies*, ii. 228,
and Frothingham, *Rise of the Republic of the United States*,
pp. 90–93.]

at the Albany Congress. The deliberations were chiefly memorable for a plan of union drawn The Albany Congress up by Benjamin Franklin which, if it had been adopted, might perhaps have averted the Revolution of twenty years later.[1] This plan would have created a true federal Union, the government of which would have operated directly upon individuals, as our present federal Union does, and not upon states only, as the Continental Congress did. Franklin's plan would have created a Continental government with taxing power for continental purposes only, leaving otherwise intact the local self-government. There would have been a president or governor-general appointed by the Crown to serve as chief executive in purely continental matters.[2]

This plan of federation was rejected with small ceremony by the colonies. In some cases no notice was taken of it; in others it was treated with contempt. There were few peo- Franklin's plan of union rejected ple as yet who saw any meaning in the demand for a closer union, and nothing but a long experience of distress and disaster would have taught them the need of it. This rejection of the Albany plan left the col-

---

[1] [Such seems to have been Franklin's opinion in 1789; see Frothingham, *Rise of the Republic*, etc., p. 149, note.]

[2] [See Bigelow, *Franklin's Works*, ii. 355–375; Frothingham, *Rise of the Republic*, etc., pp. 134–151.]

onies in a very embarrassing position. On the brink of a great war there was no single power in the country which could raise men and money for the common defence. Of course, there were but few who anticipated war, or were alive to the situation. It was at this moment that it occurred to Shirley that if the colonists could not create for themselves a continental taxing power it would be necessary for Parliament to fulfil that function. This would involve a direct tax, and while Shirley recognized the American unwillingness to submit to taxation by any other authority than that of the colonial Assemblies, he nevertheless thought that a stamp tax might be received with acquiescence because it had so few annoying features. It was by such considerations as these that the British official mind was prepared for the Stamp Act of eleven years later. As it was, the colonies had to flounder through a great war as best they could.

The representations of the royal governors and of the viceroy of Canada created some excitement both in England and in France. In England a couple of regiments, each of five hundred men, were shipped for Virginia under command of Major-General Edward Braddock. When this was learned at Versailles a force of three thousand men was started for Canada under

England and France send troops to America, 1755

Baron Dieskau.   The health of Duquesne was
failing, and with Dieskau's expedition there came
a new viceroy for Canada, the last of her French
governors, Vaudreuil, a younger son of the
former governor of that name.   The expedition
did not get clear of European waters without
adventure.   It was well understood by the British government that the squadron gathering at
Brest had troops on board destined for America.   Accordingly, a powerful force of eighteen or
twenty ships of the line was sent out to inter-
cept and capture any French vessels bound for
America.   The greater part of the French squadron, however, got away, but three of its ships,
having fallen behind through stress of weather,
Capture of   were in the neighbourhood of Cape
two French   Race when the British fleet overtook
ships   them.   As the British ship Dunkirk
came abreast of the French ship Alcide, a red
flag was suddenly hoisted upon the British flag-
ship as a signal for fighting; whereupon the
French captain of the Alcide called out, " Is this
peace or war ? "   He was answered by Richard
Howe, captain of the Dunkirk, " I don't know ;
but you 'd better get ready for war."   Scarcely
had the words been uttered when the Dunkirk and other English ships opened fire, and
the Alcide, with one of her companions, was
forced to surrender.   This little incident at

sea was the naval counterpart to Washington's passage at arms with Jumonville in the mountains.

It was in February, 1755, that General Braddock arrived at Governor Dinwiddie's house at Williamsburg. The spring was spent General in preparations for the campaign that Braddock was to wrest Fort Duquesne from the enemy and recover the Gateway of the West. The figure of Braddock has long been well known to all Americans, — a British bulldog, brave, obstinate, and honest, but more than ordinarily dull in appreciating an enemy's methods, or in freeing himself from the precise traditions in which he had been educated. His first and gravest mistake, however, — that of underrating his Indian foe, — is one that has been shared by many commanders, to their confusion, and by many writers. The fighting qualities of the red man have often been ill appreciated, and in particular he has been ignorantly accused of cowardice because of his stealthy methods Indian mode and unwillingness to fight in the open. of fighting In point of fact, his method of fighting was closely adapted to the physical conditions of the American wilderness, and it was just what was produced by survival of the fittest during thousands of years of warfare under such conditions. When white men came to America, they were at

first able to wreak wholesale destruction upon
the natives without regard to numbers or conditions. Such was the case when the Pequots,
the Stamford Indians, and the Narragansetts
were swept out of existence.[1] This was largely
because of the European superiority in arms, but
in later days, when this disparity had been done
away with, white men were apt to find Indians
quite as formidable enemies as they cared to deal
with, and in order to achieve success it was found
necessary to adopt the Indian methods, aban-
doning solid columns and lines of battle, so as
to fight in loose order and behind trees or earthworks. It is interesting to see that in these later

English
regulars
ill prepared
for such
tactics

days when the increase in the power
and precision of death-dealing weapons has greatly increased the danger-
ousness of the battlefield, there has
been a tendency to recur to Indian methods in
so far as concerns looseness of order and the
use of various kinds of cover. In the eighteenth
century there was nobody so ill fitted to fight
with Indians as a European regular, trained in
European manuals of war and inured to European discipline. Braddock's fatuity was well
illustrated in his reply to Dr. Franklin, when
the latter informed him that the Indians, as

[1] [Fiske, *The Beginnings of New England*, pp. 157–
162.]

antagonists, were by no means to be despised: " These savages may, indeed," said Braddock, " be a formidable enemy to your raw American militia, but upon the king's regular and disciplined troops, sir, it is impossible that they should make any impression." [1]

Many stories of Braddock's arrogance and illtemper have come down to us, but if we consider the obstacles that were thrown in the way of military promptness, by which zealous men like Shirley and Dinwiddie were so often goaded to anger, we need not *Braddock's difficulties* wonder that Braddock's temper was sometimes not altogether at its best. He scolded a good deal about the legislatures, and sometimes let fall exasperating remarks about the lack of zeal and rectitude in public servants. For such insinuations there was sometimes apparent ground, especially when the member of a legislature showed himself more intent upon annoying the governor than upon attacking the enemy.

The energetic Shirley made a visit to Braddock's camp at Alexandria, in the course of which a comprehensive plan of procedure was agreed upon, which involved operations on the Niagara River and Lake Champlain and the

[1] [*Life of Benjamin Franklin, written by himself.* Edited by John Bigelow, Philadelphia, 1884, i. 425.]

northeastern frontier as well as in the Alleghany
Mountains. For the present we will confine
our story to the latter.

At the outset a mistake was made in the
choice of a route. For a force like Braddock's,
wagons were indispensable, and wagons were
far more common in Pennsylvania than in Virginia. A route corresponding with the general
Braddock direction of the Pennsylvania rail-
should have
landed at road would not only have been much
Philadelphia shorter than the route through Virginia, but it would have been, at least in its earlier
stages, a route through a population which could
furnish wagons. By adopting this route Braddock would have made the Pennsylvanians feel
some personal interest in the acquisition of Fort
Duquesne; whereas, when he decided to march
through Virginia it only tended to confirm Pennsylvanians in the impression that Fort Duquesne, if conquered, was to pass into Virginian
hands. After a while Benjamin Franklin went
about among the farmers, and by pledging his
own personal credit obtained a fair supply of
horses and wagons.[1]

Braddock's force at length set out in de-
tachments and marched along the banks of
the Potomac River to the old trading station

[1] [*Life of Benjamin Franklin*, etc., edited by John Bigelow, i. 322.]

of the Ohio Company known as Will's Creek. It had lately been fortified, and received the name of Fort Cumberland. This was the rendezvous of the army. The two regiments from England had been increased by further enlistments in Virginia of nine companies of militia of fifty men each to a total of fourteen hundred men. Braddock despised these militia, and had small respect either for partisan guerilla forces or for Indian auxiliaries. The services of the chief Scarroyaddy, or of the noted frontiersman Black Jack, were at his disposal at the cost of a few civil words only, but he treated these worthies so superciliously that they went off on business of their own.

In spite of these instances of indiscretion, however, it is not correct to say, as has often been said, that Braddock neglected all precaution and was drawn into an ambuscade. Such statements are samples of the kind of exaggeration that is apt to grow up about events that create great public excitement. Braddock made mistakes enough, but he was not absolutely a fool. During the whole of the march flanking parties were kept out on each side of the creeping column, while scouts in all directions ranged through the depths of the woods. The column, which consisted of about twenty-two hundred men, sometimes extended

The march

for four miles along a road hardly fit to be called a bridle-path, on the average scarcely four yards in width. The march began on June 10, and eight days later the force had advanced only thirty miles from Fort Cumberland. By that time the rear of the column was so heavily encumbered with sick men that its power of marching had almost come to an end. It was

A detachment sent on in advance

therefore decided to leave with the rear column of about one thousand men most of the heavier wagons and other impedimenta, and to proceed somewhat more quickly toward Fort Duquesne with an advance guard of twelve hundred. But in spite of this diminution of labour, the difficulties of the road were such that the 7th of July had arrived when the advance column approached Turtle Creek, a stream that flows into the Monongahela about eight miles south of Fort Duquesne. Meanwhile, its progress had been detected and watched, as was to have been expected, by French and Indian scouts. At the fortress Contrecœur still governed, with Beaujeu second in command. The force consisted of five or six hundred Frenchmen, partly regulars and partly Canadian militia, with eight hundred Indians, some of them baptized converts from the northeast, some of them wild Ojibways led by Charles de Langlade, the

conqueror of the Demoiselle, and the rest, Ottawas under their renowned chieftain, the long-headed and ferocious Pontiac. When the approach of Braddock's column to the mouth of Turtle Creek was announced at the French fortress Captain Beaujeu volunteered to go out with a strong party and lay an ambuscade for the English. With this end in view he took some two hundred and fifty Frenchmen and over six hundred In- Beaujeu sets out to way-lay the Eng-lish
dians and stole through the woods between the fortress and Turtle Creek, but he never succeeded in preparing the desired ambuscade, nor did Braddock's force march into an ambuscade, in any proper sense of the word. So sensible was Braddock of the great danger of the road between Turtle Creek and Fort Duquesne, on the right bank of the Monongahela, that he forded the latter stream and Braddock's precautions
proceeded down the opposite bank for five or six miles, when he again crossed the river and brought his column on to a rising ground along which the narrow road ran toward the fortress. His column was then in its usual condition : a few Virginian guides in front, then the advance under Lieutenant-Colonel Thomas Gage, among whose men were two lieutenants destined in later days to play inglorious parts, — Horatio Gates and Charles Lee. Behind Gage came Sir John

St. Clair with the working party, followed by a couple of cannon, and these, in turn, by the wagons with powder and tools. Behind these came the principal part of the column, while both flanks and rear were very strongly guarded with flanking parties. The situation would not have been particularly dangerous if the British regulars had known how to separate and fight under cover. It was owing to this internal fault-iness, and not to any ambush, that Braddock's column came to grief.

When the opposing forces met it was simply the meeting of the two heads of columns in The battle a narrow woodland road. Who can ever forget that moment when Gage's light horsemen quickly fled back and those be-hind could catch a glimpse through the trees of a young Frenchman wearing a brilliant red gorget and bounding lightly along the road, till, on seeing his enemy, he turned and waved his hand? That brief glimpse of Captain Beau-jeu at the moment of his death will forever live in history. At the third volley he dropped dead. Gage's men delivered fire with admirable coolness, but its effect was slight, for the enemy, in two bifurcating columns, passed to right and to left of the English, all the time pouring in a galling fire from behind trees and bushes. Never were the conditions of a battle more simple. The English were torn to pieces because they stood in solid line where they could be seen ; and if anything were needed to make it impossible to miss them, it was their bright scarlet coats. On the other hand, no matter how diligently the British loaded and fired, they could see nothing to aim at. One officer who had been in the *The English fall before unseen foes* thickest of the fight, literally wedged in among falling bodies, said after the battle that he had not caught sight of an Indian during the whole of the battle. They were fighting simply against puffs of smoke which seemed to come from all points of the compass. For a time the cannon were diligently plied and split many tree trunks. Many of the regulars fired wildly and hit their own comrades. The Virginians, who scattered and fought in Indian fashion, suffered but little and did more than their share of execution. Some of the regulars tried to imitate these tactics, but wherever Braddock saw anything of the sort going on he would strike them with the flat of his sword and force them back into the ranks. As for the general himself, he performed *Bravery of Braddock and Washington* prodigies of valour, and was forever in the most exposed places, while he had four horses shot under him and at last fell from the fifth with one of his lungs badly torn by a bullet. Washington's fighting was equally desperate. Two horses were killed under him and his clothes were partly torn from his back by bullets. He seemed to bear a charmed life. It is needless to enlarge further upon such a scene. Let it suffice to say, that out of a total force of thirteen hundred and seventy-three all but four hundred and fifty-nine were killed or wounded ; and in addition to these, out of eighty-six officers only twenty-three escaped unhurt. The whole affair was as thickly fraught with horror as anything that is likely to happen in modern warfare. The utter fatuity of the affair, the hopeless feeling of brave men drawn up for slaughter without understanding the means of defence, has in it something peculiarly intoler-

Braddock's death

able. The gallant Braddock, as he lay half-dazed upon his death-bed, was heard to murmur, " Who would ever have thought it ? " and again, after an interval, " We shall know better how to do it next time." [1]

The skilful retreat from this field of blood added much to the credit of the youthful Washington, and marked him out as an officer likely to have a brilliant future. As for the

Dunbar's culpable retreat

rear column, which had been left under command of Colonel Dunbar, it retreated to Fort Cumberland, and presently abandoned the campaign, a most ill-judged and reprehensible proceeding which threw open the

[1] [*Life of Benjamin Franklin, written by himself*, i. 327.]

frontier to all the horrors of Indian invasion. The events of the past twelve months had done all that twelve months could do in destroying the influence of the English among the Ohio tribes. Washington's disaster at Great Meadows had gone far toward undermining their allegiance, Braddock's insolence had seasoned their contempt with a spice of anger, and now at last this headlong overthrow of an English army had convinced the red men that good medicine was all on the side of the Great White Father on the St. Lawrence.

Thus inauspiciously for the English began the mighty war that was to put an end to the dominion of Frenchmen in America, yet it must be remembered that no declaration of war had as yet been made public. These deeds of blood were the deeds of a time of so-called peace.[1]

[1] [For the literature of Braddock's march and defeat, see Winsor, *Narr. and Crit. Hist.* v. 575–580.]

IX

CROWN POINT, FORT WILLIAM HENRY, AND TICONDEROGA

WHILE General Braddock was at Williamsburg in the spring of 1755, discussing plans for the summer, he was visited by Governor Shirley, and a very extensive scheme of campaigning was laid out. While Braddock was to advance against Fort Duquesne, Shirley was to conduct a force, consisting largely of New England troops, to the Niagara River by way of the Mohawk valley and Oswego. At the same time a force commanded by William Johnson was to wrest from the French the control of Lake Champlain, and yet another force under Colonel Monckton was to proceed against the French on the Acadian frontier. The expedition against Niagara was to be commanded by Shirley himself, and he also undertook to provide a leader for the operations against Crown Point. Few royal governors had so much success in dealing with their legislatures as Shirley, who was conspicuous for moderation and tact. He knew how to make his demands seem rea-

Governor Shirley's plan of campaign

sonable in amount, and he knew how to urge
them so gracefully as to make it hard to refuse
them. In the present instance he had to deal
with the four New England colonies and New
York; and he understood very well that he
could not appoint a commander from any one of
the New England commonwealths without of-
fending the other three. But against the appointment of William Johnson nothing could
very well be said, since the aid of the Iroquois
seemed important and Johnson's influence over
them was well known. Besides, the expedition
was to be directed toward points in the Mohawk
country. For these reasons Shirley selected
Johnson to command the movement William
against Crown Point, and it proved Johnson to
attack
a good selection. It greatly pleased Crown Point
New York and the Long House, and no serious
objection was made in New England except that
Connecticut insisted that one of her own officers, Phineas Lyman, should be second in
command, and this, too, was a good selection.
There was much delay, owing to the necessity
for communicating with five different legislatures, and the larger part of the summer had
passed away before anything was accomplished.
The sad news of Braddock's defeat came like
an augury of disaster to Johnson and his men
as they were approaching the upper waters of
the Hudson in August. Along with this news

came a report from the north that the French were coming with eight thousand men to defend Lake Champlain.

Johnson's little army consisted almost entirely of New England yeomanry, many of whom

Character of
Johnson's
army were now for the first time in training for the tasks that awaited them in 1775 and the ensuing years. Among them were names afterward so important as those of Seth Pomeroy, Israel Putnam, and John Stark. The training now gained by these men and their comrades made veterans of them for the opening scene of the later war.

The movements were slow and the delays incessant, partly because the business of moving an army was so ill understood. Cannon, ammunition, and camp kettles would be forgotten and left on the way ; wagons would not arrive at the right time, either because distances had been miscalculated, or because the wagoners were disappointed of their pay and spiteful ; the stock of bullets delivered to a regiment would not fit their muskets ; stores of food were delayed until men were oppressed with hunger ; and so on through the usual list of mishaps attendant upon bad logistics. By the third week in August this New England army had arrived at a point on the Hudson River where a fortress then partly built was called Fort Lyman, a place which afterward acquired celebrity as Fort Edward. There

they were joined by three hundred Mohawks.
From Fort Lyman to Crown Point two routes
were available: one by way of Lake George, the
other by way of Wood Creek, which emptied
into the long, narrow head of Lake Champlain.
These two routes united at Ticonderoga, about
twenty-five miles south of Crown Point. After
some discussion it was decided to follow the
route by Lake George, which was then known
by its French name of Lake Sacre- Johnson
ment, but Johnson gave it the name names Lake
of the British king, partly by way of George
asserting his dominion over it. Leaving five
hundred men to complete Fort Lyman, Johnson moved with the other two thousand to the
head of Lake George, and encamped there.

Meanwhile, the French commander, Baron
Dieskau, had arrived at Crown Point with a
force of more than thirty-five hun- Dieskau's
dred men, and decided to push for- approach
ward and find the enemy. At Ticonderoga he
received information from an English prisoner
which was intended to draw him into a trap.
The prisoner informed him that five hundred
of the New England army were at Fort Lyman,
but the remainder had for some unknown reason turned back and retreated upon Albany.
This story seemed to offer to Dieskau an easy
conquest of Fort Lyman, and he pursued his
way with all haste southward by Lake Cham-

plain to what was called the South Bay, the head of which was about halfway between Wood Creek and Lake George. Thence he marched directly toward Fort Lyman, and had arrived within four miles of it when he captured a letter which disclosed the truth, that the principal body of New Englanders were encamped at the head of Lake George. Dieskau had with him six hundred Indians under Legardeur de Saint-Pierre, and these allies suggested that they would greatly prefer to attack the open camp rather than the fort. Indians, indeed, had no love for encountering cannon. When it was objected that there seemed to be more English in the open camp than in the fort, it was replied that the English were wretched fighters, and would think of nothing but running away. The victory over Braddock was cited with exultation, and several painted chieftains yelped with delight as they assured Dieskau that the more English there were in the camp the more scalps there would be to bring away. Thus persuaded, if not convinced, Dieskau gave orders to march directly upon Lake George.

The Indians prefer to attack the camp

Meanwhile in Johnson's camp, when scouts announced the approach of a large French force, its size was underestimated, and at first two parties, each of five hundred men, were ordered out by different trails to attack it. Then the veteran Mohawk chief Hendrick picked up a couple of stout sticks and tried in vain to break them, but immediately thereafter took them separately and broke them with ease. The English "Very well," quoth Johnson, "let scouting them take the same trail." But even party routed now the old red skin was not quite satisfied. "If their aim is victory," he said, "there are not enough of them; but if they are going to be defeated, there are too many to lose." The upshot was that Dieskau, receiving intelligence of this advancing party, laid an ambush and inflicted upon it a severe defeat, in which the veteran Hendrick and many well-known New England officers were killed.

Emboldened by this success, and half believing the slanders against English courage, Dieskau pressed on to attack Johnson's camp, but the latter was strongly fortified with earthworks and with trunks of fallen trees. The Dieskau most desperate efforts of the French repulsed and to carry the place by storm were fruit- captured less, and after they had fought until their strength was nearly exhausted, the New Englanders came leaping over the works in a deadly charge, and the Frenchmen were driven from the field with heavy slaughter. Among the killed was the Chevalier de Saint-Pierre, whose interview with George Washington at Fort Le Bœuf had been the opening scene of this great drama.

Dieskau was wounded and taken prisoner, and Johnson's Mohawks were furiously eager to burn him, but the Irishman treated him with great kindness and courtesy, and assured him, " They will not burn you until they burn me with you."

There is not time to go into the disputed questions which cluster about this as about most battles. New England men have claimed the chief credit for Lyman,[1] to whom they allege that Johnson never did justice; and I am inclined to think this judgment is, on the whole, well supported. The chief credit at the time accrued to Johnson, and the promptness of his reward is an index to the chagrin which was felt in England over the defeat of Braddock. Johnson was at once made a baronet. As for the victory, it would have been a very important one if Johnson had followed it up and destroyed the enemy's force. Much fault was found with him for not doing this, but, as has often happened in such cases, the reasons for his inaction are not easy to explain. With the victory, such as it was, the English were obliged to rest content for some time to come. For Shirley's expedition against Niagara was a complete failure. Shirley penetrated the New York wilderness as far as Oswego, from which it was possible to reach the Niagara

Shirley's expedition against Niagara a failure

[1] [Cf. Dwight's *Travels,* iii. 367–370.]

River in boats in the course of five or six days. But there was a French force of fourteen hundred men at Fort Frontenac. This was about equal to Shirley's full force. If he were to leave men enough at Oswego to defend the works, he would not be able to go on with force enough to accomplish his object; but if he were to proceed westward with his full force, the French from Fort Frontenac would at once capture Oswego and expose him to starvation. There was no escape from the dilemma, and it became necessary to abandon the campaign.

The winter which followed was one of such misery on the frontiers of Virginia and Pennsylvania as had never been witnessed before. Firebrand and tomahawk were *Desolation on the frontier* perpetually busy, and it proved impossible to concentrate forces in such way as to deal with the horror. It was a winter of bitter contention in legislatures, and of gloom and fault-finding everywhere.

At last, in May, 1756, nearly two years after Washington's little campaign at Great Meadows, England declared war against France, and the most memorable war of modern times was begun. Frederick of Prussia, in beginning to build up a modern Germany out of the soundest elements that had survived the general devastation of the Thirty Years' War, had contrived to enlist against himself a powerful coalition.   By his seizure of Silesia he had made a

Opening of
the Seven
Years' War

permanent enemy of Austria.   Maria Theresa, having failed to recover Silesia in the recent war, was ready to try again ; and she found a formidable ally in Elizabeth of Russia, who was ready to attack Prussia for various reasons, all of them sharpened and embittered by the deadliest of insults when Frederick had called her by an epithet that was strictly true.   To these two powers was added that of France, which was coming to forebode more danger from Prussia than from Austria. In such a combination the alliance of England with Prussia was marked out by all sound policy. From the narrowest point of view, George II.

England and
Prussia join
forces

would find his principality of Hanover thus better protected, while from the widest point of view, the contest for colonial empire could best be carried on while the military strength of France was largely absorbed in warfare on the continent of Europe. The English treasury was thus the mainstay of Frederick the Great, who put every penny of the money thus received to the best possible use by sustaining single-handed a victorious contest against Russia, Austria, and France.[1]

[1] [For the diplomatic changes which preceded the Seven Years' War, see Perkins, *France under Louis XV.*, ii. 1–84, or Tuttle, *History of Prussia under Frederic the Great*, ii. 234–321.]

While Frederick was winning some of the most astonishing victories the world has seen, and keeping his three antagonists at bay, the fight for control of the colonial world was carried on by England with great advantage against France in North America and in Hindostan.

It was not in a moment, however, that the English world reaped the advantages of this new combination of forces, for it happened that the choice made by the French minister for a commander-in-chief in America proved to be exceptionally fortunate. The appointment of Louis Joseph, Marquis de Mont- Montcalm calm, was an appointment for long-tried merit. He was forty-four years of age, having been born in the neighbourhood of Nîmes in 1712. He had an excellent education, especially in Greek and Latin classics and philology, and his literary tastes were such that one of the great objects of his ambition was to become a member of the Academy. In his leisure moments he was always engaged in reading and study. During the war of the Austrian Succession he had served with great distinction, and he was recognized by competent judges as one of the ablest officers in the French service. When he came to America he left behind him in his charming country home at Candiac, near Nîmes, a wife and six children, besides his mother. Montcalm was a man of strong family affections and intense love of home, as we see from many charming allusions in his journal and letters while campaigning in the New World.

His voyage of nearly six weeks was a rough one, and sometimes dangerous. In a letter to his wife he says: " The forecastle was always under water, and the waves broke twice over

Montcalm's account of the voyage to Canada

the quarter-deck. From the 22d of April to the evening of the 4th of May we had fogs, great cold, and an amazing quantity of icebergs. On the 30th, when luckily the fog lifted for a time, we counted sixteen of them. The day before, one drifted under the bowsprit, grazed it, and might have crushed us if the deck-officer had not called out quickly, *Luff*. After speaking of our troubles and sufferings, I must tell you of our pleasures, which were fishing for cod and eating it. The taste is exquisite. The head, tongue, and liver are morsels worthy of an epicure. Still, I would not advise anybody to make the voyage for their sake. My health is as good as it has been for a long time. I found it a good plan to eat little and take no supper ; a little tea now and then, and plenty of lemonade. Nevertheless I have taken very little liking for the sea, and think that when I shall be so happy as to rejoin you I shall end my voyages there. I don't know when this letter will go. I shall send it by the first ship that returns to France, and keep on writing till then. It is pleasant, I know, to hear particulars about the people one loves, and I thought that my mother and you, my dearest and most beloved, would be glad to read all these dull details. We heard mass on Easter Day. All the week before, it was impossible, because the ship rolled so that I could hardly keep my legs. If I had dared, I think I should have had myself lashed fast. I shall not soon forget that Holy Week." [1]

When Montcalm arrived in Montreal, his reception by Governor Vaudreuil was far from cordial. Vaudreuil aspired to military fame, and thought himself competent to direct military operations on a large scale as well as to command either Canadian militia or French regulars. He liked, moreover, to have everything his own way, and knew very well that he was not likely always to prevail over a strong-willed and energetic general-in-chief. Besides, Vaudreuil was a native of Canada, having been born there during his father's administration, and between Canadians and Frenchmen from the old country there was somewhat the same kind of jealousy that existed between Americans and British. The coldness between Montcalm and the governor

Vaudreuil not gratified by Montcalm's arrival

[1] [Parkman, *Montcalm and Wolfe*, i. 364, 365.]

sometimes had an ill effect upon the French operations.

Nevertheless the arrival of Montcalm was soon signalized by a heavy blow to the English. In a certain sense the blow was prepared by the English themselves. We have seen how Shirley's expedition had been turned back at Oswego by French demonstrations from Fort Frontenac. Such a failure was of course inevitable for any expedition directed against Niagara, unless Fort Frontenac were first captured. After Shirley's return to New York the gen-

Shirley superseded eral discontent assumed the form of a quarrel between him and Johnson, and several persons of influence in New York wrote to the minister requesting that another commander-in-chief be appointed in his stead. The ministry replied by appointing John Campbell, Earl of Loudoun, to the chief command in America; but as this particular Campbell was slow in coming, they sent General James Abercrombie in advance of him, and as Abercrombie was not quite ready, they sent Colonel Daniel Webb; insomuch that Shirley, who was just preparing a new campaign against Oswego, had to turn over the command to Webb, who turned it over to Abercrombie, who turned it over to Loudoun, — and so much swapping of horses in mid-stream, as President Lincoln would have said, was not conducive to promptness and

unity of operation.   As for the new commander-in-chief, he was as poor a choice as could
have been made. Shirley was a mere   The Earl of
amateur soldier, but he had courage, Loudoun
quickness, and discretion.   Loudoun, on the
other hand, was dull, sleepy, and irresolute,
— the kind of man who would be likely to
stop halfway in any important undertaking.
Dr. Franklin summed him up very well when
he compared him to Saint George on the tavern
signboards, always on horseback, but never getting ahead.

The effect of the arrivals of Webb and Abercrombie was to delay an expedition which Shirley would have sent to Oswego in the hope of
moving from that point against Fort Frontenac. When Loudoun arrived, late in   Loudoun
July, he determined to concentrate   plans to
attack
his efforts against Ticonderoga, where   Ticonderoga
the French had erected a new fortress, and to
content himself on Lake Ontario by merely
holding Oswego.   Having thus decided, he
allowed time to slip away without reinforcing
Oswego. This was bad generalship, since if
the French were to take Oswego, they would
not only cut off the English from Niagara but
would have their hands free to concentrate
against them at Ticonderoga and Crown Point.
After Loudoun's arrival at Albany, all operations were brought to a standstill by a silly

order of the king in council that all generals
and colonels holding commissions from the
colonial governments should rank only on the
level of senior captains.   Such an arrangement
might have put the entire provincial army under
the command of a British major.   While hot
disputes were raging over this matter, Loudoun
suddenly remembered the need of Oswego and
sent Webb in all haste with reinforcements, but
this hurry at the eleventh hour was unavailing.
When Webb arrived at the great portage between the Mohawk valley and Lake Ontario,
about where Fort Stanwix was afterwards built,
and near the site of the present city of Rome,
Fall of   he learned with dismay that Mont-
Oswego   calm had captured Oswego.   It was
even so.   While Loudoun had been dawdling,
Montcalm had been acting.   He had crossed
from Fort Frontenac, invested Oswego, and
pressed the siege so vigorously that the garrison of fourteen hundred men with two or three
hundred non-combatants surrendered, prisoners
of war.   Among the spoils were more than a
hundred light cannon.   Here something occurred which was ominous of future horror.   A
few of Montcalm's Indians began murdering
prisoners, and it was only with great difficulty
and by making lavish promises that he succeeded in restraining those painted demons.   He
reckoned that the presents to be given them

as a ransom for the prisoners would amount to
ten or twelve thousand livres.

The following winter witnessed many scenes
of partisan warfare which we need not here stop
to describe. The summer of 1757 found things
looking ill for the English cause. The French
had destroyed Oswego, which was for them an
outpost dangerously near the strongholds of the
Six Nations, but while they held Fort Frontenac they could prevent the English from reaching the Niagara River, and this fact, together
with their possession of Fort Duquesne, seemed
to have given them the victory so far as the
whole interior of the continent was concerned.
The effect of the capture of Oswego upon the
Indians was very great. One day a
party from Lake Superior came to see
Montcalm, and their spokesman thus
addressed him : " We wanted to see
this famous man who tramples the English
under his feet. We thought we should find
him so tall that his head would be lost in the
clouds. But you are a little man, my father.
It is when we look into your eyes that we see
the greatness of the pine-tree and the fire of
the eagle." [1]

It remained to see what could be done in
the direction of Lake Champlain or in that

[1] [Parkman, *Montcalm and Wolfe*, i. 475, from Bougainville's Journal.]

of Cape Breton Island. The Earl of Loudoun
Loudoun's decided that the most important thing
expedition to be done was to capture Louisburg,
against
Louisburg and to that end he started with more
than ten thousand men and seventeen ships-of-
the-line, and after wasting the whole summer
retired to the mainland because he heard that
a French fleet was approaching which outnum-
bered him by one ship. He was an apt scholar
of that worthy king of France who marched
his forty thousand men up a hill and down
again.

But while Loudoun seems to have been
incapable of achieving anything, he was able
to spoil much. These mighty preparations for
Louisburg went far towards stripping the Hudson River of its defenders, so that Montcalm
was able to entertain thoughts of advancing
southward and capturing Albany. For this
purpose there were assembled at Ticonderoga
Montcalm's in July a force of seventy-six hun-
expedition dred Frenchmen and Canadians with
against Fort
William eighteen hundred Indians, a force
Henry unusually large and unwieldy. The
story of Braddock's defeat and the fall of
Oswego had penetrated far and wide throughout the wilderness, and among the bedizened
chiefs who were gathered between Lake Champlain and Lake George were some from distant Iowa, whose language none of the white

men, not even those most familiar with the
forest, could understand. They made no secret
of the fact that they had come for feasting and
pelf. Such gormandizers the Frenchmen said
they had never seen. Long rows of oxen roasted
whole disappeared with amazing celerity, and
wild fowl vanished as if they had taken to wing
and flown down the red men's throats. When,
however, it came to eating human flesh, our
Frenchmen winced at the sight. As for brandy
and rum, it was necessary to guard the casks
with great care to prevent these thirsty allies
from breaking them open; and when Ferocity of
the Indians were thoroughly drunk Montcalm's
Indian allies
their ferocity became uncontrollable;
they quarrelled incessantly, and bit and tore
each other with their teeth like wild beasts.
It was not easy for the French to restrain these
creatures, for if they had been prevented from
eating prisoners and drinking rum, they would
have taken offence and gone trooping off on
other business, and in that wilderness they
were as necessary to the French as cavalry are
necessary in civilized warfare. It has been
said that the eyes of an army are its cavalry;
it might be truly said that the eyes of the
French force in the wilderness were its Indian
scouts.

The only English force opposed to Montcalm consisted of twenty-six hundred men at

Fort Edward, under the immediate command of General Webb, and twelve hundred at the head of Lake George, where Johnson had formerly defeated Dieskau. It was shameful mis-

The English force at Fort William Henry and Fort Edward

management on the part of Loudoun to leave this important point so weakly guarded. When Webb learned that the French were likely to make an attack, he intended to move his men from Fort Edward to Lake George, but he presently desisted from this lest the French should seize the occasion to come down by way of South Bay,[1] slip around his right flank, and move upon Albany. The expedient of withdrawing his weak advance force to the meeting of routes at Fort Edward does not seem to have occurred to him. So he sent forward a thousand men, thus raising the numbers at Lake George to twenty-two hundred. This force was protected by strong lines of works which Johnson had called Fort William Henry, and also by huge trunks of felled trees scattered in various directions.

Against this fortress Montcalm started on the 1st of August with a force of seven thousand Frenchmen and sixteen hundred Indians, leaving a garrison of four hundred men at Ticonderoga. On arriving at Fort William Henry he sent a summons to the commander, Colonel

[1] [The southern tip of Lake Champlain, about halfway between Ticonderoga and the head of Lake George.]

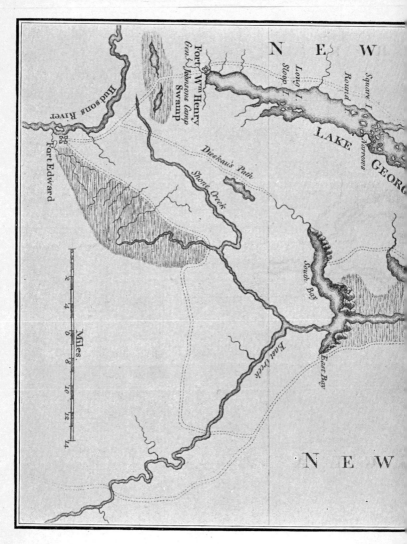

MAP OF LA

Y O R K

Sabbath Day Point

Putnam's

Narrow

Saw Mill

Crown Point

LAKE CHAMPLAIN

DROWNED LANDS

Wood

Very good

Ticonderoga

Two Rocks

Creek

Path

Path

Path

E N G L A N D

E GEORGE

Monro, to surrender, but Monro refused, and presently the French general found himself obliged to proceed by regular meth- Montcalm invests Fort William Henry ods of siege, opening parallels, planting batteries, and pounding the works. While this was going on, a letter from General Webb was captured by the French. It was written to inform Colonel Monro that General Webb would be unable to come to his assistance until further reinforcements should arrive, for which he had sent repeated requests down the river. After reading this welcome information, Montcalm kept it in his pocket two or three days until some bad breaches had been made in the English works, and then he sent it in to Colonel Monro with a flag of truce and many compliments upon his bravery. Monro politely dismissed the flag and continued to earn the compliments by holding out until the close of the eighth day ; by that time his heavy guns were all silenced, three hundred of his men were killed, and a considerable portion of the garrison were disabled with smallpox. Under these circumstances Monro capitulated. His force was to march out with the honours of war and to retain one cannon as a present in token of their gallantry. Before the articles were signed Montcalm called a meeting of the Indian chiefs, and received from them a solemn promise confirmed in every manner

known to the Indian mind that there should
be no molestation of the prisoners. The chiefs

Surrender of the forces at Fort William Henry

were unanimous in making this promise, and asseverated with much earnestness that they would restrain their
young warriors from any acts of cruelty or
plunder. No sooner, however, had the garrison
left the fort, than a rabble of Indians swarmed
in and instantly tomahawked all the men who
were confined to their beds by sickness.

This incident was like the tiger's foretaste
of blood. The Indians were too numerous to
be kept in control by their French allies. They
understood their power, and were to the last degree indignant at the prospect of being baulked
in their bloodthirsty fury. The next morning,
according to agreement, the English column
started for Fort Edward with an escort of

The Indians un-controllable

Canadian militia. At the moment of
starting, a large party of Indians
tomahawked and scalped seventeen
wounded men in the presence of an inadequate
French force that had been sent to guard them.
Not long after the march had begun another
party rushed up from under cover of the trees
and seized some seventy or eighty New Hampshire soldiers, and dragging them off under
cover, massacred them at leisure. The short
journey to Fort Edward was an evil one, for
such acts of murder kept recurring in spite of

Montcalm's persistent and furious efforts to prevent them. It is said that in the course of the march the Indians succeeded in dragging six or seven hundred persons from the column; but Montcalm was able to rescue from four to five hundred of these. The exact number of the victims has never been satisfactorily estimated, but it was enough to make The massacre of Fort William Henry a name of horror to Americans for many a long prisoners year. To Montcalm it was an abiding grief; but while we must acquit the general of any share of this atrocity, it can hardly be denied that some of the French officers showed culpable weakness, acting as if they were more than half afraid of the red men themselves, so that they were over-cautious about drawing the wrath of the murderers upon themselves. Take it for all in all, it is one of the blackest incidents in the history of our country.

Before the next season of campaigning a great change had been made in England. By a happy stroke of fortune the conduct of military operations throughout the empire had been put into the hands of William Pitt, the William Pitt greatest war minister and organizer of victory that the world has seen. It boded no good to France when the genius of Pitt was called upon to coöperate with that of Frederick of Prussia. Pitt had a supreme capacity for

administration and an infallible eye for the
selection of men to carry out his plans. He
was never confused by petty details, but saw
through them to the great underlying principles. He delighted in large ideas, as is shown
by the fact that the maritime supremacy of
England, the winning of the Mississippi valley
for English-speaking America, and the creation
of a renovated Protestant empire in Germany
were in his mind the closely allied phases of
one stupendous scheme. Along with these high
intellectual qualifications, there was in Pitt a
magnetic glow of lofty emotion which seemed
at once under his leadership to inspire the
whole English people. It was said of him that
no man ever entered his presence without going
away a better citizen and a braver man. In an
age when most statesmen looked with tolerance
upon corruption, and when domestic morals
were not upon a high plane, Pitt was absolutely
spotless in public and in private life, and the
popular faith in his disinterestedness was never
disappointed. He was a democrat, too, after
the fashion of the eighteenth century, and for
the first time since the death of
Cromwell the English people felt that
they had a leader who represented

Pitt's hold
on popular
confidence

the whole nation, from the highest to the lowest. In America the feeling toward him was
nearly as strong as in England, so that when

he began by informing the New England colonies that he should have to ask them for twenty thousand men, they replied with greater willingness than when formerly they had been asked for one fourth of that number.

One of Pitt's first acts was to recall the incompetent Loudoun and to replace him by a general of tried ability, Sir Jeffrey Amherst, and among his subordinate generals was the youthful James Wolfe, of whom we shall presently hear more. Pitt would have been glad Pitt recalls Loudoun to remove Abercrombie, but influences were brought to bear in behalf of that general of such a nature that it did not seem altogether wise to disregard them. He was accordingly retained in command of the forces on the Hudson River, while Pitt sent over to be his second in command Lord Howe, whom Wolfe called the best soldier in the English army, and who was unquestionably an officer of rare personality and extraordinary powers. This George Augustus, Viscount Howe was the elder brother of the famous admiral, Richard, Viscount Howe, and of Sir William Howe, who commanded the British army in America a few years later. These three brothers were grandsons of George I., whose daughter by the Baroness Kielmannsegge married Eman- Lord Howe uel, Viscount Howe. They were half-cousins to the reigning king, George II.

All three studied military affairs from their earliest years ; all three were warm friends to the American colonists ; but this was especially true of the eldest brother, George Augustus. In sending him to America Pitt had reason to believe that he would prove the real guiding spirit of Abercrombie's army. We have now to see how an adverse fate exacted yet one more costly sacrifice before all the benefits of the new change in administration were realized.

At the end of June, 1758, Abercrombie's army was encamped at the head of Lake George

The expedition against Ticonderoga

where Johnson had defeated Dieskau three years before, and where scarcely ten months had elapsed since the horrors of Fort William Henry. Abercrombie had collected at that spot more than six thousand British regulars and nine thousand provincial troops ; in all, more than fifteen thousand, the largest army that had ever been collected in North America. The task before him was to do what Johnson had failed to do, to move upon Montcalm at Ticonderoga and defeat him. By the 4th of July all the arrangements were completed, and next morning the whole army embarked in bateaux and canoes on Lake George. It was an imposing sight, eloquently described by more than one contemporary pen. It soon appeared that Pitt had not been wrong in supposing that Lord Howe would prove to

be the life of the army. His popularity was un-
bounded with all ranks, from the commander
down to the private soldiers. On his first arrival
in America he had seized an opportunity for
learning something about the conditions of warfare in the wilderness, for he sought   Lord Howe's
with the true insight of genius to   adaptability
adapt himself to new conditions. He would lay
aside all cumbersome baggage and trim away
all useless apparel, cutting down long coats into
jackets, making the men wear leather leggings
for protection in the brush, and carry meal in
their knapsacks, which they could at any time
cook for themselves. In all such things he himself set the example.

At noon of July 6 the flotilla had reached
the northern end of Lake George, where it narrows into a crooked river or strait communicating with Lake Champlain at the mouth of Wood
Creek. The whole force was speedily landed,
and began its march on the west side of the
river. Robert Rogers led the way with a couple
of New England regiments, but presently became
entangled in woods so dense that the   The English
rays of the sun could hardly find their   scouting party
                                            lost in the
way in. Here, after a while, they be-   woods
came confused, and were at a loss in which direction to move. A party of three hundred and
fifty French under Langy had been watching
the landing from an eminence between the river

and Trout Brook. Before they could retreat from that spot the whole English army had advanced so far as to cut them asunder from their main army at Ticonderoga, but Langy was an old hand at bushranging, and he thought that by crossing to the north of Trout Brook he could describe a semicircle and reach Ticonderoga. Thus the three hundred and fifty Frenchmen under Langy and the two New England regiments under Rogers were wandering in a forest which at midday was nearly as dark as night. And here the Frenchmen, too, soon lost their bearings. At the very head of the English column was Lord Howe with Major Israel Putnam, when all at once a rustling was heard among the branches, and a sharp cry of " *Qui vive ?* " The answer, " *Français*," was prompt enough, but some of Langy's men had sharp eyes, and even in that pitch darkness could tell the British scarlet from the French white. Langy's reply was a volley which slew Lord

Death of   Howe and wrecked the fortunes of
Lord Howe   an army. The further result of this chance collision was the defeat of Langy's party, most of which was captured, but when this densest piece of woods had been traversed, and the news of what had happened flew from rank to rank, it is said the spirit of the whole army was dashed, and high hopes gave place to consternation. So greatly had this young officer

endeared himself to people in the short time since his arrival in America, that at the news of his death there was weeping throughout the northern colonies. The commonwealth of Massachusetts afterward erected a monument to Howe in Westminster Abbey.

Nobody felt the loss more keenly than Abercrombie, who had been depending upon Howe's advice. He had need of such advice after coming within touch of the French position. Across the plateau northwest of the fortress of Ticonderoga there runs a ridge which Montcalm had fortified by felling trees in such wise Montcalm's as to make a zigzag parapet, so that defences an approaching foe could be torn between flank fires of grapeshot and musketry. On the inner side was a platform from which to fire, and the parapet was so high that nothing could be seen of the French soldiers standing upon the platform except the crowns of their hats. Along the entire front of the parapet the ground was covered with intertwisted boughs presenting a myriad sharp points to any approaching foe. Now this position was obviously one which could hardly be carried by infantry armed with muskets, but to a general who possessed the slightest inventiveness of mind it was very far from being an impregnable position. Indeed, Montcalm had been slow in making up his mind whether to try to hold Ticonderoga or to retreat upon Crown Point, and when at last he decided to fortify this position, his resolution was somewhat hastily taken. It is probable that Montcalm made a mistake in trying to defend the point of land upon which the fortress of Ticonderoga stood, for there were several ways in which Abercrombie might have defeated him. He might have sent back to the landing place and brought up all his cannon and used them to batter down these wooden obstructions before charging them with his infantry. That, one would suppose, would have been a mere ordinary precaution. And then, there was a hill in the immediate neighbourhood where Abercrombie might have planted a few batteries that could have torn the French army to pieces, and must have obliged them to change their position at once. Precisely such a use of that hill was made in 1777 by General Burgoyne, with the desired result of taking Ticonderoga, and since that occasion it has been known as Mount Defiance. Yet again, if Abercrombie had made a feint with part of his army upon Montcalm's position, while with his main force he had marched about five miles on the road to Crown Point, he would have found the lake there so narrow that he might have commanded the whole of it with batteries, and thus cut off Montcalm's retreat and left it for star-

Alternatives open to Abercrombie

Montcalm saved by Abercrombie's stupidity

vation to do the rest. It would seem, therefore, that Montcalm was rescued from a perilous
situation by the stupidity of his enemy, and it
is among the possibilities that he may have
counted upon that very circumstance. There is
a curious analogy between this battle of Ticonderoga and those of Bunker Hill and New
Orleans. At Bunker Hill the American force
was completely at the mercy of the British, and
might have been forced to surrender without
the loss of a life. This would have been done
if the British had simply gone by water and
occupied Charlestown Neck, but the brother
of the young general slain at Ticonderoga preferred to assault intrenchments and suffered accordingly.[1] So, too, at New Orleans. It was
not necessary for Sir Edward Pakenham to
assault Andrew Jackson's intrenchments, for he
might have advanced up the further bank of
the Mississippi River and turned the whole
position, but he preferred the bulldog method,
and very probably Jackson should have the
credit of having known his man.

With regard to Abercrombie, he seems to
have been influenced by undue haste. A rumour
reached him that reinforcements were on the
way to Montcalm, and therefore he was anxious
to adopt the quickest method. Besides, he seems
to have harboured that fallacious notion that one

[1] [See Fiske, *The American Revolution*, i. 167.]

Englishman can under any circumstances beat three Frenchmen. At all events, on the fore-

An assault ordered noon of July 8 the assault was ordered. The instructions to the English infantry were to carry the works by a solid bayonet charge, an order which seems almost incredible, for as might have been expected, the compactness needed for a bayonet charge was almost instantly broken up by the tangle of pointed boughs and the trunks lying in all directions upon the ground, and presently the assailants, caught in a hailstorm of grape and musket shot on either flank, could only answer by firing in turn. Again and again, with astounding gallantry, the men from New England and Old England returned to the charge. Between noon and nightfall they made six assaults of the most desperate character, sometimes almost winning their way over the parapet, but of course the situation was utterly hopeless. The

All assaults repulsed greater the bravery, the sadder the loss of life. At twilight, when the firing ceased, Abercrombie had lost in killed and wounded two thousand men.[1]

Even after all this useless waste of life, there was no reason why the English should have retreated. Montcalm was in no condition to take the offensive, and it would still have been

[1] [The killed alone amounted to some five hundred and fifty men. Kingsford, *History of Canada*, iv. 173.]

in Abercrombie's power to march down the Crown Point road and cut off all supplies from the French army ; but our accounts agree in representing the general's conduct as disgraceful. He seems to have lost his head, and thought only of escaping, as if from a superior foe. By the time he had returned to the head of Lake George, Abercrombie found himself a laughing-stock. People called him a poltroon, an old woman, Mrs. Nabbycrombie, and such other nicknames and epithets as served to relieve their feelings.

Abercrombie ridiculed

It was indeed a dark day for New England when the death of Lord Howe deprived the army of its brains. Of all the disasters of the war, perhaps none struck so near home as Ticonderoga. But the tide of misfortune had reached its height, and was already turning. We have now to take up the story of Louisburg, of Fort Frontenac and Niagara, of Fort Duquesne and Quebec, — a story fraught with good cheer for English-speaking America.

X

LOUISBURG, FORT DUQUESNE, AND THE FALL OF QUEBEC

A T midsummer of 1758 four years had elapsed since Washington's experiences at Great Meadows, and as yet little or nothing had occurred to encourage the English. It will be remembered that along the border between New France and the English colonies there were strategic points of primary importance. The first of these was Fort Duquesne, commanding one of the great central routes into the western wilderness. The French had anticipated the English in seizing this point, and the ruin of Braddock's army had been incurred in the attempt to recover it for the English. The second strategic point was Fort Frontenac at the outlet of Lake Ontario into the river St. Lawrence, for this stronghold commanded the eastern approaches to Niagara, and thus controlled the other great route to the west. Thus far its importance had been illustrated, first, by the failure of Shirley to advance beyond Oswego in the direction of Niagara, and secondly, by Montcalm's capture of

Strategic points in the contest

Oswego, a very heavy blow to the English. The third strategic point was the southern extremity of Lake Champlain with its fortresses at Crown Point and Ticonderoga, for in French hands this was an excellent base for an invasion of New York, while in English hands it would serve equally well for an invasion of Canada. This strategic point had been held from the first by the French, and in three campaigns the English had failed to drive them away. In the first of these Johnson had won a tactical victory which he failed to improve. The second had witnessed the shocking tragedy of Fort William Henry. The third had been a climax of imbecility, as shown in the useless butchery at Ticonderoga and the shameful retreat of Abercrombie after that battle. The fourth strategic point was the fortified town of Louisburg on Cape Breton Island, which not only threatened the Newfoundland fisheries and British commerce on the Atlantic in general, but also afforded an excellent base for a French invasion of the New England coast, while at the same time it made the entrance of the St. Lawrence dangerous for a hostile fleet. On the other hand, if held by the English, Louisburg afforded an excellent base for a naval expedition up the St. Lawrence against Quebec. This important place had been captured by New England militia, aided by British ships in the preceding war thirteen years before, but had been restored to France by the treaty which terminated that war.

Down to the midsummer of 1758 nothing seemed to have prospered with the English, but at all the strategic points where there had been collision, the advantage had remained with the French. The first change of fortune was at Louisburg. That town was situated on a peninsula at the south side of Cape Breton Island. To the east of it was a deep and finely sheltered bay which was defended at its northern end by what was called the Grand Battery, and on an island at the entrance, by what was called the Island Battery ; while across the peninsula, in front of the town, the entrance to the harbour was commanded by a series of four bastions named from south to north Princess's, Queen's, King's, and Dauphin's. The rear of the town was to a considerable extent protected by marshes, and the rocky coast of Gabarus Bay to the rear or west presented but few points where troops could effect a landing. At all times the sea was so boisterous as to make it dangerous for any floating thing to approach the rocks. Since the treaty of Aix-la-Chapelle the French government had spent great sums of money in perfecting the fortifications. It was now commanded by General Drucour, who had three thousand regular troops with a few Canadians

Louisburg

and Indians, while in the harbour were five ships-of-the-line and seven frigates mounting five hundred and forty guns and carrying three thousand men.

On the twenty-eighth day of May there sailed out from Halifax an English force which was to undertake the reduction of Louisburg. It was commanded by Admiral Bosca- The English wen, who had twenty-three ships-of- expedition against the-line and eighteen frigates along Louisburg with a fleet of transports carrying eleven thousand British regulars and five hundred colonial militia. The land force was commanded by the new general-in-chief for America, Sir Jeffrey Amherst. It was the 2d of June when this powerful force arrived in Gabarus Bay and scrutinized its wild coast for a place to land in the rear of the town. The prospect was not encouraging, and some officers were inclined to pronounce the attempt foolhardy, but Boscawen and Amherst saw a spot which seemed practicable, and they entrusted the task of effecting a landing there to the young brigadier-general, James Wolfe.

There were three or four places along the coast where a landing might be effected if the sea were somewhat to subside, and the plan was to make demonstrations against all these points while the extreme left wing under General Wolfe should advance against the most remote of them, known as Fresh Water Cove, with the intention of carrying it. Although this plan was matured on the 2d of June, it was not until the 8th that there was enough of a lull in the violence of the surf to admit of any approach to the shore whatever. Then the plan

General Wolfe effects a landing

was tried, and Wolfe's landing was achieved with brilliant success. Although Fresh Water Cove was defended by one thousand Frenchmen behind entrenchments supported by a battery of eight cannon, Wolfe managed his landing so as to pass by their left flank, between it and the town, and there to attack them in such wise as to cut them off. Under these circumstances the Frenchmen abandoned their works and fled to the woods, whence they made a circuitous retreat to their comrades in the town. After this auspicious beginning the remainder of the English army was safely landed, and ready for further operations. Troops were presently moved so as to threaten the communications of the Grand Battery at the north end of the harbour, whereupon the French abandoned it. The eastern side of the harbour ran in the shape of a sickle from the Grand Battery, terminating in a point opposite the point of the peninsula on which the city stood. The space of sea between these two points was the entrance to the harbour, and the small island already mentioned, with its Island Battery, lay midway between them. Considering the great superiority of the English fleet, the French had felt it rash to keep a detachment upon the opposite point, where it was liable to be cut off, and they had therefore withdrawn it. Now Wolfe, with The harbour batteries secured or reduced by the English twelve hundred men, marched past the Grand Battery and around the sickle-shaped shore and took possession of the works which the French had there abandoned, and from that point he kept up a heavy fire against the Island Battery until by June 25 all its guns were dismounted and silent.

It now became possible for the English fleet to enter the harbour, and in order to ward off such a calamity, Drucour sank six ships at the entrance. Meanwhile, General Amherst was digging his trenches and building his parallels with prodigious labour over the treacherous ground behind the town. Gradually the English drew nearer, until they approached the very walls on both sides of the peninsula, and kept throwing shot and shell into the streets. Gradual destruction of the French fleet In one adventure after another the French ships were sunk or burned until only five were left. On the 21st of July a bomb falling upon one of these penetrated her magazine and she blew up, communicating the flames to two sister ships, which were burned to the water's edge. A large part of the town had now taken fire, and the time of the besieged was largely consumed in fighting the flames; then a party of six hundred English sailors in boats rowed into the harbour and seized the two remaining French ships; one of them, a seventy-four, they burned; while the other, a sixty-four, they made a prize and towed away. On the 26th of July the last gun in the row of French bastions was dismounted and a white flag was raised. The details of the sur-

Surrender of Louisburg

render were completed next day. It was a truly great victory, for the New England coast was at last relieved of a serious danger, and the way was opened for an English fleet to ascend the St. Lawrence. There was a general feeling that the glory of the achievement belonged to the youthful Wolfe more than to any one else. While the management of the whole affair, both by General Amherst and by Admiral Boscawen, had been admirable, yet in all Wolfe's operations there had been the artistic touch, so seldom witnessed, that marked real military genius, and along with all the intelligence, the quickness and sureness, there was an electric enthusiasm that communicated itself to the whole army, and wherever that tall, emaciated form was present, there was the centre of interest.

It had been Wolfe's desire to follow up the capture of Louisburg by an immediate advance against Quebec, but the obstinate defence of Drucour had made it so late in the season that it was thought best to postpone such an enterprise for the present, and Wolfe, who was seriously ill, went home to England for the winter, while Amherst took his army to the Hudson River with intent to relieve the situation at Lake George.

Wolfe returns to England

Meanwhile in Abercrombie's camp there had been much despondency and grumbling since the terrible slaughter of the 8th of July. During the summer more or less guerilla fighting went on, in the course of which Israel Putnam was at one time taken prisoner and tied to a stake to be burned alive, but was rescued by a French officer after the tongues of flame had actually begun to curl around him. Presently one of Abercrombie's officers, Colonel John Bradstreet, accomplished something which went far toward changing the face of things on the New York frontier. Bradstreet was a native of England, forty-six years of age, but most of his life had been spent in America. Among Shirley's officers he had been recognized as very capable; he had taken part in the first capture of Louisburg, and in the present war he had been connected with the Oswego campaign. He now had reason to believe that such heavy demands had been made upon the French Bradstreet's expedition against Fort Frontenac resources in various directions that an inadequate force had been left to guard Fort Frontenac. He therefore proposed to conduct an expedition for the capture of that important place. Lord Howe had favoured this plan, but Abercrombie had not regarded it with approval. At last, after a council of war had been held to consider the case, Bradstreet was allowed to undertake the task with a force of three thousand men, chiefly militia of New York and New England. On his march through the Oneida country he found occasion to observe that Montcalm's victory at Ticonderoga had wrought more or less disaffection toward the English even in the Long House. It was high time to do something to counteract this influence. Bradstreet kept on to the site of the ruined Oswego, and thence, crossing the lake in boats, pounced upon Fort Fort Frontenac taken, August 27 Frontenac and captured it, with its garrison of only one hundred and ten men. He also took seventy cannon and mortars, nine sloops of war, and an enormous quantity of warlike material, provisions, and furs. It was impossible to make the best use of these captures without rebuilding Oswego, so as to regain a seaport on the lake;

but there did not seem to be men enough and time enough for this. General Stanwix was then building the fort known by his name, on the divide between Lake Ontario and the Mohawk valley, and that seemed to be all the constructive work that could then be undertaken. The walls of Fort Frontenac were battered down by its own cannon, and as much as possible of the military spoil was taken across the lake, whence some of it was carried away and the remainder destroyed. A thousand men were left to defend Fort Stanwix, and Bradstreet returned to the Hudson River.

In this expedition Bradstreet dealt a blow second only, if second at all, to the capture of Louisburg. It is true the success was but partial; a complete success would have meant the restoration of Oswego as a port on the route to Niagara. The building of Fort Stanwix as a means of maintaining English influence near the centre of the Long House did not quite supply the place of such a port; nevertheless, the route to Niagara was laid open, and what was of far greater importance, the communications with Fort Duquesne were cut off. That all-important fortress was supplied through the long line of communication from the St. Lawrence River to the Niagara, and thence across

The loss of Fort Frontenac weakens Fort Duquesne

Lake Erie to Presqu'Isle and Venango and down the Allegheny River. Among the munitions of war and other provisions captured at Fort Frontenac there was a great supply already on its way for Fort Duquesne. The exploit of Bradstreet left that remote strategic point in the air, and we have now to see how its conquest was completed.

Among the excellent officers sent by Pitt to America was a veteran Scotchman named John Forbes. He was a well-educated man, who had been for some time a physician before taking up the life of a soldier. He was frank, simple, honest, abounding in good sense, and very ready to learn from others. His weight of character, combined with kindliness, made him as much liked by the Americans as Braddock had been detested. It is a commentary upon Forbes's strong qualities that during his American campaign he was suffering from a severe illness which carried him off in the following spring. Among its symptoms was a severe gastric and intestinal inflammation which kept him a large part of the time in acute torture, and it was commonly necessary for him to be carried in a litter, so that this campaign might well be said to have been conducted by a man upon his death-bed. General Forbes, however, had two very active and capable lieutenants : one was

General John Forbes

The expedition against Fort Duquesne

George Washington; the other was Lieutenant-
Colonel Henry Bouquet, a native of Switzer-
land, who had seen much service on the continent of Europe and had entered the English
service in 1756. He was destined a few years
later, in Pontiac's war, to win a great reputation. The army commanded by General Forbes
with these able lieutenants consisted of about
seven thousand men, partly British regulars,
partly the ordinary provincial militia, and partly
a force known as the Royal Americans and
composed chiefly of Pennsylvania Germans. It
was among these Royal Americans that Bouquet held his commission.

The first serious question was the choice of
a route. Washington was in favour of the old
route which had been taken by Brad-   The choice
dock, but Bouquet thought it would   of routes
be better to push westward through the mountains of Pennsylvania in a course more or less
like that now taken by the railroad from Har-
risburg to Pittsburg. The opinion of Bouquet
found favour with General Forbes and that route
was chosen.

Forbes's method of advance was very different from that of Braddock. Instead of advancing through mile after mile of un-   Forbes's
known wilderness, taking with him im-   method of
mensely long baggage trains, Forbes's   advance
method was to clear the way and make some-

thing of a road as he went along, building at intervals sundry blockhouses which might serve as temporary supports and magazines. This required a great amount of digging, hewing, blasting, and building, and was a truly Herculean piece of work. Gradually, but surely, the rude road was carried over the ridges of the Alleghanies and Laurel Hill, and finally at Loyalhannon Creek the last magazine was built as a base for the final advance on Fort Duquesne, which was about fifty miles distant.

One circumstance which reconciled Forbes to this slow method of advance was his knowledge of the difficulty of holding Indian allies together for many weeks at a time without the stimulus of slaughter or plunder frequently renewed. Vaudreuil had sent parties of Hurons, Miamis, Ottawas, and Pottawattamies to the aid of Fort Duquesne, and earnestly hoped that the English would not defer their approach until these warriors should have grown tired and gone home. Forbes appreciated this point and was willing to give them time to get tired. He had much reason to expect that delay would work in his favour, inasmuch as the advance of so large a force as seven thousand men could not fail to produce a notable moral effect upon the Delawares, Shawnees, and Mingos, and he

The slow progress of the march favourable to success

entertained strong hopes of winning back these tribes to the English alliance.[1]

At this juncture it was especially important that no opportunity should be afforded the enemy of inflicting even the slightest reverse upon the English advance, since the moral effect which might thus be produced upon the Indians was likely to be out of all proportion with the importance of the affair itself.

Now there was in the English army a hot-headed and ill-balanced Scotch officer named James Grant. He was a supercilious sort of person, and looked down with ineffable contempt upon the provincial troops. It was very irksome to Major Grant to be within fifty miles of Fort Duquesne and not engage in some kind of work more exciting than that of spade and pickaxe; so he sought and obtained permission from Bouquet to take a thousand men and go forward to reconnoitre the situation. Major Grant went forward, but did not return until he had provoked a fight with the enemy, in which he was ignominiously defeated with a loss of one quarter of his force. This Grant was afterward a member of Parliament, and served in the British army during a large part of the Revolutionary War. He is

Major Grant's disastrous reconnoissance

[1] [Cf. Parkman, *Montcalm and Wolfe*, ii. 141, 142, where the letters of Vaudreuil and Forbes, describing their plans, are quoted.]

now perhaps best remembered for a remark which he made in the House of Commons in 1774, to the effect that the Americans were an undisciplined rabble who would take to their heels at the first sound of a cannon. But two years after that unlucky speech, when he met Smallwood's Marylanders at the battle of Long Island and pounded them four hours without making them give up an inch of ground, he found reason to amend his opinion.[1]

Grant's defeat near Fort Duquesne occurred about the middle of September, and three weeks afterwards a convention of Indian chiefs was assembled at Easton in Pennsylvania. This conference was brought about by the earnest persuasion of General Forbes and the wise co-operation of Sir William Johnson. It will be remembered that while the Mohawk end of the Long House, where Johnson had his home, was firmly attached to the English cause, yet through the rest of the confederacy symptoms of vacillation were sometimes seen, and at the Seneca end French interests now and then pre-vailed. The recent capture of Fort Frontenac by Bradstreet had done much to discredit the French in the minds of the Senecas, and could these Indians, with the tribes southwest of them, be induced once more to make common

[1] [Fiske, *The American Revolution*, i. 243–245.]

cause with the English, it was clear that Fort Duquesne would become untenable. To this end was exerted all the influence of Sir William Johnson over the Senecas, while at the same time a memorable triumph of diplomacy was effected by the noble Moravian missionary, Christian Frederic Post, who at the Easton conference won the alliance of the Delawares, Shawnees, and Mingos.[1] This achievement sealed the doom of Fort Duquesne. It was isolated in a hostile country without means of supply. Its French militia from New Orleans and the Illinois country departed in boats down the Ohio. Its painted and feathered allies from Detroit and Green Bay tramped off through the many-hued autumn forests in the haze of Indian summer, and presently the French commander retired with his garrison up the Allegheny River to Lake Erie and so to Montreal. When Washington and Bouquet arrived at Fort Duquesne they found it dismantled and partially destroyed. There was not time enough, so late in the season, to rebuild it properly, but around the cluster of traders' cabins that had gathered there a stockade was built, and the embryo village was named Pittsburg, in honour of the great

Christian Frederic Post wins over the Indians

The French evacuate Fort Duquesne

[1] [Parkman, *Montcalm and Wolfe*, ii. 142–150, gives interesting extracts from Post's *Journal*.]

war minister.[1] In the following year General Stanwix came there and built Fort Pitt. The gallant Forbes, after lingering all winter on the brink of the grave, died in March, and was buried in Christ Church, Philadelphia.[2]

Great were the rejoicings in Pennsylvania and Virginia, as well as in all the other English colonies, over this auspicious capture of the Gateway of the West. But neither this nor any other conquest could be deemed finally secure so long as the French maintained themselves in Canada. Pitt was one who well understood the sound military maxim that in war, until everything has been done, nothing has been done, and he entered upon the year 1759 with the firm intention of driving the French from America altogether; and what had been done on both sides of the globe was only the prelude to heavier blows. "We are forced to ask every morning," wrote Horace Walpole, "what new victory there is, for fear of missing one." Terrible was the catalogue of French defeats in

Pitt resolved to drive the French from Canada

[1] ["I have used the freedom of giving your name to fort du Quesne, as I hope it was in some measure the being actuated by your spirit that now makes me master of the place." Forbes to Pitt, Nov. 27, 1758. Kingsford, *History of Canada*, iv. 213.]

[2] [For the literature of this campaign, see Winsor, *Narr. and Crit. Hist.*, v. 599.]

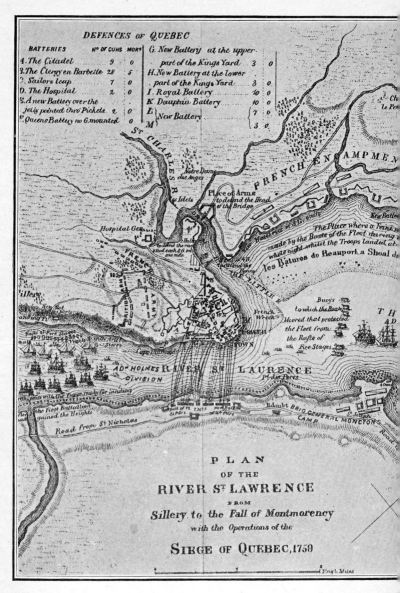

DEFENCES of QUEBEC.

BATTERIES	Nº OF GUNS	MORS
A. The Citadel	9	0
B. The Clergy en Barbette	28	5
C. Sailors leap	7	0
D. The Hospital	2	0
E. A new Battery over the jetty pointed thro' Pickets.	2	0
F. Queens Battery no. 6. mounted	0	
G. New Battery at the upper part of the Kings Yard	3	0
H. New Battery at the lower part of the Kings Yard	3	0
I. Royal Battery	10	0
K. Dauphin Battery	10	0
L. New Battery	7	0
M.	3	0

PLAN
OF THE
RIVER St LAWRENCE
FROM
Sillery to the Fall of Montmorency
with the Operations of the
SIEGE OF QUEBEC, 1759

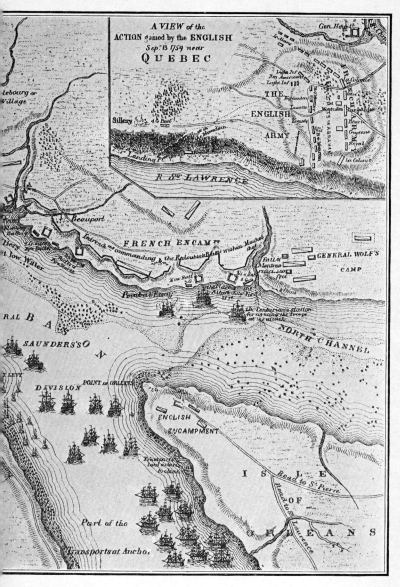

A VIEW of the
ACTION gained by the ENGLISH
Sep.ᵗ 13 1759 near
QUEBEC

Gen.ˡ Howe

Indian

FRENCH

Colvills

THE

Light Inf.ᵗʸ Roy. American
Light Inf.ᵗʸ

ENGLISH

Highlanders
Lascette

Montcalm
Repugly

ARMY

Bearn
Guyenne
Royal

Sillery 4.ᵗᵉ Post

les Colons.&ᶜ

Landing Pt.

R.ᵈᵉ LAWRENCE

lebourg or
village

Beauport

FRENCH ENCAMP.ᵗ

GENERAL WOLF'S

Intrench.ᵗ commanding y.ᵉ the Redoubts
Ball within Musket
shot

CAMP

t. low Water

New Batt.

Pail of
Montreal
retreat 800
feet

Powder i Bacoy

The Havre Du
Albancks Fire
31.ᵗˢ

NORTH CHANNEL

The Centurion's Station
for securing the Troops
at y.ᵉ attack

RAL BAS

SAUNDERS'S O

N

DIVISION

POINT D' ORLEANS

ENGLISH

ENCAMPMENT

ISLE

Road to St. Pierre

Transports
land where
broken

OF

Part of the

ORLEANS

Transports at Anchor

1759. Their army in Germany was routed at Minden by Ferdinand, Prince of Brunswick; one great fleet was defeated at Lagos Bay by Admiral Boscawen, and another was annihilated at Quiberon by Sir Edward Hawke; Havre was bombarded by Admiral Rodney; Guadeloupe, the most valuable of the French West Indies, was taken; and serious reverses were experienced in India.

In America prodigious exertions were made. Massachusetts raised seven thousand men, and during the year contributed more than a million dollars toward the expenses of the war. Connecticut raised five thousand troops; New Hampshire and Rhode Island furnished one thousand between them; New York raised twenty-six hundred and eighty; New Jersey, one thousand; Pennsylvania, twenty-seven hundred; Virginia, two thousand; and South Carolina, twelve hundred and fifty. These, together with twenty-two thousand British regulars and other special levies of provincial troops, made an aggregate of somewhat more than fifty thousand collected for the overthrow of the French power in America.

Preparations for the campaign of 1759

With regard to the strategy with which this force was to be used, it bears the marks, of course, of the pre-Napoleonic age. The weak points in eighteenth-century strategy were the insufficient concentration of resources and the persistence in advancing against objective points Weak points by means of converging lines. Such of eighteenth- century errors were often enough repeated in strategy the nineteenth century with less excuse. Since now, for the first time in the great war, the capture of Quebec entered into the plan of campaign, the more modern method would have been to concentrate everything upon that one point and to avoid expending energy in subordinate matters, however important, such as the capture of Fort Niagara, or the reëstablishment of Oswego, inasmuch as success in the greater undertaking would carry with it success along the whole line. Nevertheless, the policy of diffused attack was more in accordance with the mental habits of that time, and Amherst, the commander-in-chief, though a capable general, was not a man of great originality. His plan was to complete General Am- the victories at the west and insure herst's plan the safety of Pittsburg by sending an of campaign expedition westward to restore Oswego and take Niagara. At the same time the principal blow should be struck at Quebec by General Wolfe, assisted by the fleet under Admiral Saunders. As for Lake Champlain, Amherst undertook to clear the French from there and proceed against Montreal, in the hope either of taking that city and advancing against

Quebec, or, at least, of creating a diversion that would lighten Wolfe's task. The subordinate parts of this scheme were carried out with a creditable measure of success, yet not such as to take away from Wolfe the necessity for doing the impossible. As often happens in warfare, the shortcomings of the average intellect were repaired by the presence of some heaven-sent genius.

We may first note the fortunes of the western expedition which started from Albany under General Prideaux, with Sir William Johnson second in command. The work to be accomplished by this force was important, and five thousand men were prudently allotted to it. General Prideaux was to garrison the new Fort Stanwix, and proceeding thence to the shore of Lake Ontario was to leave half of his troops under Colonel Haldimand [1] to restore and defend Oswego, while he himself with the remainder of the army should move against Fort Niagara. The wis-

General Prideaux's expedition against Fort Niagara

[1] [On Haldimand's interesting career and invaluable services to American history, see Kingsford, *History of Canada*, iv. 317, 318. Like Bouquet, he was a Swiss by birth. He gathered together two hundred and thirty-two volumes of manuscripts relating to American history for the years 1758–1785, which are now in the British Museum. They have been copied for the Canadian Archives, and have been calendared in Brymner's *Reports*. Cf. Winsor, *Narr. and Crit. Hist.*, viii. 461.]

dom of leaving a strong force at Oswego was presently demonstrated when the French came across Lake Ontario to attack it. The pressure upon Quebec had become so heavy that it was not easy to find men enough for this western work, and one thousand men were all that could be gathered. This party, commanded by the partisan chieftain La Corne, made a demonstration upon the camp at Oswego, but was repulsed with considerable loss, and retired from the scene.

Fort Niagara, situated at the mouth of the Niagara River, was bravely defended by its commander, Pouchot. In the course of the engagement Prideaux was killed by a shell, and the command devolved upon Johnson. Cut off, as Pouchot was, from all help from the east, his fate was only a question of time unless something could be done in his behalf by the militia and Indians of the west. A force had been gathered together from Detroit and the Sault Ste. Marie, from Green Bay and the Illinois Fall of Fort River, consisting of about eleven hun-Niagara dred Frenchmen with two hundred Indians under command of the able leaders Marin, Aubry, and Ligneris, who had been the last commander at Fort Duquesne. The original object of this western muster had been to retrieve the last autumn's disaster and take Pittsburg from the English ; but the Frenchmen had only advanced as far as Presqu'Isle and Le Bœuf when a message from Pouchot summoned them to come to the rescue at Fort Niagara. They made all haste in that direction, but on arriving in the neighbourhood were encountered by Sir William Johnson and totally defeated, losing all their principal leaders, who were taken prisoners. Nothing was left for Pouchot but to surrender his fortress and men. This surrender, which was made on the 24th of July, was the final blow to the French in the west.

While these things were going on at Niagara, General Amherst with thirteen thousand men was advancing from the Hudson River upon Ticonderoga. The terrible defences which Montcalm had built, and which had cost Abercrombie two thousand men in his attempt to carry them by storm, were still in position and once more confronted the brave men who returned to the spot. Montcalm was no longer in command, having been called away to Quebec to defend that supreme position against the expedition led by Wolfe. Ticonderoga was now commanded by General Bourlamaque, who made as few signs of life as possible. Amherst was a man not given to erring on the side of rashness. Such an attempt as Abercrombie's he would never have thought of making; so he drew up his army

General Amherst marches against Ticonderoga

before the works and studied the situation. His meditations were interrupted by a stupendous explosion which scattered one of the forts in Ticonderoga deserted and blown up fragments through the air, like a gigantic Roman candle. This explosion represented the partial success of the Frenchmen's attempt to destroy the fort. Bourlamaque had been instructed by Vaudreuil not to offer serious resistance at either Ticonderoga or Crown Point, where a defeat would endanger his being cut off; but, on the other hand, he was to withdraw the whole length of Lake Champlain to the river Richelieu, and there make a determined stand, where his line of retreat would be tolerably secure. In these prudent instructions we see how great had been the change of animus in the French commanders during the past twelve months. They had ceased to despise their adversary.

The faults of Amherst as a commander now come into the foreground. He was a safe and prudent commander, not likely to commit any startling blunder, but his movements were marked by excessive deliberation. Instead of pushing and harassing Bourlamaque with might and main, he devoted too much attention to the restoration and repair of the forts at Ticonderoga and Crown Point, a kind of work which might have been left for another season. Am-

herst was the commander-in-chief, whose objective point was some position where he might
coöperate with his subordinate, Wolfe, Amherst's
in what all agreed to be the crowning ineffective
operation of the war, if it should prove activity
successful. If he could not directly coöperate
with Wolfe, his next best course was to compel
Montcalm to weaken his own force for the sake
of helping Bourlamaque; and the only practicable way of doing this was to push Bourlamaque
with all possible persistence and fury; but this
Amherst was far from doing. His conduct of
the campaign was busy, but languid, and the
month of September arrived before any progress had been made in disturbing the French
lines at Isle aux Noix.

Thus the problem of taking Quebec was left
for Wolfe to solve alone, and after his own
fashion. It seems hardly necessary to cumber
the narrative with the numerous details of the
summer's disappointing work. The principal
elements in the problem were as follows : —

The city of Quebec stands on the summit of
a cliff at least two hundred feet in height at the
junction of the St. Charles River with Quebec
the St. Lawrence. It occupies the
apex of the cliff between the two rivers, and
looks eastward down the St. Lawrence. Below
the St. Charles the distance down the north side

of the St. Lawrence to the Montmorenci is six miles. The bank is rather low, but precipitous, with a low beach at its foot, and for some distance from this beach the river is shallow. Nearly opposite the magnificent cataract of two hundred and fifty feet by which the Montmorenci discharges itself is the island of Orleans in mid-stream. Between this large island and the city of Quebec six miles up-stream the width of the river is not less than two miles, and it is often called the Basin. In passing Quebec, a name which means "The Narrow Place," the stream narrows to less than twelve hundred yards, so that in Wolfe's time the city could be reached by batteries planted on the south side of the stream at Point Levi, although the French had been disinclined to believe this.

When Wolfe came up the river in June he encamped his army upon the island of Orleans and upon the mainland at Point Levi and surveyed the situation. The French army, fourteen thousand strong, was encamped behind entrenchments along the six miles of low cliff between the St. Charles River and the falls of Montmorenci. The lofty cliff above the city had small sentry parties posted at intervals along the summit, while eight miles above, a force of twenty-three hundred men under Bougainville was posted at

The position of the French forces

Cap Rouge. The purpose of this latter detachment was to check and give timely warning of any possible movement from above on the part of Amherst, should he succeed in getting into that part of the world. Now Wolfe was good enough general to know that Montcalm's army was his chief objective point in a deeper sense than Quebec. Unless he should crush the French army, the position of Quebec would be of small use to him, while with the army once disposed of, Quebec would drop into his hands like a ripe apple. The difficult question was, how to get at the French army. Their position between the St. Charles and the Montmorenci was simply inaccessible. They could not be reached from English batteries south of the river, and it was impossible for any English force to turn their left flank without putting itself into a very dangerous position, where it would be liable to be cut off from the fleet which served as its base. The greater part of July was spent by Wolfe in inspecting the eastern bank of the Montmorenci to see if there were any means of attacking there; but no available place was found, and with all his dare-devil courage, Wolfe was not the man to risk useless sacrifice of life. Besides, even if a vigorous attack could have been made at that point, the French could easily withdraw, for their supplies came to them from the west. A flank attack on the west of their

line by the St. Charles River would have compelled them to stand and fight, where defeat meant ruin. But for the English to land in that locality was simply impossible. On the last day of July, apparently for the sake of doing something or other, Wolfe landed a considerable force on the low ground just above the Montmorenci. That he did not intend to storm is obvious, for when some of his brave regiments rushed forward, it was entirely without orders, in pursuit of a sudden impulse, and a deadly fire from the French infantry soon made them recoil. A large part of the month of August was spent by the young general on a sick-bed, attacked by a complication of diseases from which there was small hope of recovery ; he begged only to live long enough to solve the problem which Pitt had laid before him. To his physician he exclaimed, " Oh, Doctor, just patch me up enough for this business and I 'll ask no more ! " It was

probably while tossing on that feverish couch that his mind began playing with the thought which presently developed into a stern resolve. If a landing could not be effected at the St. Charles in face of a greatly superior force, how might it be with the heights above the city, which were watched only by small parties of sentinels ? Wolfe went up the river with boats and inspected the bank for himself, and about two miles above the city, at a place called Anse du Foulon, he detected a zigzag path which he rightly judged led to the summit of the well-nigh perpendicular cliff, though its course was in great part hidden by stout bushes. At the summit of this cliff the point of land upon which the city stood opened out into a wide plateau, known from some old settler as the Plains of Abraham. If a force could be landed here it would *Wolfe plans to scale the heights* compel Montcalm to come and attack, for otherwise his food supply would be cut off. With this end in view Wolfe increased the activity of his men in all directions. The batteries at Point Levi had been throwing shot and shell into the city for several weeks, and had reduced large portions of it to ruins. The bombardment now became more furious than ever. One move which he made quite puzzled Montcalm, but conveyed no hint of what was really contemplated ; the greater part of the British force was moved up the river to Cap Rouge, where such demonstrations were made as completely to absorb the attention of Bougainville. Montcalm was inclined to regard the movement as the final embarking of the British army preparatory to sailing down-stream and away, for his mind could conceive no possible alternative for Wolfe except the abandonment of the enterprise. With regard to Wolfe himself, while his attitude was one of grim determination, it can hardly be said to have been hopeful. The expedient was one from which success might come, and was therefore preferable to a confession of failure. One circumstance upon which he rested some hope was the fact that boats now and then succeeded in stealing down under the black shadow of the lofty bank with provisions for the French army below. On the 12th of September all was in readiness, and Wolfe made such demonstrations below the city that Montcalm began to think that a landing at the mouth of the St. Charles might be intended, and that thus the Lord was delivering his enemy into his hands. At the

Final preparations — same time, the demonstrations against Bougainville were redoubled, and English ships kept moving from point to point in such wise as to strain every nerve of the watchful and bewildered French. In the course of the day Wolfe called to him his friend Jervis, afterward celebrated as an admiral, and told him that he had a presentiment of impending death; and taking from about his neck a small chain with the miniature of the lady to whom he was betrothed, he gave it to Jervis to be returned to her in case he should not survive the anticipated battle. As midnight approached, all was silence at Cap Rouge, but such demonstrations were made below the city that Montcalm was on horseback all night, expecting an attack at the St. Charles. Meanwhile, at the gleaming of a lantern at the masthead of one of the ships, sixteen hundred men dropped into their boats and waited for the ebb of the tide. Then, at the momentary flash of another lantern, all began rowing down-stream in the The start dark shadow of the cliff. Twice they were challenged by sentinels above, but an officer who spoke French fluently replied that they were boats with provisions for Montcalm.

Wolfe sat buried in thought, occasionally repeating aloud verses from Gray's "Elegy," which had been published a few years before, and one line,

"The paths of glory lead but to the grave,"

betrayed what was passing in his mind. "Gentlemen," he said to the officers with him, "I would rather be the author of that poem than take Quebec." When they reached the landing-place, the head of the column went ashore, under the lead of Wil- The ascent liam Howe, youngest brother of the general who had been killed at Ticonderoga. As the sixteen hundred landed, the zigzag path was overcrowded, but there were so many bushes as to afford an abundance of handles and footholds on that steep precipice. The height of the climb was a little over two hundred feet, or about the same as that of Bunker Hill Monument. But at length it was safely accomplished, and just as the first streaks of dawn glimmered on the eastern horizon, the gallant Howe with his men leaped upon the summit and scattered the French sentinels, who were seized with panic and stood not upon the order of their going. It was still early dawn when the sixteen hundred were drawn up in order on the Plains of Abraham. Other boats were following close behind, and by six o'clock three thousand more had climbed the rocky wall. The alarm was now spreading in many directions, but it was a long march for any of the French forces to reach the spot where Wolfe stood. When the tidings came to Montcalm his countenance fell. "This is a very serious business," he said, and instantly put a large portion of his force under marching orders. Not a moment was to be lost, for Wolfe on the Heights of Abraham was in possession of his line of communication. Nothing was to be done but to go and fight the English in a position where defeat meant destruction. By nine o'clock in the morning Montcalm had about five thousand men on the plateau, while Wolfe was waiting for the numbers of the French to reach a point where their defeat might be final ; for now Wolfe had good grounds for confidently expecting victory.

Complete surprise of the French

Only two thousand of the force opposed to him were French regulars. The rest were Canadian militia, unsurpassed in bush fighting, but hardly fit to withstand a charge of British grenadiers. The attack was made by the French, who rushed forward with great spirit. The battle Wolfe's orders to his men, like those of Prescott in later days at Bunker Hill, were to withhold their fire until the enemy were within very close range. This order was strictly obeyed. When the volley was delivered, it made sad havoc in the French ranks, and when the British followed it with a solid bayonet charge on the double-quick, the French line was hopelessly broken. The firing in some parts of the field remained very brisk on both sides. In crossing an exposed place Wolfe received a ball in the wrist which shattered the arm, but he tied it up with his handkerchief and kept on. Presently a second ball struck him in the groin without causing him to stop, and almost immediately afterward a third passed through one of his lungs. As he staggered, he was seized by four men, who carried him to the rear and laid him upon the ground. He was already somewhat comatose, when one of the officers exclaimed, " My God ! see how they run ! " " Who run ? " exclaimed Wolfe, rousing himself. " The enemy," replied the officer, " is giving way everywhere." The young general's

eyes lighted up once more as he eagerly cried
out, " Go, one of you, my lads, to
Colonel Burton and tell him to march
down to the Charles River Bridge and cut off
their retreat;" then, turning upon his side, he
murmured, "Now, God be praised, I will die
in peace."

Death of
Wolfe

For Montcalm, too, the final summons had
come, and he was no more to see the beautiful
Provençal home for which he had so wearily
yearned. As he was approaching one of the
gates of the city, mounted on his black horse,
a bullet was lodged in his chest, which in the
intensity of excitement he seemed hardly to
feel. As he passed through the gate a party
of women, seeing the blood stream-
ing down his waistcoat, burst into
loud lamentations: "He is killed! The Marquis is killed!" "Do not weep for me, my
children," said he; "it's nothing." But, as he
said the words, he fell from his horse and was
caught in the arms of his officers. When the
surgeon informed him that the wound was mor-
tal, his reply was, "So much the better. I shall
not live to see Quebec surrendered."

Death of
Montcalm

Thus came to a close one of the greatest
scenes in the history of mankind, the final act
in the drama which gave the North American
continent into the keeping of the English race
instead of the French; and perhaps there has

never been a historic drama in which the leading parts have been played by men of nobler stuff than Montcalm and Wolfe. After the fall of Quebec there could be no doubt that the fate of Canada was decided. The capture of Montreal by Amherst in the following summer was like an appendix to a tale already told.

INDEX

THE END

The Riverside Press

Electrotyped and printed by H. O. Houghton & Co.
Cambridge, Mass., U. S. A.

WRITINGS OF JOHN FISKE

Historical

THE DISCOVERY OF AMERICA

With some Account of Ancient America and the Spanish Conquest. With a Steel Portrait of Mr. Fiske, many maps, facsimiles, etc. 2 vols. crown 8vo, gilt top, $4.00.

The book brings together a great deal of information hitherto accessible only in special treatises, and elucidates with care and judgment some of the most perplexing problems in the history of discovery. — *The Speaker* (London).

OLD VIRGINIA AND HER NEIGHBOURS

2 vols. crown 8vo, gilt top, $4.00.
Illustrated Edition, 2 vols. 8vo, $8.00.

History has rarely been invested with such interest and charm as in these volumes. — *The Outlook* (New York).

THE BEGINNINGS OF NEW ENGLAND

Or, the Puritan Theocracy in its Relations to Civil and Religious Liberty. Crown 8vo, $2.00. Illustrated Edition. Containing Portraits, Maps, Facsimiles, Contemporary Views, Prints, and other Historic Materials. 8vo, gilt top, $4.00.

Having in the first chapters strikingly and convincingly shown that New England's history was the birth of centuries of travail, and having prepared his readers to estimate at their true importance the events of our early colonial life, Mr. Fiske is ready to take up his task as the historian of the New England of the Puritans. — *Advertiser* (Boston).

THE DUTCH AND QUAKER COLONIES IN AMERICA

With 8 Maps. 2 vols. crown 8vo, gilt top, $4.00.

The work is a lucid summary of the events of a changeful and important time, carefully examined by a conscientious scholar, who is master of his subject. — *Daily News* (London).

NEW FRANCE AND NEW ENGLAND

With Maps. Crown 8vo, $1.65, net. Postage extra.

This volume presents in broad and philosophic manner the causes and events which marked the victory on this continent of the English civilization over the French.

THE AMERICAN REVOLUTION

With Plans of Battles, and a Steel Portrait of Washington. 2 vols. crown 8vo, gilt top, $4.00. Illustrated Edition. Containing about 300 Illustrations. 2 vols. 8vo, gilt top, $8.00.

Beneath his sympathetic and illuminating touch the familiar story comes out in fresh and vivid colors. — *New Orleans Times-Democrat.*

THE CRITICAL PERIOD OF AMERICAN HISTORY, 1783-1789

With Map, Notes, etc. Crown 8vo, gilt top, $2.00. Illustrated Edition. Containing about 170 Illustrations. 8vo, gilt top, $4.00.

The author combines in an unusual degree the impartiality of the trained scholar with the fervor of the interested narrator — *The Congregationalist* (Boston).

THE WAR OF INDEPENDENCE

In Riverside Library for Young People. With Maps. 16mo, 75 cents.

THE MISSISSIPPI VALLEY IN THE CIVIL WAR

With 20 Maps and Plans. 1 vol. crown 8vo, $2.00.

A HISTORY OF THE UNITED STATES FOR SCHOOLS

With Topical Analysis, Suggestive Questions, and Directions for Teachers, by F. A. Hill, and Illustrations and Maps. Crown 8vo, $1.00, net.